CATULLUS

A POET IN THE ROME OF JULIUS CAESAR

D1434880

CATULLUS

A Poet in the Rome of Julius Caesar

Aubrey Burl

With a selection of poems
translated by Humphrey Clucas

AMBERLEY

Dedicated to Philip Burton,
lover of poetry,
for his yearly Spring Rhythms.

This edition first published 2010

Amberley Publishing Plc
Cirencester Road, Chalford,
Stroud, Gloucestershire, GL6 8PE

www.amberley-books.com

ISBN 978 1 84868 391 4

British Library Cataloguing in Publication Data.
A catalogue record for this book is available from the British Library.

Typeset in 10pt on 12pt Sabon.
Typesetting and Origination by FonthillMedia.
Printed in the UK.

CONTENTS

Frater Ave atque Vale

Row us out from Desenzano, to your Sirmione row!
So they row'd and there we landed – 'o venusto, Sirmio!'
There to me through all the groves of olives in the summer glow,
There beneath the Roman ruin where the purple flowers grow,
Came that 'Ave atque Vale' of the Poet's hopeless woe,
Tenderest of Roman poets nineteen hundred years ago,
'Frater Ave atque Vale' – as we wandered to and fro
Gazing at the Lydian laughter of the Garda lake below
Sweet Catullus's all-but-island, olive-silvery Sirmio.

Lord Alfred Tennyson

Maps and Diagrams

ILLUSTRATIONS

Bust of Catullus, Sirmione
Airport car parking sign, Verona
Arena (Colosseum) in Verona
Villa of Catullus (Sirmione)
Roman wall in Verona
Statue of Can Grande above the church, Verona
Tablet listing executions in Tullianum prison
The condemned cell, Tullianum
Paul Getty's replica of Piso's villa, Herculaneum
    Courtesy of the J. Paul Getty Museum, Malibu, California
Across Basilica Sempronia to the three pillars of the Temple of Castor & Pollux
Temple of Vesta, Rome
Drawing 'Death of a sparrow/Clodia's sparrow'
    From the illustrated edition of Burton and Smithers, 1928
First page of Codex 'O'
    *Courtesy of the Bodleian Library, University of Oxford, MS. Canon. Class.
    Lat. 30, fol. 1r*

ACKNOWLEDGEMENTS

Many people have helped me with this book. Four undertook the erudite search for a linguistic Greek/Latin brassière and the classical references to it: Professor Jasper Griffin, Public Orator of Balliol College, Oxford, my brother-in-law Russell Lawson and my classically-educated son Geoffrey. Neil Mortimer discovered Pliny's obsession with the health-giving faculties of that underwear.

There has been other assistance: the Bodleian Library for the photograph of the Catullan manuscript, 'O'; the Paul Getty Museum in California for the photograph of the reconstructed Piso's villa; and Robert Harris for information about that villa and its recent excavations.

I am delighted that Humphrey Clucas has agreed to have a selection of his translation of Catullus printed in this book. Their variety and clarity will provide the reader with a keen taste for the virtuosity and delicacy of the Roman poet.

Much appreciation is due to the staffs of the library of the Society of Antiquaries of London and of the University of Birmingham for their assistance in tracking down ageing volumes on dark shelves.

Since the first edition of *Catullus* in 2004 revisions have been made to include new material such as the discovery of a completely 'new' poem by the Greek poetess, Sappho, and the manner in which it was treated by Catullus many centuries later.

A considerable debt is owed to my publisher, Sarah Flight of Amberley Publishing, for resurrecting that old poet from the limbo into which the publishing world had allowed him to drift.

The Bibliography has been updated.

As always, my deep gratitude to Judith, my wife, for accompanying me to Rome, Verona and Catullus' villa near Sirmione. She has also tolerated a study's 'library' of books, ancient and modern, of Catullus, Caesar, Cleopatra, Spartacus and all that compelling company of ancient Rome.

Verona provided us with a fine hotel and very good local meals. Rome did not, only poor accommodation near the Forum. Disappointing food. Sirmione near the ruins of Catullus' villa on the shores of Lake Garda is a tourist town of tawdry tat with no mention of Catullus. But whether in Verona, Rome or Sirmione there were always echoes of his music.

Finally, my very belated thanks to the stall-holder in Leicester's open-air market who many years ago sold four pristine leather-bound volumes of a complete Plutarch to a threadbare student, generously reducing the asking price of one pound ten shillings (£1.50) to an affordable pound. The books are still pristine but well-read and well-used.

CHRONOLOGY OF EVENTS

(The suggested dates of some of the poems of Catullus are conjectural.)

BC

753   Traditional date for the foundation of Rome.

620?   Birth of Sappho, Greek poetess, on island of Lesbos.

218-03   Second Punic War. Hannibal crossed the Alps. His Carthaginian army defeated Roman legions and ravaged Italy for sixteen years.

216   Battle of Cannae. Eight Roman legions annihilated by Hannibal.

215   Statue of Cybele brought from Phrygia to Rome.

191   Temple of Cybele dedicated on the Palatine Hill.

108   Marius, Roman soldier fighting against Jugurtha in Numidia, returned to Rome, elected consul.

107   Marius back to Numidia. The patrician, L. Cornelius Sulla, on his staff

100   Birth of Julius Caesar.

91-89   The Social War. Italian tribes compelled Rome to give them citizenship.

88   Sulla elected consul, given command against Mithridates. Marius usurped the post. Sulla entered Rome by force. Marius outlawed.

88-4   First Mithridatic War fought by Sulla.

87   In Sulla's absence, his rival, Marius, returned to Rome. Murder of enemies.

86   Death of Marius. Sulla captured Athens.

84?   Verona. Birth of Catullus.

82   Sulla defeated the Samnites at the battle of the Colline Gate. His 'proscriptions' led to deaths of enemies and of rich landowners.

78   Death of Sulla.

73-71   The Third Servile War. Slave revolt of gladiator Spartacus. Finally defeated by Crassus. Crucifixions along the Appian Way.

70   Pompey and Crassus elected consuls. Birth of poet Virgil. Early poems of Catullus, [11, 67]?

68   Birth of Cleopatra.

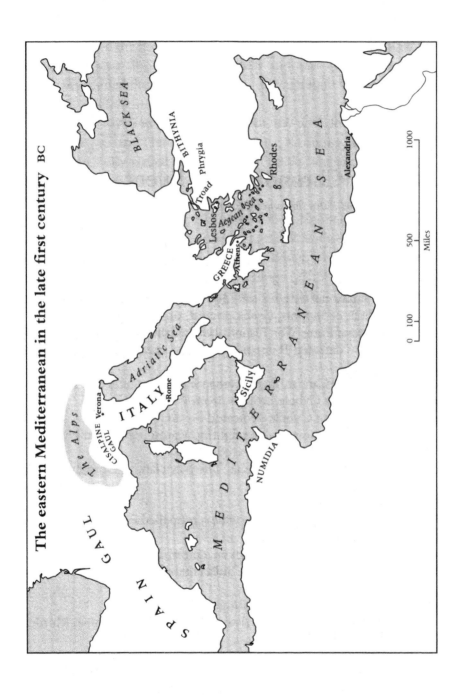

The eastern Mediterranean in the late first century BC

67	Pompey's successful war against pirates in the Mediterranean.
65	Birth of poet Horace.
63	The consul, Cicero, suppressed the Catiline conspiracy. Plotters executed. Caesar elected Pontifex Maximus. Octavian, later Augustus, born.
62	In Rome Clodius Pulcher profaned the rite of Bona Dea. In battle near Pistoria Catiline defeated and killed.
61	Trial and acquittal of Clodius Pulcher. Despite Pompey's overseas triumphs he was snubbed by the Senate.
60?	Catullus to Rome? First Triumvirate of Pompey, Crassus and Julius Caesar.
59	Caesar elected consul. Catullus, beginning of his affair with Clodia. His earliest poems to her [2, 3, 5, 7, 51]? Death of Metellus Celer, husband of Clodia. Caesar given military command of Cisalpine Gaul for five years. Livy, historian, born.
58	Clodius Pulcher as tribune effected the banishment of Cicero.
58-51	Caesar's victories in Gaul, Germany and Britain.
58	Ptolemy XII and his daughter Cleopatra came to Rome asking for the pharaoh to be restored to the throne of Egypt.
57	Catullus in Bithynia. Grief for brother [101]? Inspiration for *Attis* [63]. Cicero recalled to Rome. Dio, Egyptian ambassador, murdered.
56	Trial of Marcus Caelius Rufus, defended by Cicero. Catullus returned to Rome [4, 10, 31]. Bitterness against Clodia [11, 37 and others]?
55	The poems of Catullus against Mamurra, Gellius and others [74 onwards]? Caesar given five years' command in Gaul. His first invasion of Britain. Pompey and Crassus consuls for the second time. Pompey given five years' command of Spain; Crassus five years in Syria. Catullus: completion of *Peleus and Thetis* [64]?
54	Death of Catullus? One of last poems [1]? Caesar's second invasion of Britain.
53	Death of Crassus at the battle of Carrhae.
52	Killing of Clodius Pulcher at Bovillae. Pompey made sole consul.
51	Cleopatra joint-ruler of Egypt with half-brother, Ptolemy.
49	Caesar and Mark Antony crossed the Rubicon. Pompey fled to Greece.
48	Pompey defeated at the battle of Pharsalus. Murdered in Egypt. Cleopatra deposed by brother's guardians.
47	Cleopatra restored to the throne of Egypt. Library at Alexandria burnt.

46	Caesar's Julian calendar of 365¼ days introduced. Caesar made dictator and consul for ten years.
44	Caesar assassinated in Rome. Helvius Cinna, friend of Catullus, mistaken for an assassin and killed by a mob.
43	The Second Triumvirate: Mark Antony, Octavian and Lepidus. Cicero killed. The poet Ovid born.
42	At battle of Philippi Mark Antony and Octavian defeat Cassius and Brutus, assassins of Caesar.
37	Mark Antony married Cleopatra.
31	Battle of Actium. Mark Antony and Cleopatra defeated by Octavian.
30	Suicides of Mark Antony and Cleopatra.
27	Octavian became the first Roman emperor, Augustus.

PREFACE

Catullus might have become no more than a legend. Even for a poet of genius there was no promise that his works would survive indifference, neglect and decay. Before books and before printing, a poem was as fragile as words written on a cloud or whispered to the wind.

> Beauty is but a flower
> Which wrinkles will devour,
> Brightness falls from the air ...[1]

wrote Thomas Nashe. The elegiac sadness was true for Catullus who knew the danger. 'May my little book last for more than a generation,' he wrote to his friend Cornelius Nepos, adding, 'if anyone happens to be a future reader of these trivial indecencies and finds that he can touch them without disgust I'll be pleased.'

That was not a generation but more than two thousand years ago. And, as he feared, Catullus was lost for over a thousand of them. By a literary miracle he was rediscovered. Now scholars analyse him, argue over translations, find this word misspelt, that one misunderstood. The critics are necessary but they are the men outside.

'The common man has been enjoying Catullus behind the scholar's back,' wrote E. G. C. Levens, and he was right.[2] Catullus' is a short book, hardly more than two thousand lines, just over a hundred poems. But some of those poems are lyrics of enchanting loveliness, others are invective of such vitriol that even today they shock. More are so sexually explicit that editors omit them from sixth-form schoolbooks.

Most enticing to many readers of Catullus is the collection of poems about his passionate affair with an anonymous, married woman. There is gentleness, laughter, despair, beauty in them. The words sing and burn. The world is fortunate to have them.

Yet physically Catullus has almost disappeared from Italy. In Rome there is nothing to see. In Sirmione there are the ruins of his villa but the authorities are reluctant to state that it was his. In the tiny town there is a bevy of shops for tourists and just one bust in the Piazza Carducci against Lake Garda. It is wrongly dated.

In Verona, his birthplace, there is a statue of the poet but it is inconspicuous, one of five poets and historians high on the roof of the Loggia del Consiglio, 'the finest Renaissance building in Verona'. Far more prominent is the three times life-size statue of Dante in the Piazza dei Signori below. Otherwise Catullus is ignored. Far better known is the fraudulent balcony of the spurious Juliet in the Via Cappello.

It is ten miles away at Villafranca that Catullus is acknowledged. The airport is called 'Valerio Catullo' with 'Catullo Parking' signs everywhere for drivers. The symbolism is apt. Disregarded on the ground, a great poet is honoured in the skies of northern Italy.

There has never been a full-length biography of Catullus and the times that he lived in. The nearest was the 124-page essay by Jack Lindsay appended to his translation of the poems in *Gaius Valerius Catullus* of 1929. It was printed by the Fanfrolico Press, a publisher 'that came dangerously close to scrutiny by the [Australian] police censor'.

Almost unobtainable in a limited edition of 325 signed copies, despite its scholarship, Lindsay's 'life' is dated. Today there are many translations of the poems of Catullus, even more literary criticism, but there is still little about the man.

This book tells the story of a poet and his marvellous poetry, set against the background of years of unrest, violence and death in ancient Rome.

Note to the Reader

Where a poem is quoted in the text it is followed by its bracketed number in the corpus, e.g. [14]. Except where stated translations are by the author. For others, the names of the translators and their dates are given: e.g. Richard Lovelace (1618-57).

Poems quoted in the chapters are not in chronological order, that being uncertain, but have been selected to illustrate some aspect of the poet's life – his friends, emotional attachments, external events.

Most of the poems are undatable; a few offer clues. Poem [10], mentioning Bithynia, may have been composed around 56 BC after the poet's return from that province. Poem [55], with Catullus searching 'as far as Pompey's portico', must be of 55 BC or later after Pompey's theatre had been dedicated in that year. Poem [11], with its reference to 'the dreadful Britons at the world's end', was probably written after Caesar's second invasion of Britain in 54 BC. The precise date of most of the others in the corpus remains speculative because they exist in a rearranged collection of verses written from perhaps as early as 68 BC to 54 BC or later.

The poems were contained in three 'books' or *Libri* written on separate papyrus rolls. *Liber I* consists of poems [1-17] and [21-60], numbers [18-20] usually being omitted because of their dubious authenticity. The fifty-seven accepted poems are short, personal and written in a variety of metres. *Liber II*, poems [61-4], contains four long poems in various forms about marriage. They are the most ambitious of Catullus' pieces. *Liber III*, poems [65-116], are elegies and short epigrams, a body of varying worth, seemingly rather scrappily arranged.

Amongst them are poems that no Victorian editions would print.

The following lines from Poem XVI perfectly illustrate this:

... nam castum esse decet pium poetam
ipsum, versiculos nihil necesse est;

which can be translated as

... a poet may be a decent and pure-living man
but, even so, some of his verses can be foul and scurrilous

No proper edition of *Catullus* will omit those verses.

Details of his corpus, its origins, editor or editors and the significance of the poems are discussed in the chapters that follow.

A selection of translations of Catullan poems into English from Elizabethan times to the present day can be found in Gaisser, 2001.

For more detail the edition by Goold (1989), with a scholarly translation facing the complete Latin text and explanatory notes, provides a good introduction to the poems. Any reader wanting more will find the translation by Martin (1979) is admirably supplemented by the same author's (1992) discussion of the problems surrounding Catullus. An indispensable general background to the period, persons and poems is provided by T. P. Wiseman's *Catullus and His World. A Reappraisal*, (1985, paperback, 1987).

Other rich pickings are listed in the Notes and Bibliography of the present book.

INTRODUCTION

It is only by chance that we are able to read the marvellous poems of Gaius Valerius Catullus today. They have survived, by the grace of his gods and simple good luck, whereas the works of talented friends and poets Bibaculus, Calvus, Cinna, Cornificius and Ticidas fill little more than three meagre pages of print.[1]

Catullus was remarkable. He dined with Julius Caesar, moved in Rome's most privileged circles, mixed with rich and raffish young men of the world, and enjoyed the high-class and costly company of women of the world. It is all in his verse. He was a great poet.

It is pessimistically but mistakenly believed that we have very few facts about his life. In 1472 there was a brief biography by Gerolamo Squarzafico in the first printed edition of his poems. 'Valerius Catullus the lyric writer was born at Verona in the 163rd Olympiad [87 BC], the year before Sallustius Crispus, in the terrible times of Marius and Sulla, on the day Plotinus first began to teach Latin rhetoric at Rome. He loved a girl of high rank, Clodia, whom he called Lesbia in his poetry. He was very playful and in his time he had few equals, and no superior, in versifying. In jests he was especially charming, but in sober matters very serious. He wrote erotic poems, and an epithalamium to Manlius. He died in the thirtieth year of his life and was buried with public mourning.'[2]

What this vague and incomplete account does not mention is that Catullus lived during some of the most violent decades of Roman history. The years of his childhood were those of the aftermath of the ruthless civil war between Sulla and Marius when a name casually added to a public list meant another person to be killed. As a young man he was in Rome when Caesar, Pompey and Crassus were struggling for power, and when Cicero was at the height of his oratorical powers. It was also the period when Catiline and his conspirators were plotting to overthrow the Senate and the government of Rome and when Clodius, patrician turned plebeian rabble-rouser, and the brother of the woman that Catullus loved, was inciting the resentfully impoverished citizens to riot.

The Rome of Catullus was not only the romantic glory of temples of immaculate white stone and occasional marble. Temples did exist on the high Capitoline Hill, with the Forum stretching below them, but lower still the

Subura district was a ramshackle of slum tenements, such badly-built death-traps that no cooking could be done for fear of fire. Outside, the streets were sludges of filth.

Rome was not today in a toga. It was dirty, dangerous and pregnant with beliefs that are alien to the modern mind. When the Capitoline Hill with its Temple of Jupiter was hit by lightning in 65 BC it was not experts on weather that were summoned but a special group of priests, who deduced the reason for the calamity by examining the entrails of sacrificed victims. 'They declared that, if the gods were not appeased, conflagration and civil war and the end of the city and the Roman world were at hand. They recommended that expiatory games often days' duration should be celebrated for Jupiter and that a new and bigger statue of Jupiter should be set up on the Capitol, facing the east, that is, the Forum.'[3]

The gods were respected, feared and had to be placated. After Hannibal's appalling annihilation of eight Roman legions at Cannae in 216 BC, people in Rome believed that religious rites had been improperly performed. Priests consulted the Sibylline Books. Those oracular sayings from Greece, kept in the Temple of Jupiter, proclaimed that there had been corruption and that human lives were demanded. Two men and two women, slaves from Greece and Gaul, were sacrificed in Rome's oldest market, the Forum Boarium, alongside the River Tiber.

There was worse. The holy Temple of Vesta had been defiled. Two of her priestesses, sworn to chastity, had taken lovers and the penalty for that was death by being buried alive. One man was flogged so severely that he died. A Vestal Virgin committed suicide. The other was executed as the law demanded. When Hannibal failed to attack Rome it was clear to every citizen that the sins had been expiated and that the gods were appeased.[4]

It was a different world. 'Studying ancient Rome should be like visiting some teeming capital in a dangerous and ill-governed foreign country; nothing can be relied on, most of what you see is squalid, sinister or unintelligible.' With no collection of household rubbish, garbage and filth were just thrown out of windows. It was sometimes worse than rubbish. Suetonius mentioned that 'a stray dog picked up a human hand at the crossroads and brought it into the room where the [emperor] Vespasian was breakfasting and dropped it under the table'.[5]

Yet during those turbulent times Catullus wrote some of the finest poetry ever known. He could be regal, witty, lyrical and frequently obscene. Born of a wealthy and highly regarded family he could confidently insult Caesar.

I am quite indifferent, Caesar, about being in your favour,
I don't care if you're white or black, good or bad. [93]

He became so popular that even twenty years after his death people were still declaiming his verses, irritating the poet, Horace:

... that ape
whose only artistic achievement is to croon Calvus and Catullus.[6]

Yet Catullus almost disappeared as a poet when copies of his poetry on their dry papyrus rolls were destroyed in the burning of the famous library at Alexandria in 47 BC. The building was badly damaged when Julius Caesar, staying near the harbour in the city with Cleopatra, was besieged for almost six months by a mob. Cut off by Egyptian vessels he sent fire-ships into the port, the flames flared, igniting a dockside laden with inflammable stores and setting fire to the library. About 300,000 of the irreplaceable rolls, including those on parchment brought from the port of Pergamum, modern Bergama in north-west Asia Minor, were saved. But it was to be a brief respite: they were finally destroyed in AD 641 when Arabs overran Alexandria and for six months the documents provided fuel for thousands of baths in the city.[7]

Writers of this period survived by sheer luck. A book about 'fragmentary Latin poets' lists almost a hundred writers, including Julius Caesar and Cicero, who survive only in a few, disconnected lines with the result that they seem banal. One of them, Volumnius, a patron of the actress Lycoris, seems to have written an invitation to a modest meal of 'shoots of cabbage put in bubbling, boiling water', while another, Vernus, enters posterity only as the author of 'The soothed pain will be treated with gentle skill', neither line likely to be a candidate for anyone's book of evocative verse [8]

Even the emperor Augustus, writing when he was the patrician, Octavian, is known by only one complete epigram, a remnant that he may not have wished as his sole relic. It was an explicit account of the sexual rivalry between him, his rival, Mark Antony, Antony's disenchanted wife Fulvia, Antony's beautiful mistress Glaphyra and Manius, Antony's military agent. The lines are an uncensored account of the commonplace adulteries and homosexuality, whether pleasurable or humiliating, of Rome and they are a blunt revelation of the relaxed morals and uninhibitedly coarse language of the privileged classes.

Antony's shagging Glaphyra. So his wife, Fulvia, vows
revenge by screwing me! No chance! I loathe these lustful cows!
And Manius, Antony's companion, waggles his stiff rod
at my defenceless arse. Unwanted bliss, by god!
'Screw, or fight', says Fulvia. 'Is your cock so proud?
Rather death than me? To bed! Horns triumphant, blare out loud!'[9]

The aftermath of this uneasy *ménage à quatre* was predictable. All four were sensualists. Mark Antony was an easy-going philanderer, enjoying many women before meeting and marrying Cleopatra of Egypt. Manius, his procurator and a pederast, 'seems to have played a large part in stirring her [Fulvia] up'. Octavian/Augustus was a sexual hermaphrodite who found pleasure in making love to women and being loved by men. He was, remarked Suetonius, 'accused of a variety of improprieties ... jeered at for his effeminacy. Mark Antony alleged that Julius Caesar made him submit to unnatural practices in return for adoption into the Julian family, and after surrendering his virtue to Caesar he sold himself to the Governor-General of Spain for 3,000 gold coins'... None of his friends could deny his adulteries. On one occasion, deep in the abandon of a banquet, he beckoned his host's attractive wife to follow him. It was much later with gown rumpled, hair-style and reputation in ruins, that red-faced she returned to the wine and whispers of the dining-room. Mark Antony sent him a mocking letter. 'Does it really matter so much where, or with whom, you perform the sexual act?'[10]

As for Fulvia, a woman to be met on other occasions in this book, three times married and a near-insatiable nymphomaniac, she was also cruel and vindictive, on one occasion piercing a dead enemy's tongue with her long and sharp hairpin. Understandably, any threat from that sadistic matron would concern any man, even Octavian.

The lovely Glaphyra, also thrice married, appears a contented participant in the revels. An Egyptian philosopher, Dio, later to be murdered by an erstwhile friend of Catullus, termed her a *hetaira*, a courtesan of superior quality. A hedonist is likelier. Being the wife of the wealthy ruler of Judaea it is arguable that it was a longing for carnal-versatility rather than venality for cash that tempted her to the pleasures of Mark Antony's love-making.

Octavian's is one short verse of six lines, but it is a realistic picture of the society that Catullus was to know. He could be just as candid about the cheerful immorality of his acquaintances – and as worried about the survival of the poems he wrote about them.

A writer was susceptible to the loss of everything he had written. Falling out of fashion could also result in neglect. Papyrus could decay but it was the best that a writer had. After composing with a stylus on to a tablet of wax, a poem would be copied on to a roll of papyrus. The roll was clumsy to read. If it already contained work it had to be unrolled backwards to the last piece of writing and the first blank space. Reading from it was even more awkward, turning forwards with the left hand, unwinding with the right as verse followed verse. However, to an educated Greek or Roman it was every day practice. Catullus' collected work was not large, some 2,300 lines of 116 poems, of which only eight were long, and the corpus existed only on the ephemeral rolls that could be lost, damaged, destroyed or mislaid somewhere, almost irrecoverable.

They were. For a millennium of silent years the poems were no more than legends. Catullus was forgotten. His epigrams had lost their meaning and his popularity faded. Many of his witticisms were so topical that later readers could not understand them because their human targets were unknown figures of the past.

The same incomprehension affected the light-hearted 'legacies' of the medieval French poet, François Villon. His editor Marot, writing in 1533, less than eighty years after Villon's death, discovered that although there were still people who could recite whole passages, much had been forgotten. 'For a man rightly to understand all the meaning of the legacies of Villon he should have lived in Paris and in his day, and should have known the places, the things and the men of whom he speaks; for the more the memory of these fades away, the less shall a man apprehend the meaning of the aforesaid legacies.'[11] The same truth affected Catullus.

Just as Parisians puzzled over people that Villon mocked: Cardon, Grigny, Laurens and others, so over the years Romans found the jests about Gellius, Egnatius and Mamurra jokes without significance. Readers preferred the undemanding eroticisms of Ovid and the witty but less forgotten targets of Martial's epigrams.

Within a hundred years of his death, there was not even a mention of him amongst the indecent graffiti on the walls of Pompeii. There were only bawdy quotations of Ovid, Martial and Horace.[12]

However, the fear of the extinction of his poems concerned Catullus and he devised a means of survival.

Who's to receive my debonair, brand-new booklet,
sleekly bound and freshly pumice-polished?
You, Cornelius, you who have always thought
my trifles of some lasting worth.
You, my countryman, the only person
with courage to write a three-roll *History*,
scholarly, by Jove, and laborious to compile.
Take this gift. I gave this triviality to you
although it's nothing. Let my Muse safeguard it
for more than one quickly-perished generation.

[1]

Cornelius Nepos was an esteemed correspondent of Cicero's, a celebrated historian who in his later years enjoyed the favours and patronage of Augustus.

As well as erotic love poems and anecdotes he compiled the earliest set of biographies, *De Viris Illustribus*, 'Lives of Famous Men', in sixteen volumes of which just one survives, a compendium of foreign generals including Hannibal. He is less respected today. An 'intellectual pygmy', was one unkind assessment.[13]

To ask a man as respected and famous as Cornelius Nepos, so notable in his lifetime, to look after his poems was like requesting Alfred, Lord Tennyson, aristocrat, Poet Laureate, acquaintance of royalty, to protect one's work. But Nepos was another poet of Cisalpine Gaul, from Hostilia, modern Ostiglia, some twenty miles south of Verona, almost a neighbour of Catullus, and even though he was more than ten years older the two were close friends.

But despite his precautions Catullus vanished. He was almost forgotten for over a thousand years until the unexpected discovery of a single manuscript in his hometown, Verona. That near-miracle swiftly disappeared but two copies had been made. They also vanished but not before there were three more transcriptions. From them the entire body of poems was finally printed in 1472. But problems remained: the unique manuscript, known as 'V' for Verona, had contained a thousand mistakes caused by the faulty copying of already imperfect earlier drafts with misspellings, poems run together, errors caused by the dubious Latin of medieval scribes. It was only by the nineteenth century, after long years of study and correction by scholars across Europe, that a reliable edition was issued.[14] And even today there are still 'a much larger number of cases (between fifty and a hundred) where editors continue to be divided on the need to emend or on the choice between variant readings or rival conjectures'.[15] (For the history of the manuscripts see: Appendix II.)

In his poem, 'The Scholars', W. B. Yeats, to whom Arthur Symons had read entrancing passages of Catullus, scorned those painstaking pedants who worried over words, seeking for meanings amongst confusion. In poem [11] they corrected 'V's meaningless *horrible aequor*, 'horrible (unknown in Latin) flat surface' into what Catullus had written, *horribiles quoque*, 'and also the terrifying' [Britons], referring to Caesar's invasion of Britain. To Yeats such men removed the magic.

> Bald heads forgetful of their sins,
> Old, learned, respectable bald heads
> Edit and annotate the lines
>
> That young men, tossing on their beds,
> Rhymed out in love's despair
> To flatter beauty's ignorant ear.
> All shuffle there; all cough in ink;
> All wear the carpet with their shoes;

All think what other people think;
All know the man their neighbour knows.
Lord, what would they say
Did Catullus walk that way?

The Scholars

Yet without the meticulous exegesis Catullus would not walk at all, just shuffle and stumble lamely into the present century.

A sharp example of how one misread word could alter the entire meaning of a poem occurred in [95]. In it Catullus praised the dedication of his friend Helvius Cinna, who had spent nine meticulous years revising and improving his mini epic, *Smyrna*, about a woman who had fallen in love with her father.

Commending such effort Catullus apparently contrasted it with the slipshod and ephemeral offerings of three other versifiers. One of them, astonishingly, was Quintus Hortentius Hortalus, elegant, softly-spoken orator, dandy, epicure and composer of risqué verses, such a respected friend of the poet that at a time when Catullus was mourning the death of his brother, he honoured a promise by sending Hortalus a translation of Callimachus [66]. The generous gift makes the attack in [95] all the more inexplicable.

More puzzling still is the fact that in a short poem of only ten lines Catullus criticized two more versifiers, Volusius and Antimachus. Three victims were too many, diluting the contrast between the diligent creativity of one man and the slipshod rubbish of others, an unlikely fault in a poet as fastidious as Catullus.

Three lines, 3, 7 and 10, explain. Line 3 accused Hortentius of reeling off half a million tawdry lines a year. Line 7 told Volusius that his *Annals* would die on the banks of the Padua. Line 10 dismissed the vulgar taste of the hoi polloi who admired the turgid monstrosities of Antimachus. But he, Hortentius and Volusius were not three separate targets. They were one.

Superficially poem [95] is a technical failure but its contradictions vanish with the realization that the scrawled black thick Gothic lettering of one medieval copyist had been misread by another. Recognizing the letters 'H.. T..E..N..S' the copyist must have guessed 'Hortentius', the middle name of a known associate of Catullus. It was a bad guess. The real word was 'Hatriensis', 'from Hatria', a geographical allusion to a person just as recognizable as the 'bard of Avon', 'outlaw of Sherwood Forest' or 'Whitechapel murderer' are to Shakespeare, Robin Hood or Jack the Ripper.

Hatria was a town on the Po delta, one mouth of which was the Padua river into which Volusius' *Annals* were to disappear, their abundant sheets of parchment fit only as wrappings for cooked mackerel. Line 3 was not about Hortalus, as Catullus would have called his friend, but the despised Volusius of Hatria whose thousands of lines are long forgotten. He was a nonentity, a prolific but untalented rhymester whose outpourings were as verbose as those of the fifth century BC Antimachus, another vapid buffoon whose works were described by Callimachus as 'fat writing and not lucid'.

That Volusius, a pseudonym for Tanusius Geminus, was indeed the butt of [95] is proved by his presence in another, [36], in which his *Annals* are condemned as 'brimful of lavatorial clumsiness', a criticism made against another native of Padua, Livy. Nor would Catullus have called the orator 'Hortentius'. 'Hortalus' was the usual form of address as [65] showed. But the copyist's blunder left the friend of Catullus an unintended recipient of the poet's scorn. He has remained so almost everywhere. Of twenty-one versions of line 3 known to the author, seventeen use 'Hortentius'. Whigham offered 'Hortalus'; only Goold preferred 'Hatriensis'; Lindsay in 1929 came close with 'hatrian' and then, in 1948, 'Hatrian', adding that Cinna's *Smyrna* 'is contrasted with the *Annals* of Volusius'.[16]

'Hortentius' for 'Hatriensis' was one of the myriad misreadings that Yeats's 'bald heads' had to contend with. In codex 'V' nearly 700 were amended in the fifteenth century, and century by century more were recognized: first eighty-five, then thirty-seven diminishing to sixteen more until in the nineteenth century German scholars found a further 147. With so many corrections it was inevitable that tiny subtleties like 'Hortentius' instead of 'Hatriensis' remain in four-fifths of modern editions.

At the end of the fourteenth century Catullus lingered in three precarious manuscripts, all of them with numerous contradictions and omissions. The frail poems teetered at the edge of extinction for almost a century until 1472 when the first printed edition of his poems was published in Venice.[17] Even then his work was not immediately accepted in the literary circles of Europe. Critics appreciated his longer poems with their heroic lines and vivid imagery. They liked the lyricism of his poems of love:

> My woman says there is no one she would rather wed
> Than me, even if Jupiter himself were her suitor.
> So she says. But what a woman will say to an imploring lover
> Should be written on the wind and engraved on running water.
>
> [70]

But there were many verses that were quite unacceptable. The early eighteenth-century French priest and writer, Fénelon, complained of 'Catullus whose name one can't utter without experiencing horror at his obscenities', perhaps thinking of the uninhibited coarseness of the poem in which Catullus begged Ipsitilla, a highly paid courtesan, to welcome him because

Lying here in bed I've had enough to eat
But hunger for you is causing something
To make a tall pyramid of my sheet.

[32]

Repression of many poems continued well into the late nineteenth century, especially in the sitting-rooms of Victorian England. Sir Richard Burton, explorer and translator of the *Arabian Nights*, was determined to publish an unexpurgated version of the poems. To him the Roman poet was not to be converted into a Victorian gentleman in a 'boiled shirt, dove-tailed coat, black-cloth clothes, white pocket-handkerchief and diamond ring'. But four years after his death in 1890, his sixty-year-old widow published the *Carmina of Gaius Valerius Catullus* with a scurry of asterisks replacing scurrilous lines. As the joint translator, Leonard Smithers, complained, 'Sir Richard laid great stress on the necessity of thoroughly annotating each translation from an erotic (and especially a paederastic) point of view, but subsequent consequences caused me to abandon that intention.'

Lady Isabel Burton burnt the original manuscript in disgust, not having been allowed to see it in preparation. 'NEVER SHEW HALF-FINISHED WORK TO WOMEN OR TO FOOLS,' her husband had decreed. Nor did she show it to Smithers. 'She consistently refused me even a glance at his MS,' he wrote. Unsurprisingly the result was frustrating. In poem [28] part of the verse was published as:

Memmius! Thou didst long and late
*** me supine slow and ***

which told the reader nothing.[18]

A faithful translation of the two lines would read:

Memmius, you had me down, and properly buggered,
Slowly, with the entire length of your tool.

One can understand Lady Burton's repugnance. Ironically, however, Catullus was not admitting homosexuality. He was writing metaphorically about the unscrupulous manner in which Memmius had 'shafted' him financially over the profits from Bithynia.

In 57 BC Gaius Memmius was appointed annual governor of Bithynia on the shores of the Black Sea and took Catullus and a friend with him as members of staff. It was the custom for such appointments to be profitable to everyone by means of taxes, bribes and deals. Thirteen years earlier Gaius

Verres had been made governor of Sicily for an unprecedented three years. He boasted that the first year had made his fortune, the second enough money to hire the best defence lawyers, and the third sufficient to bribe the jurors. He was over-optimistic. Cicero prosecuted him for corruption so successfully that Verres abandoned his trial and retired to Marseilles taking the bulk of his wealth with him.[19]

Memmius was not as rapacious but he was ungenerous. The unrewarded Catullus did not forget but his whimsical revenge did not appeal to Lady Burton.

The censorship continued for years. In 1925, Hugh Macnaghten's *The Poems of Catullus* was addressed to 'Dear men and women, girls and boys' urging them 'to open it, and just to glance, whate'er the page on which you chance ... Catullus is a starry lad', but not telling his readers that forty-one of the 116 'stellar' poems had been excluded.

Not included, of course, was Ipsitilla's [32] but also excluded was [68B] with its entirely decorous references to an affair between Catullus and the married woman that he loved. Waiting alone in a secret house that a friend had found for him, waiting for the first time for her to arrive, waiting in hope and apprehension, he heard

> ...the soft steps of my shining goddess,
> Hesitating at the door's worn sill, pausing there
> With the faint tap-tapping of her sandal
> > (lines 70-2)

And then:

> in that house fragrant with the scents of Assyria,
> during that wondrous night she gave me pleasures
> filched from the lap of her token husband.
> > (lines 144-6)

The unsuccessful obscenity trial of *Lady Chatterley's Lover* in 1960 and the very successful production of the semi-pornographic revue *O Calcutta!* in 1969, with its bold use of the notorious four-letter word, showed how taste was changing. Now there are translations of everything that Catullus wrote, sometimes so intent on defying convention that they diminish the poetry to the standard of lines scrawled on a lavatory wall. Catullus merits gentler treatment. He was a genius. In Ezra Pound's words, even 'the Greeks might be hard put to find a better poet among themselves than in their disciple; Catullus'.[20]

1

CHILDHOOD, YOUTH AND WAR – VERONA, 84-63 BC

Gaius Valerius Catullus is always called a Roman but in reality he was half-Celtic with the mystically poetic imagination of that race. He was born of a wealthy family in Verona, probably in 84 BC.[1] Verona was an important city in Cisalpine Gaul, 'Gaul south of the Alps', a vast region extending southwards to the river Rubicon and northwards to the Alpine mountains, fertile and prosperous and taken under the protection of Rome five years before the poet's birth. It became a full Roman province in 49 BC.

On 28 May, two years after the birth of Catullus, and two hundred or more miles south of Verona in Interamnia, not far from Rome, Marcus Caelius Rufus was born. He was to be a senator, an orator, a man accused of murder, and a rival to the poet over a woman of enviable loveliness. His affair ended bitterly when she had Rufus put on trial, accused of attempting to poison her. The orator Cicero spoke in his defence.

The eighties turned into a decade of violence when two successful generals, Marius and Sulla, turned against each other. Gaius Marius, ageing, half-mad, six times consul, fled from Italy, fearing assassination. Then, campaigning in Sulla's absence in Asia Minor against King Mithridates, he returned to Rome in 87 BC for revenge. Accompanied by hundreds of armed slaves known as *Bardiaei* he marched through the streets. Nervously citizens saluted him. If the greeting was not returned the man was killed. For five days and nights the massacre continued, with the slaughter of hundreds of patricians.

'Headless trunks thrown on to the streets and trampled underfoot' horrified the defenceless city. 'But the people were most provoked by the licence of the *Bardiaei*, who murdered fathers of families in their houses, defiled their children and raped their wives.' The plundering and murder went on until even Marius was sated. Then the slaves 'were killed by Gauls with javelins as they slept'.[2] Marius died the following year.

The first century BC was a time of continuing unrest. At the end of the second the Republic had suffered two vicious rebellions of slaves in Sicily, the Servile Wars of 135 and 104 BC. Overseas, Roman legions were fighting against Jugurtha in Africa and Mithridates in Asia Minor. Even earlier there had been a brutal civil war between well-to-do diehards in the Senate, landlords with great estates – the *optimates* – determined to retain power and privilege, and their rabble-rousing opponents, usually tribunes such as the Gracchi brothers, who appealed directly to the popular assemblies – *populares* – to assist the impoverished citizens and farmers dispossessed of their land.

Everywhere there was struggle. To the savagely repressed slaves and the impoverished peasants was added the discontent of tribes in central and southern Italy, who rebelled in the so-called Social Wars of 90-88 BC, resentful that they had not been granted Roman citizenship. The first year went so badly for Rome that in 89 BC the Senate did offer citizen status for any tribe that laid down its arms. Only the Lucanians and Samnites continued to resist. Short-sightedly but predictably the senators cheated. Citizenship was given to no more than ten of the thirty-five tribes involved, so that even if they were near enough to Rome to attend an election they could always be outvoted by the citizens of Rome itself.

One outcome of that conflict was that the people of Cisalpine Gaul became Latins but not full Romans, awarded the *ius Latii*, 'Latin right', a halfway stage to Roman citizenship with a status equivalent to the Latin colonies.[3]

Verona was a town loyal to Rome but it was a loyalty based on self-interest. Just over a hundred years before the birth of Catullus it had sided with Hannibal as he destroyed Roman army after army in a series of brilliant battles.

By 89 BC the city, lying between the Alpine foothills and the river Po, was already an important trading centre. Its 'latinization' may have been incomplete but for centuries it had been hellenized and Greek influence was strong. Originally an Etruscan settlement it was invaded in the early fourth century by a mixture of Celts from Brixia, modern Brescia, and Rhaetic Gauls from the Retiche Alps near Zurich. Under Brennus they descended from the mountains to occupy Verona, overrunning the Etruscans. Brennus went on to sack Rome in 390 BC.

Verona was small. Built inside the cramped ox-bow bend of the river Adige it was no more than two-thirds of a mile from north to south and only half that across. But it was well fortified with high walls, stretches of which still stand. And it quickly adopted Roman customs. Towards the end of the first century BC there was a theatre on the far side of the river, one of the best preserved in northern Italy. Class distinction provided semicircles of comfortable stone benches near the stage. High above them was the cramped seating for ordinary citizens.

Decades later a gigantic amphitheatre was raised outside the city's southern gate. It was the finest outside Rome, second only to the Colosseum in size. Today its well-preserved exterior, galleries and arena form one of the most impressive of these spectacles of death.

Pliny called Verona the town of Raeti (Gauls) and Eugani (Etruscans). Verona became Celtic-Etruscan, a place where fair-haired Celts in leggings were commonplace. Togas were the exception. By the time of Catullus the majority of Verona's people were 'tall, husky blue-eyed celts, dressed in breeches and blankets. On market-days the long-haired raetic tribesmen, girded with daggerbelts, came down from the Alps and the Venetic peasants plodding in with their donkey-packs of wool and wheat and copperware. Here and there was a burly teuton trader, who had brought amber and furs and war captives all the way over the Brenner Pass to trade for wine, steel blades, glass beads and pretty scarves, or a group of short stocky etruscans from their mountain refuge, over Lake Garda where the celts three centuries before had driven their ancestors.'4

Catullus was born into riches. In three or four generations his prospering family was steadily elevated from the social status of *equites*, businessmen, to the highest, reaching senatorial rank under Augustus and consular under Tiberius. By then they had a palatial villa at Sirmio. Towards the end of the second century BC, Valerius, soldier and grandfather of Catullus, chose a strongly defensible site at the far end of the narrow peninsula, a villa that was enlarged ,and aggrandized within a century. The father of Catullus was one of the wealthiest, most prominent citizens of Verona, entertaining Julius Caesar when he was governor of the province.5

The family had interests in Italy and abroad. In his *Catullus and His World* Wiseman speculated that their wealth came from tax-farming and exporting from Bithynia south of the Black Sea in Asia Minor, explaining Catullus' brother's presence there and the poet's own willingness to visit the country. Such business transactions would explain the poet's familiarity with the method of counting money, fingers flicking beads across an abacus. One can almost hear the clicking.6

> Kiss me a thousand kisses, then a hundred,
> A second thousand succeeded by a hundred,
> Yet count a thousand more, one more hundred,
> Again a thousand and again a hundred,
> Until with all the thousands we collected
> Our kissing is concluded...(p. 223)
>
> [5]

It was a well-to-do social background that ensured a good education and an upbringing of luxury and privilege. But it was not a time of peace. When Catullus was two years old a reign of terror across the whole of Italy resulted in almost 5,000 enemies of Sulla being put to death. Years before that, two dangerous opponents of Rome had been defeated.

Jugurtha, king of Numidia (now Tunisia) had offended Rome but had resisted all efforts to defeat him. After three generals failed Marius was sent in 107 BC but was just as unsuccessful. It was Sulla two years later who captured the king by persuading his father-in-law to betray him in exchange for a bribe. Jugurtha was taken to Rome, paraded in chains to Marius' vainglorious and unjustified triumph, and then, on the first day of the new year, 104 BC, was lowered down the shaft of the foul, domed, subterranean chamber of the Tullianum prison where executioners waited to strangle him.[7]

Two decades later, king Mithridates of Pontus, now eastern Turkey, rose against Rome. Conquering neighbouring kingdoms, invading Greece where he had 80,000 Italians put to death in reprisal for the exorbitant taxes levied by Rome, his armies were finally overcome by Sulla in an incisive campaign and in 85 BC the king was compelled to give up his foreign lands, surrender eighty galleys and pay a fine of 3,000 gold talents. Asia Minor was even more unlucky. For its part in the revolt a tribute of 20,000 talents was demanded, a ruinous and unpayable sum. The dilemma was solved by Roman money-lenders at an outrageous profit.[8]

Years later, by 63 BC, Mithridates was dethroned and deserted. He tried to commit suicide by poison, but found it impossible: for years, fearing assassination, he had been taking draughts of toxic herbs such as rue to immunize himself. In the end he was slain by his guards.[9]

It was a century of conquest. By the end of the century Rome would dominate the Mediterranean and Europe: Spain, France, Yugoslavia, Bulgaria, Greece, Asia Minor, Syria, northern Egypt, the northern coastline of Africa, all were hers. Grain, food, luxuries, taxes and slaves were gathered in for the benefit of Rome. Following the truce there was a millionaire's fortune in plunder for Sulla to bring to Rome. Meanwhile, in 83 BC, laden with ransacked booty and attended by his legions, Lucius Cornelius Sulla, patrician and social superior to the 'knight' Marius, landed at Brundisium and marched up the Appian Way to Rome. There was one last battle at the Colline Gate on the Quirinal Hill in 82 BC when Samnites and their tribal allies attempted to storm the city but were overcome and butchered. Then, while Catullus was still an infant, the terror began.

Sulla proclaimed himself dictator and was addressing the Senate in the Temple of Bellona, explaining the constitutional changes he proposed to introduce, when shouting and screams could be heard from the Circus Flaminius nearby. Sulla reassured his audience. 'They are only a few rebels I have ordered to be chastised.' The 'few' were several hundred dead.

It was the beginning, not the end. Lists of proscriptions were drafted against 'outlaws and enemies of the State', not only political rivals but names of anyone disliked by Sulla's friends or of anybody who owned a desirable property. A military colleague of Sulla, Crassus, acquired sprawling estates for almost nothing.

The first list of those to be exterminated contained eighty names. The second, 220, the third the same number as more candidates entered Sulla's vindictive mind. Forty senators were slain, 1600 *equites*, killed by Sulla's 10,000-strong 'bodyguard', the Cornelii. 'Slaves brought the heads of their masters, sons had no compunction in killing their fathers.' A computed total of 5,000 deaths is conservative.

One who escaped was the seventeen-year-old Julius Caesar, who was married to Cornelia, daughter of Cinna, colleague of and co-consul with Marius. Sulla commanded him to divorce her, he refused and was proscribed. Caesar fled to the anonymity of the Sabine Hills where he contracted malaria as he skulked from hiding-place to hiding-place in the marshy countryside. He reached safety only in 81 BC when he joined the staff of Minucius Thermus, governor of Asia Minor, who was ordered to take his army to Mitylene on the island of Lesbos to besiege Mithridates, who had started yet another war against Rome, his second of three.[10]

These were brutal yet creative years. Throughout Italy men feared for their families and their lives. However, Gaius Licinius Macer Calvus, poet and close friend of Catullus, was born, Italy's first gladiatorial amphitheatre was erected at Pompeii around 80 BC, and the twenty-four-year-old Marcus Tullius Cicero attended lectures on public speaking. In 80 BC Cicero defended Sextus Roscius, who was accused of his own father's murder. This must have taken courage as the accuser was Chrysogonus, ex-slave and protégé of Sulla. But the orator proved that the freed man was guilty of corruption, of wanting Roscius dead to acquire his father's estate. Nevertheless it could have been a death sentence for Cicero, who subsequently withdrew to Greece until Sulla died.[11]

Sulla ignored the matter, concentrating on reform and giving more power to the Senate, reducing the power of the people's tribunes and limiting debates in the popular assemblies to subjects permitted by the Senate. Then, abruptly, in 79 BC, he resigned, abandoning everything to retire to Puteoli between the resort of Baiae and Naples. For a year he led a life of debauchery, with drunken feasting in the disreputable company of actors, actresses, musicians, prostitutes, the notorious female impersonator Metrobius, and the comforts of the beautiful and rich courtesan, Nicopolis. In 78 BC, suffering from phthiriasis, an infestation of lice, and very ill, Sulla was enraged to learn that a magistrate had deliberately delayed the payment of a debt in the hope that Sulla's imminent death would save him. Sulla had him choked in his presence and promptly died himself of a burst blood vessel.[12]

Almost immediately his reforms were undone. Struggles between the landed aristocracy and the landless commoners resumed against the background of renewed military threats from which the unarmed senators were defenceless. An imaginary picture of the men known to Catullus in Rome might be likened to a nineteenth-century oil painting of a society wedding – bride, groom and parents in the foreground, relatives and colleagues behind them, and at the rear the lesser guests and the vitally important but almost unrecognizable caterers and servants.

For Catullus, the first group consisted of his closest friends and poets: Licinius Calvus, with whom he passed a laughing afternoon exchanging erotic verses, Helvius Cinna, who spent nine years on the composition of an epic poem, Cornelius Nepos, who was entrusted with the 'littlenbook' of Catullus.

Behind those intimates were acquaintances such as Caelius Rufus, orator, lawyer and rival for the woman Catullus loved. There was also Clodius Pulcher, patrician, tribune and demagogic rabble-rouser, who was involved in an irreligious sexual scandal shortly before Catullus came to the capital around 60 BC.

It is the third group that intrigues – almost in shadow, the four men standing there were the great figures of the middle of the century, dominating politics, commanding armies, yet hardly mentioned by Catullus in his writings: Pompey the Great; Crassus, known as Dives, 'the rich'; and Cicero whose career was different. The fourth man, Julius Caesar, was the exception.

Gnaeus Pompeius, nicknamed Magnus, 'the Great', by Sulla for his military exploits, had been a distinguished lieutenant of the dictator, defeating his enemies. Later, appointed governor of Spain, he proved himself a competent general and a man of ambition. From his conquests a succulence of fruit trees was sent to Italy.

Marcus Licinius Crassus, more than ten years older than the others,[13] had commanded Sulla's right-wing against the Samnites at the Colline Gate in 82 BC. During the proscriptions he bought cheaply everywhere, accumulated extensive areas of cultivated farming land, *latifundia*, invested in blocks of slum tenements, owned silver mines, and astutely recognized that burning buildings were benefits. He offered derisory sums to owners of neighbouring properties as they waited for their own houses to catch fire. Crassus haggled with the helpless men, won, paid, and sent in his fire-fighting teams of 500 specially trained slaves to quell the blaze.

In the late sixties Crassus was accused of the serious crime of immorality with a Vestal Virgin, Licinia, in whose company he was frequently seen and whom he visited privately. He was put on trial and prosecuted by Plotinus. If found guilty the penalty for him was death, for her to be buried alive. But his attentions were caused by lust not for her body but her belongings. She owned an attractive estate in the suburbs of Rome that Crassus coveted, although only at an uninviting price. He was so well-known for his avarice that he was instantly believed and acquitted. He continued visiting Licinia and eventually persuaded her to sell.[14]

Marcus Tullius Cicero had also fought in the Social War against the Samnites as a military tribune under Pompey's father. He was to become famous as an orator and notorious for his conceit and venality, willingly defending a client one year and just as willingly prosecuting him the next if there was any political advantage.

Towering above these exceptional men was Gaius Julius Caesar. He had not fought in the wars. He was, wrote the historian Suetonius, 'tall, fair and well-built, with a rather broad face and keen, dark-brown eyes. His health was sound ... He was something of a dandy, always keeping his head carefully trimmed and shaved.' He became bald but 'used to comb the thin strands of hair forward from his poll'.[15]

Caesar and the three others were men whose decisions and actions affected the development of Roman institutions, men whose deeds resulted in the collapse of the Republic and the beginning of the empire and the tyranny of emperors. To the poets, living in their dreams, however, it was inconsequential.

They lived in an age of turmoil. Wars were being fought in Africa, Asia Minor, in Spain and Gaul, and there was a third uprising of slaves. The frustrations of an unelected patrician, Catiline, caused a blood-drenched rebellion. There were illegal executions, trials for corruption and murder. Yet none of this appeared in the poetry. Political matters affecting the life of every Roman citizen were the disregarded items of an unread news bulletin.

The poets were like men preoccupied in conversation who happened to be passing through a riot in the streets, oblivious to the sounds of doors being smashed down, the smoke of burning tenements, the shrieks of the injured, the crashing of stones ricocheting off walls, engrossed in a debate as to which metre was most suited to an epigram, interested in the latest gossip but ignoring the history of the world. To them Great Men were no more than wraiths, far away and voiceless unless their private lives encouraged a scurrilous quip, and some did.

Crassus was ignored. Cicero merited one ambiguous verse from Catullus. Calvus did refer to Pompey but only to ridicule his homosexuality. In translation there are two very different interpretations of his quatrain. Both are derogatory.

There stands the Mighty Man, we see,
Concerned, bewildered in his head.
What troubles his Pomposity?
How to get a man to bed!

Pompey's an attractive girlie,
With a 'how-about it?' air too.
Ruffling breezes make him surly
They muss his scented, curly hair-do.[16]

In poem [57] Catullus accused Julius Caesar of the same perversion – with some justification.

Calvus and Catullus felt able to broadcast their libels with no fear of the assassin's dagger. Within three decades that impunity vanished. When the emperor Augustus wrote insults about him, the poet Asinius Pollio was asked why he did not retaliate. 'It's hard to write a poem about a man who can write your death warrant,' he replied. The danger was real. In AD 23 Aelius Saturninus was thrown off Rome's Tarpeian Rock for his scurrilous verses against the emperor Tiberius. Yet Catullus had no such concern when he described the sexual foibles of Julius Caesar.[17]

Caesar had the enviable reputation of attracting beautiful women, usually married ones. But on the expedition with Minucius Thermus in Bithynia such fame turned to infamy. There was derisive laughter amongst the common people of Rome and disgusted contempt amongst the morally upright patricians.

In 80 BC he had been sent to Bithynia to demand that its king, Nicomedes IV, 'Philopater, a sad creature, greedy and cruel', should send a promised fleet to blockade the port of Mitylene on Lesbos against Mithridates. The court of Nicomedes was debauched, corrupt and filled with a harem of lipstick-painted youths. The youthful Caesar enchanted the king, who was so enamoured that he insisted that the Roman should sleep in the royal chamber with its golden bed and luxurious hangings. Next day, against austere Roman tradition, Caesar acted as the king's attentive cup-bearer during a long, voluptuous banquet. At its conclusion he retired, but not alone. Cicero wrote about it in a letter. 'Caesar was led by Nicomedes' attendants to the royal bedchamber, where he lay on a golden couch, dressed in a purple shift ... So this descendant of Venus lost his virginity in Bithynia.'[18]

News of the sodomy reached Rome: it was not the overt homosexuality that scandalized people, although it was unpopular, but for an official representing Rome 'to prostitute oneself with a barbarian' was a social crime. Caesar was unabashed and having gone to Mitylene with the ships he returned to Bithynia 'on the pretext of having to deliver a sum due to some client of his who had been set free'. Rome jeered. The incorruptible senator, Curio the Elder, condemned Caesar as 'every woman's husband, and every man's wife'. During Caesar's victories in Gaul his legionaries had a marching-song:

Caesar is triumphant. Gaul is screwed and dead.
Nicomedes' only triumph – screwing Caesar in his bed.

The insult by Catullus was at another time and named another man, Mamurra, Caesar's *Magister fabrum*, chief engineer in Gaul.

What a fairy pair of faggots, what a thorough
Brace of buggers, homo Caesar, gay Mamurra.

[57]

But that was in years to come. In 80 BC Catullus was four years old and about to begin his formal education.

There were schools but their teachers demanded fees and so most Italians remained semi-literate. For those families that could afford it education at these *ludi* began around the age of five and continued until eleven. Girls finished their formal instruction then, many marrying a year later. Children of the rich remained at home with a private tutor, often a scholarly slave.

It was rote learning, and consisted of the fundamental three 'Rs' of reading, writing and arithmetic, chanting the twenty-two letters of the Roman alphabet, I and J, U and V being interchangeable; there was no W or Y. Both Latin and Greek were taught, through conversation, learning their grammar and writing on wax tablets with a metal stylus, the better-off having the luxury of papyrus and a reed pen, using ink of gum and soot. For the wealthy there could also be a bronze inkwell coated with black niello and engraved with mythological scenes in silver and gold. Arithmetic was limited to the awkward Roman numerals still to be seen on many town-hall clocks: I, V, X, L, C, D, M, clumsy, slow for addition and subtraction, very difficult for multiplication and division. Children learned to use the counting-frame of an abacus, pushing its *calculi*, the stone beads, to and fro as they added or took away. It was a repetitive means of teaching but effective for willing students. Each day sons would recite to their fathers, painfully wary of mistakes.

For the older boys education was more interesting, though just as demanding. It included history, philosophy, geography, geometry, music and astronomy. From the age of fifteen a boy could remove the child's medallion from his neck, exchange the scarlet-hemmed toga for the plain white, and start to study literature: classical Greek authors such as Homer, Aeschylus, Sophocles, Euripides and Menander; and Latin works, such as: the *Annales* epic of Quintus Ennius, the *Poem of the Punic War* epic by Naevius about the first war between Rome and Carthage, and other solemn writers of solemn subjects. Only Plautus, comic poet and playwright, with his perfect use of metre, offered any lighthearted relief.

Finally there was rhetoric, the art of public speaking, an essential ability for any ambitious man. The richest families sent their sons to Athens or Rhodes to be 'finished' by the very best Greek rhetoricians. Training could last years; Cicero continued studying until he was thirty.

And so it was – in Verona during the colder months, at the villa at Sirmio in summer – that Catullus steadily became a scholar proficient in his studies, involved in the business concerns of his family.

West of Verona, stretching almost three miles from the southern shores of Lake Garda, is the long, narrow Sirmione peninsula. Sirmio in Roman times was an important posting-station and one of the largest granaries in Cisalpine Gaul. Today it is a lucratively crowded tourist resort. Northwards the land is hillier and more wooded, with splendid views across the lake, the ridge of Monte Baldo to the east, jagged peaks to the west, mountains far to the north. Catullus loved the cliffs above the lucidly blue waters.

Of almost-islands and of islands
Sirmio is the loveliest of Neptune's waters
in lakes or in the spreading seas

...

Salutations, Sirmio, from your master,
delighting to be home once more. (p. 226)

[31]

It is not always peaceful. Winds blow off the Dolomites and the still waters of the lake can be whipped up into waves as surging and as dangerous as those at sea, and then subside as suddenly. 'The violent and abrupt changes of mood which characterize the lake are also characteristic of Catullus' poetry,' observes one translator.[19] Immense ruins rise here at the end of the peninsula. There are stone and brick rooms, archways, cellars, walls twenty feet high [6m], a confusion so complete that fifteenth-century explorers thought that these were subterranean dwellings. Knowing of the associations with Catullus they called the underground bewilderment the 'grotte di Catullo', the cave of Catullus.

Much lay buried until the end of the eighteenth century. By the middle of the next it was decided that these were the remains of a Roman spa. Excavations in 1939-40 and 1948 proved that these were not baths, nor a monastery, below-ground homes or a theatre but the gaunt skeleton of the 'biggest Roman villa in the north of Italy' – a huge L-shaped complex almost 200 yards long by 115 yards wide (167 x 105m), with a spacious garden and olive orchard between its arms, a building that had been constructed in the early first century BC and extended early in the next. The early dates coincide with those for Catullus and the long oral tradition supports the likelihood that this was where the poet lived.

Visitors stroll through the roofless rooms, along verandas, on terraces around the rectangular garden, see the adjacent hot, warm and cold baths to the south. To the north is the domestic area, the *atrium* or reception room, the *triclinium* for dining, the bedrooms, a study. Everywhere among the tall, bleached walls are the faded remains of frescoes and murals, weathered mosaics, everything of considerable, costly quality.

At the entrance to the site is a small museum. Amongst the artefacts on display is a broken fresco labelled '10. Poeta', depicting a young man, dark-haired, in an ankle-length toga, bare-footed. His left hand holds a scroll. Popularly and understandably it is known as a 'portrait' of Catullus. Possibly it is, 'Handsome ... strong mouth, gaiety in the eyes, nut-brown complexion... could even be a likeness of the poet.'[20]

In 76 BC, when Catullus was eight, Caesar sailed for Rhodes to study under the famous 'rhetors' but was captured by pirates, always a threat in the Mediterranean. For over five weeks he was a comfortable and confident captive, joking, rebuking his captors when he wished to sleep, mocking them because their demanded ransom of twenty *talents* was an insult to his social standing. Fifty would be appropriate. He added that when he was released he would crucify them.

He meant it. The ransom was paid, he went to Miletus, obtained a ship, knew that the pirates would be drunkenly celebrating, caught most of them and had them crucified. Before erecting their crosses 'he first mercifully cut their throats'.[21] Suetonius remarked on his clemency.

Piracy was finally eliminated ten years later when Pompey, 'a man of consular rank', was proposed as an admiral with 'absolute power and authority in all the seas within the Pillars of Hercules'. That any citizen should be elevated to the status of near-dictator shocked many senators and there was furious opposition to the recommendation in the *Curia*, the Senate House. Protests ceased when a crow flying over the Forum fell dead. Pompey was appointed.

In March 66 BC he divided the Mediterranean into thirteen segments, each with its own squadron of forty fighting-ships, heavy quinqueremes with five slaves to an oar, and faster, more manoeuvrable triremes with three banks of oars. Straits were blocked. Strongholds and island settlements were attacked. It was all over in three months.[22]

Pompey had already distinguished himself, defeating rebels in Italy and then conducting a long, victorious campaign in Spain before returning to Italy in 71 BC. Crassus had contentedly made himself a millionaire. Cicero's career was different. Widely respected for his daring defence of Sextius Roscius, Cicero stood for the post of *quaestor* in 76 BC and was elected. For an ambitious man hoping to reach the highest post in the Republic, a consulship, two difficult offices had to be attained first. The first was that of quaestor, a junior magistrate and finance officer. The second was to become a *praetor*, one of two senior judges. Only a praetor could become a consul.

A quaestorship, for men over twenty-five years of age, was the lowest and the easiest office to achieve because there were twenty positions, elected annually. The appointment was for a year, and led to automatic membership of the Senate and, at the end of the twelve months, appointment to an overseas province for a further year to assist the governor in the administration of finances and the collection of taxes. Cicero was sent to western Sicily, where he worked meticulously and honestly and was proud of his work. He was taken aback on his return to Rome to find that no one had missed him nor knew of his achievements.[23]

Of the praetors, they were second only to the consuls in importance and power and took their place if the consul was absent on military duty. At the end of his year a praetor became a *propraetor* or governor of a province for another twelve months. Many ex-praetors stood for election as a consul. Few were successful.

Consuls were pre-eminent in power, in responsibility and appearance, at least thirty-six years old, usually forty to forty-five. Whereas senators wore the traditional plain white toga, a consul's had a broad purple band. He wore red sandals and when in the streets was accompanied by an escort of *lictors*, attendants, each carrying the *fasces*, the axe bound in rods that symbolized the weapons used to execute malefactors. A consul was supreme both in civic and military power, riding at the head of legions marching against an enemy. With so many foreign wars and civil conflicts, most consuls already had experience of troops and fighting. This was true of both Pompey and of Crassus.[24]

The four years from 76 to 73 BC were vibrant with history but a history hardly affecting the boy Catullus as he neared the end of his first period of learning. Battles in Spain, the second Mithridatic War were important but remote. The events of the three years that followed brought danger much closer to Verona.

The year 73 BC began undramatically. Cicero's dominating but wealthy wife, Terentia, nagged him to prosecute the patrician Catiline because he had seduced Fabia, who was both half-sister to Terentia and a Vestal Virgin. As a young man Catiline had been involved in various scandalous episodes but what had happened with Fabia or with Cicero remains unknown. He survived.

It was not suspected sexual peccadilloes in Rome that alarmed Cisalpine Gaul. It was the escape of a Thracian shepherd from the gladiatorial barracks at Capua near Pompeii, 350 miles south of Verona, and the beginning of the third Servile War. The shepherd's name was Spartacus.

Over the entrance to a house in Pompeii there is a sketch of two mounted gladiators with lances and round shields. The name of one begins 'Phili ...'. The other is complete – 'Spartaks' – and the date of the writing and the unusual Thracian name, Spartacus, could mean that this is a drawing of the man who would defeat Roman army after Roman army over three years. As Pompeii is less than thirty miles from Capua it is feasible that he had been taken there to fight in the arena.[25]

With seventy-four others, armed with kitchen knives, they slashed and stabbed their ways to freedom, seized wagons laden with weapons for the barracks and took refuge in the crater of Vesuvius. Runaway slaves joined them. An unconcerned Senate sent a praetor, Gaius Claudius Glaber, to end the nuisance. He camped at the foot of the volcano. Spartacus and his half-trained rabble clambered down the steep slopes using vines, surprised the Romans and routed them. More men joined the uprising. They defeated another army and began to enjoy the success and freedom. They took towns and ravaged them. The fifth-century historian Orosius recorded that 'wherever they went the slaves indiscriminately mixed slaughter with arson, theft and rape'. They trained new arrivals until there were over 100,000 men in their ranks. But they were weak. Like an eighteenth-century pirate captain in the West Indies Spartacus had total power in battle but off the battlefield he was just one more man.[26]

Realizing that the 'nuisance' was a threat, the Senate followed tradition and sent two consuls to suppress the rebels. One of the two, Lucius Gellius Poplicola, encountered a breakaway army of Germans led by Crixus and massacred them. The other consul, Gaius Cornelius Lentulus, met Spartacus and was badly beaten. The son of Poplicola, also Gellius, was later viciously lampooned by Catullus in epigram after epigram:

> What can the vile Gellius be doing? Wriggling in bed,
> naked one night, with mother and sister,
> another being the 'husband' in place of his uncle ...
> [88][27]

Spartacus, his better-organized troops equipped with legionary armour and weapons, went northwards towards the Alps and the security of Gaul. Frightened farmers, families and villagers rushed to the walls of Verona. When Catullus was twelve, half-attentive to history, astronomy and geometry, the horde reached Modena, only fifty miles away. Then news came that the murderous mob had turned back. Legions and danger lay ahead. Plunder and pleasure lay behind.

In the absence of Pompey in Spain the Senate put the militarily ambitious Crassus in charge of six legions. He made an astonishing misjudgement, as there was neither honour nor respect to be gained from defeating slaves.

Against Spartacus, however, he was decisive. A legate, Mummius, disobeyed orders and recklessly attacked Spartacus with savage losses. Crassus picked 500 of Mummius' disgraced troops, divided 'them into fifty groups of ten and had his centurions choose one from each to be cruelly and publicly executed.

Spartacus went to the south of Italy, hoping to reach Sicily and raise another rebellion there. The ships promised by pirates and paid for were never sent. There was one final battle at the river Silanus in 71 BC. Crassus was victorious and took prisoners, but the corpse of Spartacus was never found. (In London on April Fool's Day, 1865, the daughter of Karl Marx asked her father the name of his greatest hero. 'Spartacus', the Communist replied.[28])

Five thousand of the slaves had fled from the field but were rounded up by Pompey on his timely return to Italy. For that, and for his achievements overseas, he was awarded a triumph through the applauding streets of Rome. Crassus, who had actually won the war, was permitted a mere *ovatio*, the meanest of concessions because he had overcome only slaves, not proper soldiers. His crown was myrtle, not the prestigious laurel.[29]

But Crassus fashioned his own triumph. The Appian Way, that great highway engineered by the orders of Appius Claudius Caecus in 312 BC, was a splendour of cemented octagonal blocks of granite and basalt, stretching 136 Roman miles from Capua to Rome.

Capua, the chief town of Campania, on the river Volturno a few miles from the sea, was famous for its perfume factories. Oils and essences for its luxurious and costly scents were shipped in from the Mediterranean: oil of roses from Egypt, lilies from Sheba, poppies from Galilee, oil of ambergris, rinds of lemons and oranges, the fragrance of sage and mint, of rosewood and sandalwood, pungent odours, subtle aromas. Capua smelt of paradise and its creations were the expensive indulgences of an opulent Rome.[30]

But in 71 BC that delightful air was fouled with the sickly stench of rotting human flesh. Crassus had his 6,000 captives crucified along the Appian Way on either side of the road, his commercial mind having them arithmetically spaced every fifty Roman paces, hanging, slumping, writhing on their crosses until the flesh decayed and the bones fell apart.[31]

In 70 BC Pompey and Crassus, loathing each other, were elected joint consuls. It was an uneasy partnership and partly illegal. Pompey was too young for the office but with two armies camped outside Rome the Senate did not quibble over a nicety. The new consuls instituted changes. Sulla's constitutional reforms were minimized, the people's tribunes were reinstated. Jury courts, once the sole right of senators, were opened to the *equites*, the businessmen or traders. The rank of censor was reintroduced, with two ex-praetors assuming this role as guardians of public morality, organizers of population censuses and critics of unworthy senators. Sixty-four senators were expelled. This was welcomed and made even more pleasing by the allocation of free corn to 40,000 male citizens. Crassus made himself even more popular by paying for an enormous free banquet of 10,000 tables.[32]

It was an appropriate year for Cicero to impeach the former governor of Sicily, Gaius Verres. As a dishonest praetor in Rome he had been disgracefully guided by the courtesan, Chelidon. During his unprecedented three years as governor in Sicily he followed the even greedier advice of another courtesan, Tertia. Verres had to flee from Rome before the end of his trial. The following year Cicero became a *curile aedile*, a commissioner of public buildings, temples and markets. One year later, prospering, he purchased a villa in Formiae and another in Tusculum.[33]

It was also the time when Catullus was old enough to exchange the boyish toga praetexta, with its purple hem, for the man's white toga. His toys, childish things and clothes were burnt as offerings to his family's household gods, the *lares*, at the shrine at the centre of his home. Slaves dressed him carefully in his new, proud toga over a belted tunic. Trousers were thought to be unmanly.

A toga was large, difficult to put on and ungainly unless properly arranged. Too high and too tight, it proclaimed its wearer a clumsy bumpkin. Too loose and too long suggested effeminacy in an age when manliness and virility were indispensable attributes of a Roman. Only will-power prevented Sulla from hitting the foppish Julius Caesar, whose floppy gown had a belt hanging 'fetchingly around the hips'.[34]

A toga was a sartorial challenge that only the rich could meet successfully. A capacious semicircle of wool perhaps eighteen feet across and seven feet deep (5.5 x 2.1m) it was draped from behind, its left end hung over the left shoulder to fall in front of the body. A large fold from the centre of the right was taken around the right hip and passed over the left shoulder to lie behind the back. What remained of the right also went over the left shoulder. Finally, the straight edge of the left end was tucked into the tunic's belt. Every pleat, every fold had to be perfect, the right shoulder left exposed in its tunic.

Understandably togas were disliked. They were heavy, difficult to put on, costly to clean, but they were distinctive and proclaimed citizenship. For funerals, togas were black. Tunics were preferred for every day wear, a woollen cloak, the *pallium*, over them in cold weather. In the early second century AD Juvenal wrote sarcastically, 'We may as well face the truth. In most of Italy no one puts on a toga until he's dead.'[35]

Still, none of this would have bothered a young man in his first proper toga. And there were also additional delights for a well-educated youth in the form of poetry and girls:

> I put on the white toga. I was a man,
>   those were the young green years of a Spring

when I discovered girls, and the sweet but bitter
companionship of the Muse of poetry.

[68A]

As for the girls, he learned from willing participants. For the poetry it is
probable that he had the guidance and encouragement of the famous 'neoteric'
or new poet, Publius Valerius Cato of Verona. A contemporary of Catullus,
Furius Bibaculus, praised him.

Cato grammaticus, Latina Siren
qui solus legit ac facit poetas.

Cato, teacher, singer of the Latin song, who
alone knows talent, he alone can make a poet.

Cato, a freedman, had prospered but suffered under Sulla, having to sell
his Tuscan house to pay off debts, and by 40 BC, very old, he died in poverty.
During his career he attracted many students, some of them to become
distinguished. To them he preached the virtues of Alexandrian brevity rather
than the tedium of long drawn-out Roman epics.

Before the time of Cato's influential teaching, an aspiring Roman poet
was expected to follow the accepted forms of epic and tragedy with some
comedy and satire. But now there came the innovations of love poems and
wit in the sharp epigrams of poets such as Callimachus of Cyrene, librarian
at Alexandria in the mid-third century BC. That poet's advice was to keep
the Muse, his inspiration, slim and slender, and the poetry slight and closely
woven. Some had their doubts.

Critics everywhere! It's me they dog,
no poet, him, a jumped-up clever-clog,
a line a day, then another, one by one
until the 'mini epic's done.

...

Ignore them. Keep poems short,
melodious, light, length's a disaster.
Leave saga-verse to Zeus. He's the master!

Aetia, I.[36]

This was new. It was personal. And Catullus was to excel in this unusual kind
of poetry. From him came delightful lyrics, lovely verses and obscenity. At first
his was poetry with a Veronese accent, with Celtic words, but those words were

controlled and by the time that he reached Rome they had almost gone. What grew was confidence, craftsmanship and laughter. Bitterness came later.

It is unlikely that many lines of these early 'five-finger exercises' are included in today's editions of Catullus. One or two of the better ones may have been revised and improved but of the 116 poems that we have maybe only three have come from this period. They were perhaps the results of challenges set by Valerius Cato to test Catullus' ability to translate from Greek [66], to write in a difficult metre [17] and to use an Alexandrian elegy to comic effect [67].

Poem [66] is a direct translation of the elegant couplets of Callimachus about the 'Lock of Berenice'. Married to the pharaoh Ptolemy III, who was at war in Syria, his queen Berenice vowed to cut off all her hair if he returned safely. She kept her promise and her tresses were reverently placed in a temple. They then vanished. The astronomer Conon ingeniously explained that they had been transformed into a lovely constellation he had just discovered, the *Coma Berenices* between Virgo and the Great Bear.

The poem was a conceit but a light-hearted one. E. A. Havelock (1939), who could only visualize Catullus as a lyric poet, dismissed the translation as 'a piece of hack-work written to order', which it might have been if Cato had asked for it. If hack-work then many good poets would envy its quality. The fortunate survival of the poems of Catullus has been described. There was another means of avoiding oblivion. The translation by Catullus contains ninety-four lines. Of the original Greek there are only a few lines surviving from two imperfect papyri and one or two scraps. But Catullus had used the complete poem and line for line his translation was faithful. Years later, maybe added to and polished, it remained good enough for Catullus to send it to a friend, Quintus Hortensius Hortalus, who had asked for a poem [65].[37]

Other early examples of a young man learning his profession can be seen in items of local interest in Verona. K. P. Harrington thought so and translated Catullus, 'When my blooming youth was enjoying its merry springtime I made merry enough in light verse', and added that poems [17] and [67] could 'belong to this youthful period. They certainly exhibit the intimate knowledge of the gossip of the day that we should expect to find in a young man about town.'[38]

Poem [17] concerned a complacent husband and a decaying bridge in the city. It is a clever piece, displaying conscious wit, technical proficiency and an anxiety to prove that provincial Verona did have links with civilized Rome. There must have been local tittle-tattle about the gullible old man who never bothered about his young wife's extramarital engagements. In Roman times it was quite common for young women to marry much older men but the majority were not allowed the licence of the one in Verona. Charles Badham, nineteenth-century classicist, caught the mood if not the metre and length of line of Catullus:

There's a bride
That is tied
To this nincompoop fellow;
A neat little thing
In her bloomiest Spring
As soft as a kid,
To be guarded and hid
Like grapes that are mellow.
But he's blind to the risk,
Lets her gambol and frisk ...[39]

(Badham, 1813-84)

Catullus might have wished for some personal involvement. He fantasized about a rustic festival in the city with people dancing on the treacherous bridge and of the husband tumbling into the marsh below. 'Catullus, evidently not unmoved by her charms, would like to see the town's rickety bridge collapse under him.' It was a direct association with a ritual in Rome in which straw puppets were thrown into the Tiber, itself a half-forgotten memory of a superstitious custom, the *sexagenarios de ponte deiere*, when sixty-year-old men were sacrificed as offerings to the river-god to ensure the continuing strength of the bridge.[40]

Cato might have asked his pupil to write something in a very rare metre, the Priapean, and this allowed Catullus a subtle in-joke. He used the metre of Priapus, a god notorious for his voracious sexual appetite, in a poem about a husband incapable of sex. The metre, like others in classical languages, was expressed in the length, not the stress, of syllables: long (——) and short (U) in lines of:

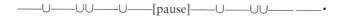

J. Michie translated it perfectly as the first line shows:

Verona, you possess an ancient bridge on which ...
                    (Michie, 1981, p. 45)

Whereas the di-dah, di-dah of the English iambic pentameter,
./././././

Verona has a very ancient bridge ...

gives a totally different sound.

The Priapean was a metre of jerks, stops and slitherings, ideal for creating the empathic creakings and crackings of a rotting bridge. It also reproduced the squelch of mules losing their shoes in the mud. Roman horses and donkeys were shod with metal-soled leather socks tied to their legs, easily lost on boggy ground. Technically poem [17] is brilliant.[41]

The third of the poems, [67], is a typical back-street muttering about the scandalous behaviour of a woman, but the tittle-tattler is not a priggish neighbour but a bedroom door who has overheard the unfaithful wife from Brixia giggling to her servants about her unconsummated marriage. But she was not a virgin.

> Her former husband left her quite a maid;
> his languid manhood couldn't bloom one inch
> to lift his shirt and make a virgin flinch.
> And so the father jumped ahead and tried,
> incestuously, the soundings of the bride . . .
>   (Lindsay, 1929, LXVII)

Once she was in Verona the door betrayed his master, the second husband, by admitting adulterer after adulterer into the room.

It was a sordid story, a variation on the bawdy 'Milesian' tales of which the *Golden Ass* of Apuleius is the best-known, a crude anthology for men to guffaw over in a tavern. A copy was found in a Roman's baggage after the battle of Carrhae in 53 BC between Crassus and the Parthians, away from-home reading for a soldier during the dreary nights of a campaign.[42]

Havelock considered 'The Door' an early attempt to imitate the Alexandrian elegy. What is significant is its placing among the poems immediately after [66], about 'Berenice'. In poem [67] a lustful woman enjoys men in her husband's absence whereas Berenice had loyally waited for Ptolemy to return from the wars. It is a contrast in construction that was to be a feature of the 'book' of Catullus.

He may have been sufficiently pleased with the poem to save it and add a reference to his friend, Caecilius, who bought the infamous house years after the affairs between the unnamed woman and Posthumus, Cornelius and several others, but there may be more to it than that. 'Though Catullus does not assert an interest, his defamation is most naturally explained as coming from the lips of a rejected suitor.'[43]

It was springtime for Catullus and luxuries abounded in Italy. Already in 110 BC oysters had been cultivated at Baiae by the local merchant, Sergius Orata, who made a fortune selling the bivalves to the luxury trade. By 69 BC cherry trees were being sent by Lucullus to Rome from the Black Sea region.

Trees and bushes for Armenian apricots, Persian peaches, Damascus plums, Mount Ida raspberries near Troy, Sidon quinces – all were exported by Pompey on his Mediterranean campaigns.

In 64 BC the Pontifex Maximus, head of the official Roman religion, died and Julius Caesar stood for election to a post of little power or money but considerable prestige. It was a gross presumption: the position was traditionally held by illustrious, elderly men. Already highly popular, however, from the extravagantly spectacular gladiatorial games he had staged in 65 BC, and helped by the tribunes and widespread bribery, Caesar was comfortably elected on 15 March in 63 BC. He became the guardian of the twenty Vestal Virgins.

Those women had been chosen from patrician families and sworn to virginity for thirty years in the service of Vesta, guarding her sacred flame. They were highly respected. A lictor went before them in the streets. Consuls gave way to them. For one to lose her chastity meant condemnation by the high priest of the goddess, and then to be stripped, flogged in a darkened room, dressed as a corpse, carried in a closed and muffled bier to the Campus Sceleratus, 'field of the accursed' just inside the Colline Gate, and entombed alive in a subterranean chamber with a couch, a lamp and a little food. To elect Caesar as High Priest of the Vestal Virgins could have been likened to choosing a wolf to look after lambs, but he had too much ambition and sufficient discretion to avoid accusations of impropriety.

He moved from his unpretentious home in the noisy, dirty district of the Subura to the prestigious area of Rome's great Forum and the even more prestigious sacred precinct of the circular Temple of Vesta at its south-east corner. Adjacent to it was his official headquarters of the Regia with its walled garden, the ancient palace of the legendary Numa Pompilius, Rome's second king. On the far side of the temple was the large, rectangular house of the Vestal Virgins and behind it was Caesar's new residence, the *domus publica* on the Via Sacra, 'the Sacred Way'. It was only a quarter of a mile from the Subura but, it was an elevation to nobility.[44]

At the end of the following year his home was to be the scene of an ungodly intrusion.

2

NEW POETS, OLD ENEMIES AND SCANDAL – ROME, 65-62 BC

These were the years when Catullus exchanged the mercantile dullness of Verona for the artistic enticements of Rome. Valerius Cato knew many writers there and it may also be that Quintus Metellus Caecilius, better known as Metellus Celer, 'the swift', during his stay as governor, offered him introductions to families who would put a young, rather gauche man from the provinces at ease.

The family of Catullus is an empty page, even their names. His father was a businessman but little more is recorded. Nothing is known about his mother. He had a brother, perhaps older and more involved with the family's commercial interests, but he is also nameless. With such a vague social background it is no more than guesswork to speculate whether there was objection to his departure for Rome. What is probable is that there was concern about news coming from that city.

Four more years of disruption had followed – political, domestic and artistic. There was to be uproar in the Senate, civil war and judicial murder. Caesar's wife was to be the subject of maliciously gleeful gossip. During these years also, new, sometimes outrageous forms of poetry appeared in Rome, brought there by young poets inspired by Callimachus, Valerius Cato, and a contemporary, Philodemus of Gadara.

There was an outburst of talent from northern Italy, some famous names among them: Gaius Longinus Cassius, future assassin of Caesar, from Parma; Titus Livius, Livy the historian, from Patavium, modern Padua; Gaius Plinius Secundus, Pliny the Elder, naturalist, from Como; Publius Virgilius Maro, Virgil the poet, from Andes near Mantua; Catullus of Verona, and friends such as Caius Helvius Cinna of Brixia, Brescia; Cornelius Nepos, Caecilius, also of Como, and the disliked but capable fellow poet, Furius Bibaculus, from Cremona.[1] With backgrounds that were as much Gallic as Italian the poets were lyrical revolutionaries experimenting in unusual verse-forms and exploring the rhythms of unfamiliar metres.

Their poetry came to Rome. Distractingly. It was as though guests at a soirée, expecting a programme of Vivaldi, Palestrina and quietly decorous chamber music, were suddenly confronted by a Chicago-style jazz band of trumpet,

clarinet, trombone, double bass and drums, beating out ragtime, dixieland and foot-dragging blues. The new verse was exciting, sharp, lovely, corrosive, alluring. But it did not endure. The propriety of the following Augustan Age turned from the jitterbugging to the measured orderliness of ballroom dancing. The reformed poetry was excellent but staid. 'How lucky it is for us therefore that we have to deal with the Spring season of Roman poetry since it died in its first summer.'[2]

Traditionally Roman poets had written in lines of six metrical feet – hexameters – and in a limited range of metres, the short-long, ∩ ——, iamb, 'the moon'; the —— ∩ ∩, dactylic, 'lunatic', and the —— ——, spondee, 'bright moon'. The new poets also used them but added a crusade of others – choliambs, iambic senarii and iambic trimesters often in Phalacean hendecasyllables, lines of eleven syllables, and with a flurry of Alexandrian variants: Priapean, galliambics, lightly floating metres, more French than Latin, revealing the Gallic mixed-ancestry of the young poets. There were lyrics and lampoons, some epics, more epigrams, Sapphic strophes, but very few didactic lectures.[3]

Cicero disparagingly referred to the men as *'Cantores Euphorionis'* (idle singers) like Euphorion of Antioch whose third century BC lyrics had an abstruse charm that appealed to Catullus. Cicero also scorned the poets as 'Neoterics', new poets. He was not alone. Centuries later, in Stuart England, the royal physician, William Harvey, advised John Aubrey to improve his classical education by studying 'the Fountain head, and read Aristotle, Cicero, Avicenna, and did call Neoteriques shitt-breeches'.[4]

In a letter to his friend, T. Pomponius Atticus, Cicero wrote sarcastically of the Neoterics' obsession with the new and the discarding of the old. 'You can sell these worn-out spondees to any of the New Poets you choose, keep the profits.'[5] In 63 BC, however, it was not Catullus but Catiline that preoccupied Cicero and the Senate.

Lucius Sergius Catiline, Catilina in Latin, came from an impoverished patrician family. He had fought valiantly with Sulla, was elected a quaestor in 77 BC and a praetor in 68 BC. He became a governor in Africa in 67 BC but was accused of corruption in the province and put on trial in 65 BC, 'a year of signs and portents, of murder, fire, the destruction of law and civil war'.[6]

The trial was a farce. The prosecutor was Publius Clodius Pulcher, the same man who, eight years earlier, had accused Catiline of seducing a Vestal Virgin. Internal politics decided the verdict. The ever-wealthier Crassus was antagonistic to the smug conservatives of the Senate and apprehensive of the power and popularity of Pompey, who was winning battles overseas – a man who supported the Senate and the status quo. Proposals for reform by Crassus were foiled by a censor, Lutatius Catulus, and Cicero. In retaliation, Crassus and Julius Caesar turned to Catiline, with his ambitions to become a consul with its considerable legal advantages. Widespread bribery persuaded the jurors and Catiline was acquitted – to the disgust of Cicero.[7]

Two candidates had already been accepted for election as consuls. With his associates Catiline plotted to have them killed. The plan was discovered, the pair were given bodyguards and were duly elected. Undeterred, Catiline put himself forward with a colleague, Antoninus Hybrida, for the consulships of 64 BC. Cicero also stood but he was not a patrician, 'a mere immigrant', sneered Catiline, and for the previous thirty years only aistocrats had been chosen.

The election was unpleasant. All three men, in togas liberally sprayed with pipe-clay, the *Toga Candida*, 'dazzlingly white' (from which the English 'candidate' is derived), were unscrupulous in their use of promises and money. Cicero denounced Catiline as guilty of tyranny, extortion, adultery, incest and murder. Despite being supported by Caesar and Crassus, Catiline was narrowly outvoted. In 63 BC he stood again, this time with a sensational and populist programme that promised widespread land resettlement for the poor, the proscription of enemies, and the cancellation of debts, a threat that so alarmed Crassus that he abandoned Catiline who, once again, was defeated.[8]

Resentful, desperate, impossibly in debt, Catiline made plans, collected weapons, borrowed money and gained the support of well-to-do women. The contemporary but biased historian Sallust corrupted the facts, stating that the plot began a year earlier than it really did to make it appear more sinister.[9] He described one of the women, mother of the assassin, Brutus: 'Amongst their number was Sempronia, a woman who had committed many crimes that showed her to have the reckless daring of a man. Fortune had favoured her abundantly, not only with birth and beauty, but with a good husband and children. Well educated in Greek and Latin literature, she had greater skill in lyre-playing and dancing than there is any need for a respectable woman to acquire, besides many other accomplishments such as minister to dissipation. There was nothing that she set a smaller value on than seemliness and chastity, and she was as careless of her reputation as she was of her money. Her passions were so ardent that she more often made advances to men than they did to her. Many times already she had broken a solemn promise, repudiated a debt by perjury, and been an accessory to murder. At once self-indulgent and impecunious, she had gone headlong from bad to worse. Yet her abilities were not to be despised. She wrote poetry, made jokes, and conversed with decorum, tender feeling or wantonness; she was in fact a woman of ready wit and considerable charm.'[10]

According both to Cicero and Sallust, the intention of Catiline, encouraged by Crassus and Caesar, was to overthrow the state, kill his enemies and 'as many senators as convenient' and set up a fresh government.[11] Legions in Etruria under Manlius would march on Rome in October. Cicero was to be murdered. Two men would call at his house early on 7 November, since it was the custom of clients to visit patrons shortly after dawn. But with so many discontents involved, the plot was discovered. Cicero's door was bolted. Foreign ambassadors handed over letters that proved that a rebellion was planned. On 8 November in the Senate, Cicero in a fierce speech, 'In the White Toga', proclaimed Catiline a traitor and to weaken him he offered Antoninus, Catiline's colleague, the governorship of the rich, loot-bountiful Macedonia which had been allotted to Cicero. Antoninus accepted. Catiline outwitted Cicero. He offered to prove his innocence by going into voluntary custody in the home of Lentulus, even Cicero himself or the praetor, Metellus Celer, a man that Catullus was to know well. None accepted. Catiline left Rome and joined the army in Etruria.[12]

Five conspirators – Cornelius Lentulus Sura and four others – were arrested. In the Senate on 5 December Cicero as consul demanded the 'Extreme Penalty', death, for them. Only Caesar argued against him. Marcus Porcius Cato, a heavy drinker but an incorruptible and uncompromising Roman, spoke ferociously against leniency. During his speech he saw a note being passed to Caesar. Suspecting it was connected with the conspiracy he demanded to see it. It was handed to him. It was from one of Caesar's many mistresses, Servilia, Cato's own half-sister. 'Take it, you drunken idiot,' he shouted

The death-sentence was approved. The condemned men were led to the Capitoline prison behind the Senate. In it was a former cistern, the underground Tullianum, 'the spring'. Lentulus was lowered into the cell and the executioners strangled him with a noose. The other four followed. Their bodies were dragged through a doorway opening on to Rome's major drain, the Cloaca Maxima, and thrown into it. In the Senate the word 'death' was forbidden. Cicero was euphemistic, *Vixerunt*, 'they have lived', he announced. Senators named him *Pater patriae*, 'Father of his country'. But he had violated the constitution. In Rome there could be no capital punishment except by consent of the people in legal assembly.

In Etruria, Catiline recruited men. He is an enigma today because his actions were only recorded by men hostile to him – Cicero, a political rival, and Sallust, a moralizer of whom 'very little of what is known reflects any credit upon him'. Gaius Crispus Sallustius was licentious, had been expelled from the Senate, had had an affair with Fausta, daughter of Sulla, and been thrashed by her husband, Milo. Restored to the Senate by Caesar he became governor of Numidia, which he plundered thoroughly, marrying Terentia, the divorced wife of Cicero, and retiring to write a history of Rome (now mostly lost).[14] His style was elegant, but his descriptions preposterous.

To Sallust, Catiline was a man of a 'vicious and depraved nature', enjoying unnatural practices with youths, notorious for defiling respectable women, dishonouring a Vestal Virgin, and lusting after Aurelia Orestilla, 'a woman in whom no respectable man ever found anything to praise except her beauty'. To obtain her, Catiline murdered his own son, after which crime 'his complexion was pallid, his eyes hideous, his gait now hurried and now slow'.[15] Sallust accused him of 'a criminal enterprise...fraught with unprecedented danger to Rome'. Yet that criminal had stood three times for consul, debarred in 66 BC on a technicality, narrowly defeated in 64 BC only to lose again in 63 BC. It could have been after that humiliation that the resentment of an insulted patrician drew him into anarchy. The evidence is so partial that the truth becomes elusive.

Usually accusers are counterbalanced by defenders and a modern historian is at liberty to choose between them – whether Richard III was a good king or a child-killing opportunist, or Mary, Queen of Scots, a saint or a sinner. In the famous/infamous 1881 Gunfight at the OK Corral in Tombstone, Wyatt Earp and his partners were defended in the town's newspaper, the *Tombstone Epitaph*: 'The marshal and his posse acted solely in the right.' In opposition, the town's other paper, the *Daily Nugget*, argued that 'hard-working cowboys ... had been rubbed out by a ruthless police force'.[16]

Catiline had no Roman equivalent of the *Epitaph*. Doubts remain. He could have been a sincere reformer hoping to restore justice to the oppressed, exploited and impoverished citizens of the Roman Republic. He did stand three times for election to the consulship, applying for elevation to a lawful position in which his proposals for justice could be put forward. Conversely, when his plans were thwarted by enemies his uncomplicated solution was not the futility of debate but the finality of daggers.

Ancient historians were propagandists presenting the best picture for their own side and the worst for their enemies. Faults were ignored. Heroes were impeccable. Romantics delight in the arboreal peace of Sherwood Forest and the social policy of robbing the rich for the profit of the poor, yet even the democratic Robin Hood and his Merry Men such as Little John and Much the Miller were not always kind-hearted as a monk and his little assistant discovered in *Robin Hood and the Monk*.

John smote of the monkis hed,
No longer wolde he dwell;
So did Much the litull page,
Ffor ferd lest he wold tell.

Stanza 52

And chivalrous Robin himself, immaculate in Lincoln green, could behave in a manner far from the ideals of Hollywood. In *Robin Hood and Guy of Gisborne*, having killed the knight:

Robin pulled forth an Irish kniffe,
And nicked Sir Guy in the fface,
That hee was never on a woman borne
Cold tell who Sir Guye was.

Stanza 42[17]

It is never mentioned, little known. Robin Hood may have been unglamorously cruel but his reputation stands proud, unblemished by the truth.

With Catiline it is the reverse. There is so much black that one cannot see the white. It is not only Sallust, semi-hysterical as he was. Cicero was no better. Addressing Catiline in the Senate there was, he claimed, 'no imaginable form of dishonour which does not stain your private affairs, no bounds can be set to the lecheries your eyes have witnessed, the atrocities your hands have committed, the iniquities with which every part of your body has been plunged'.

Even the mild Plutarch added his own denunciations, of the abominable Catiline having 'unlawful commerce with his virgin daughter, and of murdering his own brother'. That the satirist Juvenal could think of nothing worse than that the villain had 'conspired to attack our homes and temples at night, with steel and flame', seems almost frivolous.[18]

Whatever the truth about Catiline, and he was probably better than his detractors claimed, after he had left Rome to join the legions of Manlius he was threatened by two Roman armies on either side of the Apennines, one under Antoninus, the other commanded by Metellus Celer, who had been sent to Piconum with three legions to prevent Catiline reaching the Alps. Catiline turned back and in January 62 BC confronted Antoninus at Pistoia near Florence. Antoninus complained of gout, perhaps reluctant to fight his old comrade, and left the conduct of the battle to his legate Marcus Petreius.

The fighting was bitter but after a long struggle Petreius won. Few of his opponents ran away. 'They all had their wounds in front.' Catiline's body was far ahead of his men, cut down but still breathing when it was found. 'Catiline was afraid of nothing. Antoninus trembled at his own shadow.' As proof of Catiline's death his head was sent to Rome. His tomb there was decorated with flowers.[19]

Fugitives from the battlefield were captured and executed by Metellus Celer. He became proconsular governor of Cisalpine Gaul and stayed in the province for months in 62 BC.[20] In Verona it is likely that he met the father of Catullus. Having taken troops from Rome on a campaign that promised to be bloody it is improbable that he took his wife with him. Her name was Clodia.

These were savagely fascinating events, matters that concerned the stability of the state and the upholding of the laws. They were brutish years. There had been homicidal plots, suspects had been put to death, there had been carnage on the battlefield. Yet in his poems Catullus never mentioned a single incident, not even a hint. Politics were for other minds. Far more important than Catiline to Catullus was Callimachus. Far more fascinating than Cicero to him was Sappho of Lesbos, the finest poetess of the ancient world, a musical singer of the heart.

Sappho lived around 600 BC, during a period when Jeremiah, woeful prophet of Israel, was foretelling Nebuchadnezzar's capture of Jerusalem in 597 BC. It was a distant age but the fame of Sappho endured and spread. Two centuries later Plato insisted that 'some say there are nine Muses...but, how careless, look again...Sappho of Lesbos is the tenth'. Three hundred years after Plato, the Greek geographer and Stoic, Strabo, thought her 'a miracle of a young woman' although she may have lived until old age, even been sacrificed to Apollo or executed by being thrown over a cliff. And almost 2,000 years after Strabo she had not been forgotten, although only two other poems were known at that time. Lord Byron called her 'Dark Sappho' of Lesbos, singer of loveliness:

The isles of Greece, the isles of Greece!
Where burning Sappho loved and sung...[21]

Born to a rich aristocratic family on Lesbos, the third largest of the Aegean islands, lovely with woods and meadows, abundant with vineyards for which it was famous, 'one of the jewels of early Hellenistic civilization', Sappho married a prosperous merchant and had a daughter, Kleïs.

Hers was a life of privilege but it allowed the world the privilege of her poetry, emotional, personal, direct, almost effortless in the manner in which it spoke to the reader in words of every day speech, conversational chatter whose deceptive ease appealed to Catullus. Her verses had pace 'like the onflow of a never-resting stream' and it was uncomplicated, 'luminously direct', wrote Jenkyns. Ernst Morwitz agreed. 'She uses the simple words of every day life in simple uncomplicated sentences. The stronger the emotion, the fewer the adjectives. One of her most intense poems contains not a single adjective.' It was musical, lyrical, literally to be accompanied by a lyre. It appeared without art. It was all art.[22]

The moon has set.
and the Pleiades, it's mid-'
night, the hours go by.
I sleep alone.

[Fragment 168B][23]

There were inferences of female homosexuality as the *Suda* hinted, a late tenth-century lexicon of Byzantium, originally known as *he Suidas*, 'fortress', a valuable though untrustworthy encyclopedia of facts, hearsay and trivia. Uniquely it included a list of the works, most now lost, of Callimachus.[24]

Of Sappho the *Suda* said, 'A lyric poetess. She had three companions and friends, Atthis, Telesippa and Megara: she was also accused of shameful love with them.' The *Suda* provided a joke. Sappho 'was married to Kerkylas, a very rich man who came from Andros', an Aegean island near Corinth. It seemed matter-of-fact. It was not. It was a sexual pun. 'Andros' was Greek for 'man', 'Kerkylas' in Greek was χερχοζ, 'male sexual organ'. Sappho's unlikely husband was 'a man's penis'. She became a popular 'subject of comic plays in the fourth century BC (bawdy and heterosexual)'.[25]

The speculation about lesbianism came from her poems about Aphrodite, goddess of physical love.

> If she flees you now, she will soon pursue you,
> If she won't accept what you give, she'll give it;
> If she doesn't love you, she'll love you soon now,
> even unwilling.

[Poem 1]
(Powell, p. 3)

The reaction to such poems has altered over time. In the nineteenth century Sappho was envisaged as a kind of headmistress of a girls' seminary. In the later twentieth century she was the leader of a lesbian harem. There were almost desperate attempts to discover evidence of unnatural practices in her verses, '...wearing a phallus of leather...' which perhaps reveals more about the researcher than the poetess. Certainly it is the poetry that matters.[26]

In his 'Sapho to Philaenis' of 1633, 'the first female homosexual love poem in English', John Donne did not doubt her love of a woman:

> ...Thy body is a naturall *Paradise*
> In whose selfe, unmanur'd, all pleasure lies,
> Nor needs *perfection*; why shouldst thou than
> Admit the tillage of a harsh rough man?
> ...
> Likeness begets such strange selfe flatterie,
> That touching myself, all seemes done to thee.[27]

To Catullus she was an inspiration. He knew and used her works in two of his poems, [11] and [51]. He admired one of her fragments:

Like the wild hyacinth flower which on the hills is found
Which the passing feet of the shepherds for ever tread and wound
Until the purple blossom is trodden into the ground.

[Fragment 105B]
(Dante Gabriel Rossetti, 1870)

He alluded to it in his own keen lament for the woman he had lost:

Unlike past years my love for her is perished,
Through her harsh fault it's broken like some wild flower
At a field's edge, flicked by a passing plough,
Felled, fading into death. (p. 226)

[11][28]

Time and linguistics were traitors to the works of Sappho. Her nine books of lyrics were completely lost and her epigrams and elegies forgotten. Only two poems and a hundred or so disconnected lines were known until late in the nineteenth century. But unlike the unfortunate vanishing of poets like Catullus her disappearance was more intentional.

Geography was to blame. Her island of Lesbos was hardly ten miles from Asia Minor, modern Turkey, and the mainland could be seen on clear days, but the island was over 150 sea-miles of the Aegean from Greece and Athens. Over the years her provincial language became difficult to understand, her archaic Aeolic dialect unfamiliar to modern Athenian ears accustomed to the purity of Attic speech.

If not as unintelligible as Robert Burns'

I gie thee meal and fee
And yet sae meickle muck ye tine
Might a' be gear to me!

her words were certainly as pidgin-Greek as William Barnes's idiomatic

Since I noo mwore do zee your feäce

in its Dorset vernacular of 'bold and broad Doric'. Readers of classical Greek could not be bothered and Sappho's poems became so neglected that until recently they were no more than fragments and guesses.[29]

Chance has many disguises. It was a lottery with Catullus until three flimsy copies of an ephemeral copy of a fragile copy were sent to the safekeeping of libraries. It was a translation from Greek to Latin for a poem of Callimachus. It was a rubbish-dump for Sappho.

In 1895 the Egypt Exploration Society sent Bernard Grenfell and Arthur Hunt, classical scholars of Queen's College, Oxford, to Egypt in search of papyri. In 1892 a public archive of the reign of Marcus Aurelius had already been discovered at Mendes in the Nile Delta and there could be other rewarding sites. The explorers went to Oxyrhynchus in the Nile Valley, an insignificant provincial capital a hundred miles south of Cairo, where they noticed some untouched low mounds. They were the sand-covered remains of a municipal refuse-tip with household scraps, old bills, accounts and masses of papyrus, torn into strips to be mushed into papier-mâché for wrapping mummies and stuffing crocodiles, the discarded tatters of centuries.

It was not all trivia. Amongst the ripped fragments were parts of a lost play by Sophocles and some poems by Sappho, a few complete, most in half-lines, the tantalizing right-hand or left-hand sides of torn pages strewn haphazardly in the layers of rubbish, but Sappho nevertheless. The pieces were packed in Huntley & Palmer biscuit tins and sent to England. Since 1906 the chore of deciphering, translating and linking the disordered fragments has proceeded tediously. Much of Books I, II and IV of the original nine has been restored, but it will be years before the work is concluded.

Minor miracles do happen. In 2004 a papyrus at Cologne University was found to contain snippets of three Sappho poems. Two were no more than the expected bits and pieces but the third was the almost complete other half of the torn Fragment 57. Before that discovery only a word here, a phrase there, were preserved of the original twelve lines:-

....fair gift
....children/ song/ clear-sounding lyre
...old age already/ all skin
...and/ hair/ from black
...knees do not carry
...like young fawns
...What could I do?
...not possible to become
...rose-white Dawn
...carrying/ the earth's end
....yet/ seized
...wife.

Gratifyingly, when coupled with the Cologne extract a gently, mournful poem of two verses could be reconstructed. [Words still missing are shown in brackets].

For the fragrant-bosomed [Muses bring] fair gifts,
[Be generous] young girls [and sing] to the clear, melodious lyre.
[But of my once-tender] body old age already has now
[destroyed]. My hair's turned [white] from black;
My heart's grown heavy, my knees will not carry me
That once were as light for dancing as young fawns.
....
This condition I regret, resent, but what could I do?
Being human it's impossible not to become old.
Tithonus was, myth says, by the rose-white dawn-goddess
Seduced, and carried to the world's far distant end.
Handsome and young then, yet, over time, grey age
Decayed him, a human husband of an immortal wife.

[Fragment 57]

A legendary handsome young Trojan, Tithonus, was enticed by the goddess of the dawn, the Greek Eos, Roman Aurora. Luring him, but fearful of losing him, she begged Zeus to give him everlasting life but forgot to ask for unending youthfulness.

Tithonus slowly but inexorably withered into a croakingly decrepit husk. Knowing his irresistible fate, Sappho wept that she too could never be young again. But, finally, after 2,500 years of absence a poetess is being reincarnated.[30]

Copies of copies, translations, piles of unwanted litter, all were unlikely literary treasure-houses. Quite differently, it was the destruction of Herculaneum that saved another favourite model for Catullus, his contemporary Philodemus, a poet from Gadara near the Lake of Galilee, a town better known for its lemming-like swine than its lyricists.

Philodemus, philosopher, wit and epigrammatic versifier, wrote with brevity and charm, qualities much admired by Catullus.

Charito is sixty!
but her hair remains dark,
her unpadded bosom firm.
Unwrinkled, graceful,
she is a temptress without age.
Men come to her
unmindful of her years.[31]

It is brief, uncomplicated, quiet. Even translated from the original Greek it has a delicacy, typical of the poet's light touch.

Philodemus stayed quite frequently at a villa just outside Herculaneum, whose owner Calpurnius Piso Caesonius had been the governor of Macedonia from 57 to 55 BC. Despite enriching himself by plundering the province ruthlessly, not a *denarius* of the spoils reached the purses of Fabullus or Veranius, members of his staff, and friends of Catullus who chuckled at the meanness:

Admirable Veranius, and you,
dear Fabullus, of the retinue
of the governor, Piso, you profitless
lackeys whose empty luggage is no struggle
to bring home ...

[28]

For his dishonesty and corruption the ex-governor was denounced in the Senate by Cicero. But as Piso was the father-in-law of Julius Caesar, who had taken his daughter Calpurnia as his third wife, there was no trial. Piso retired to his luxurious villa by the sea. The virtual palace housed a glory of precious objects acquired in Macedonia: sculptures, jewellery, mosaics, fine vases, tapestries, amphorae and 'the greatest single collection of ancient bronze statuary ever found. So fine were the pieces...that they were a prime object of Herman Goering's thievery during World War II.'[32] The villa also contained at least one, probably two or more, extensive libraries of thousands of papyrus rolls containing philosophical works, plays by Greek dramatists and the writings of Philodemus. All were preserved by a volcanic miracle.

A hundred years after the death of Piso, Herculaneum and Pompeii, eight miles away, were destroyed when the volcano of Vesuvius, green with trees, its lower slopes widely cultivated with vines, erupted on the afternoon of 24 August AD 79. The sky was split by a grotesque cloud like a pine tree from a world of giants, twelve miles high, its trunk supporting a blotchy cloud of spreading branches that turned the afternoon into night. Pompeii, a market town, its streets rutted with the wheels of carts and wagons, and already damaged by an eruption seventeen years earlier, was submerged under fine pumice, falling rocks and a flow of red-hot lava. The air was poisonous with lethal fumes.

Herculaneum, a fashionable resort, closer than Pompeii to the volcano, but unaffected by the prevailing wind, suffered in a different way. There was a light fall of pumice, maybe only eight inches thick. But then with hurricane-force winds howling between the houses, toppling anything weak, there were molten surges of pumice, limestone, ash and gases, bubbling and scorching downhill, oozing like plastic into rooms, cupboards and pots, not as hot as lava but up to 400°C, hot enough to carbonize any organic article, charring but not burning them. And it moved gently, leaving a coil of rope hanging on a wall, creeping around kitchen utensils, leaving eggshells unbroken. It slurped up the sides of houses, over walls and into Piso's villa outside the town. Slowly the mass cooled, setting like a fist of iron, covering the ruins. Weeds grew, rotted, earth and mould developed and Pompeii and Herculaneum became the world's most famous buried cities.[33]

After some Roman looting they remained undisturbed, gradually forgotten, for over 1,600 years. Then in the eighteenth century, while digging for wells and tunnelling for an underground canal, excavators chanced upon marble slabs and works of art and the cities became the target not of archaeology but of those greedy for beautiful antiquities. Herculaneum was known about as early as 1594 but was methodically searched only from 1750. Mining began at Pompeii in 1748, and was halted then resumed in 1754. Sadly the director appointed by royalty to supervise the investigations, a colonel of engineers, was insensitive, arrogant and obstructive. Rocque Joachin de Alcubierre was the man whose archaeological incompetence was famously described 'as familiar with antiquity as the moon is with crabs'.[34]

Fortunately in 1750 the 80-foot [27m] deep shaft of a well being dug on a terrace overlooking the Bay of Naples exposed marble paving surrounding an immense garden. The person put in charge of the exploration of Piso's villa was Karl Weber, a Swiss architect. His systematic tunnelling was constantly hindered by the jealousy of his incompetent superior.

The years 1750 to 1764 were an excavator's nightmare: a long shaft down to head-high tunnels had to be hacked out through the solid sediment and conditions were like those of a mine with water seeping everywhere and walls greasy with slime. This heroic task had to be abandoned in 1765 before the eastern end was reached because ventilation shafts and tunnels became choked with toxic carbonic gases.[35]

Yet they were also years offering magnificent rewards. The miners exposed the extravagance of an indulgent millionaire whose low, red-tiled villa was at least 1,000 Roman feet long built on an embankment parallel with the coast, and standing above a terraced slope overlooking a private harbour with boathouses on the shore of the Gulf of Naples.

At the north-western end of the villa was an impressive entrance with a vestibule leading to the atrium and smaller reception rooms. To its left was an enormous garden surrounded by covered walks and with a huge central pool fed by hydraulic piping. There were living-rooms, bedrooms, dining-rooms, everywhere signed with the tastes of a man with uncountable wealth, finely painted murals and frescoes, exquisite mosaics, and nine valuable bronze statues, nearly all of them undamaged.

The millionaire J. Paul Getty, who had visited and been fascinated by Pompeii and Herculaneum, collected his own private treasury of ancient pottery and statues and built a museum to house the pieces at Malibu in California, whose design was based on the plan of the villa by Karl Weber. In it were mosaics, marble inlays, hand-made lanterns, all meticulously copied, and the garden itself was reproduced with acanthus, myrtle, roses, anemone, camomile, hyacinth, narcissus, violets, oleander, box-hedges – a garden fragrant and colourful all year round with water features to produce cooling sounds. It was opened in 1974 at a cost of $17 million. It was remodelled and was due to reopen in 2004.[36]

For Karl Weber the greatest prize came in October 1752. From the imposing portico with its tall columns a vestibule led to the atrium with a colonnaded court beyond it. In a corridor to the right were two little rooms. The smaller was stacked high with shelves laden with charcoal briquettes. At the centre of the room was a wooden stand with more of the blackened objects. In the dim light of the tunnel Weber's tunnellers thought they were blocks of wood and threw them away. Then it was noticed that they were consistently cylindrical and of the same size, perhaps bundles of burnt cloth or fish-nets. When they were broken nothing could be seen and again they were discarded. It was only when one was taken into the open air that faint signs of writing could be detected. The 'briquettes' were rolls of papyrus in wooden cases, and this library was to be the largest collection ever found, with 800 recovered in 1752 rising to almost 2,000. Many of them were dull treatises by Philodemus, but others his light-hearted poems. Recent but unarchaeologically supervised excavations have shown that the villa extended downhill towards the sea and that during the eruption slaves may have been carrying rolls from a second, even a third, library to safety.

Those papyri, if they exist and can be recovered, if opened and transcribed, may contain the richest collection of classical literature since the destruction of the famous libraries in Alexandria. Among them could be the missing three-quarters of Livy's *History if Rome*, or unknown plays by Sophocles, Euripides and other Greek dramatists; perhaps a definitive arrangement of the three 'books' of Catullus; maybe, a dancing-girl of a thought, the entire, uncorrupted poems of Sappho. In 2002 proper archaeological excavations began. Classical scholars await the results with bated breath![37]

From the beginning the challenge was to read the hard-baked 'lumps of charcoal' whose outside skin was so hard that it had to be sliced through on either side. During this crude process many were ruined. An eighteenth-century specialist in the handling of ancient manuscripts, Father Antonio Piaggio, was more successful. With a contraption similar to a wig-making machine and with a concoction of string, fish-glue and gut it became possible to unwind three inches [8 cm] of a roll in a working day. After four years of trial, error and damage three entire papyri could be read, one by Philodemus.

Today technology is replacing the surgical methods. Digital cameras, scanners, X-rays and computer enhancement make the recovery of the fragile material less hazardous, particularly for carbonized rolls like those in the villa where the black writing is only just discernible against its carbon-black background.

There is a grace note: Sappho and Philodemus are being joined in death as they never were in life. At the Bodleian Museum in Oxford rolls from the Villa of the Papyri, and torn papyri from the Oxyrhynchus rubbish-dump are being examined by an identical process. It is as though the ghost of Philodemus were addressing the wraith of Sappho in his famous poem:

He: Excuse me, lady.
She: Who? Me?
He: If you don't mind.
She: Not at all.
He: Something to eat?
She: For me? Lovely.
He: Afterwards?
She: With pleasure.
He: Just so. And the price?
She: Later. If it's good, whatever you think.
He: Brilliant. When? Eight o'clock, nine?
She: Whenever.
He: Now?
She: Your place or mine?

In that fictitious romance Sappho, having been born five centuries before Philodemus, might have replied, very graciously:

But if you love us
Choose a younger bed.
For I cannot bear
To live with you when I am the older one.
                    [Fragment 121][38]
                    (Carson, p. 247)

That imaginary encounter between a man and a woman never occurred but another in Rome was very real and very serious.

The Festival of Bona Dea, the Good Goddess, was celebrated at the beginning of December and held in the official dwelling of the Pontifex

Maximus, Julius Caesar, who in 62 BC was also a praetor. The goddess was so chaste that after marriage no man except her husband saw her. Her feast day to increase the fertility of women scrupulously excluded men. It was held at night, attendants at the door of the dimly lit incense-burning house ensuring that only women were admitted. Inside, everywhere, anything masculine, be it painting or statue, was veiled.

The rituals were conducted by the mistress of the place, Aurelia, mother of Caesar. Married women and Vestal Virgins came, there was a coffer filled with curative herbs, there were sacrificial fires and esoteric objects from the east in readiness for the orgiastic rites after midnight when the chaste Vestal Virgins had departed. Only rumours exist. Nakedness is mentioned, an altar ornamented with representations of phalli, abandonment to the goddess, but no details. It was said that what in earlier times had been pious supplication by the time of the late Republic had corroded into depravity. 'The sanctity of these mysteries was profaned by the introduction of lasciviousness and debauchery.'[39]

A hundred and fifty years later, Juvenal, tongue in cheek, deplored the corruption in his *Satire VI*:

> The secrets of the Good Goddess are scarcely a secret. The pelvis
> is stirred by the pipe, and Priapus' maenads are swept along
> frenzied by horn and wine alike, swinging their hair
> in a circle, and howling. Then what a yearning for sex erupts
> in their hearts; what cries are emitted as their lust pulsates, what rivers
> of vintage liquor comes coursing down their drunken legs!
> Tossing her garland in, Saufeia challenges harlots
> trained in a brothel and takes the award for undulant hips;
> she in turn admires Medullina's rippling buttocks.
> ...
> Would that the ancient rites, or at least the public observances,
> might take place without such vile desecration!
> ...
> Today what altar is without a Clodius skulking around it?
> Nowadays, all of them, high or low, have the same lust.
> The woman who treads the black stone blocks is not any better
> than the one who rides on the shoulders of tall Syrian porters.
>
> (lines 314-51)

The black stones, discovered in 1899, were a holy pavement of marble close to the Temple of Vesta. Rumour had it that the largest stone covered the burial place of Romulus, legendary founder of Rome, but no body was found.[40]

There was outrage long before Juvenal's time. On 1 January 61 BC, Cicero wrote to his friend Atticus: 'I imagine you have heard that P. Clodius, the son of Appius, was caught dressed up as a woman in Caesar's house at the national sacrifice and that he owed his escape alive to the hands of a servant girl – a spectacular scandal.'[41]

Publius Clodius Pulcher, cynical prosecutor at the farcical trial of Catiline three years earlier, was a patrician and a populist, a rabble-rouser savagely opposed to the self-perpetuating avarice of Rome's well-to-do conservatives. In his early thirties he was arrogant, intelligent and reckless with the assurance of a well-born and privileged young man. He was a member of the proud and wealthy Claudian family, whose ancestor Appius had built Rome's first aqueduct and was responsible for the construction of the great Appian Way along whose sides the followers of Spartacus had been crucified by Crassus.

Clodius was also the brother-in-law of Metellus Celer, governor of Cisalpine Gaul in 62 BC, who had married the eldest of Clodius' three sisters, all called Clodia.

Perhaps as a dare, perhaps from curiosity or just defiant devilment, possibly from a sexual assignment all the more attractive because of its danger, Clodius entered the forbidden house disguised as a flute-player. It was foolhardy. A serving-girl recognized his masculine voice and screamed. There was panic, hysteria; he ran away, hid, was discovered and recognized but managed to escape.

This was desecration of a sacred place. There was also a popular suspicion that an illicit, rendezvous with Caesar's wife, Pompeia, had been arranged. Caesar divorced her, announcing to the general mirth of Rome that 'Caesar's wife can do no wrong'. She had to be above suspicion. Cicero chuckled about the fiasco to his friend, Atticus: 'I am sure it will distress you!'

Less amusingly, the Senate concluded that there had been *nefas*, a wickedness committed against the religion of the state, a sacrilege made worse by having occurred not in a private house but in the public dwelling of the Pontifex Maximus. There was no precedent for such a crime. The matter was referred to the Vestal Virgins and the priests who declared that there had been an affront to the gods. It was decided that a special court with a hand picked jury should be appointed, before which Clodius would be tried for his impiety.[42]

It was some time around 61 BC that Catullus made the long journey from Verona to Rome. It is not possible to be more exact, nor is it necessary to guess. It is known that he had lived in Verona. His poetry proves that he went to Rome. The chronology suggests that 61 BC is the likeliest year for that move. Caution is advisable.

Pessimism, the brother of literary cowardice, is not. A recent book about Sappho 'provided' a chapter about the facts of her life. It was a cynically blank page. Facts exist. She was a woman and she lived in the sixth century BC. She was born on Lesbos, to an aristocratic family. She had three brothers. She was married to a wealthy merchant – but not 'Kerkylas!' – and had a daughter. Many ofher friends were women. She was a poetess and lyricist; her poems filled nine books and were written in a local Aeolic dialect. Some complete poems and many fragments survive.[43]

In comparison, the life of Catullus is much more detailed. Any narrative of the life of Catullus, wrote Martin warily, 'would be problematic for a number of reasons, the most important of which is the almost total absence of reliable biographical data.'[44] The present writer would agree if 'precise' came before 'reliable'. Quite a lot is known about Catullus – his birthplace and the year he was born, his friends, the woman he loved, her name and family, his visit to Bithynia, the death of his brother, his acquaintance with Caesar and Cicero, his intimacies with both the socially acceptable and the grossly unacceptable people of Rome.

Because of these facts E. A. Havelock's ironical 'biography' with its constant reservations is droll but over-stated. 'The result is an elaborate structure of ingenious hypotheses,' the critic teased. 'We may suppose (so runs the reconstructed story in its most complete form) that Catullus spent his boyhood at Verona and on Lake Sirmio [Garda!], a youth of good provincial family, but, *we must assume*, living a life close to that of the Gallic frontiersmen. His education, *no doubt*, received at Verona, was, *we can readily imagine*, assisted by tutors and grammarians of the district ... At Verona (*it is tempting to assume*) he was introduced to Metellus, the husband of his future love, during Metellus' governorship of Cisalpine Gaul in 62 BC. Armed (*we may imagine*) with letters of introduction, he comes, a young unsophisticated provincial, to the capital [and] ... (*it is safe to guess*) he obtains entry, despite his provincialism, to the most exclusive circles of fashion and politics in Rome.'[45] One smiles but as a reconstruction it is flimsy.

Around 61 BC Catullus travelled from Verona to Rome, first along the local roads through Hostilia (modern Ostiglia) to Mutina (Modena) where he joined the better-laid surface of the Via Aemilia, built in 187 BC. It led to Bononia (Bologna), Ariminia (Rimini) and Fanum Fortunae (Fano). Here it linked with the prestigious highway of the splendid Via Flaminia, its 220 Roman miles constructed in 220 BC by the consul Gaius Flaminius, who was killed three years later fighting against Hannibal at the battle of Lake Trasimene. The great road extended through Spoletum (Spoleta) and Narnia (Narni) to Rome.[46]

Altogether it was a distance of well over 300 Roman miles and it may be assumed that Catullus did not walk. He could have ridden, used a carriage, even been carried in the comfort of a cushioned litter. The litter or *lectica* is perhaps least likely, being such a luxury. One could read, even write in its curtained privacy, smoothly borne along by its shoulder-strapped bearers, the best ones coming from Bithynia, but it was expensive and it was slow, covering perhaps fifteen miles on a good day.

A horse is equally improbable – fast but incapable of carrying much luggage and exposing its rider to the weather. For a moneyed young man, anxious to give a good impression, bringing clothes, writing materials, domestic equipment supervised by servants and slaves, a hired carriage would be the sensible means of transport, either the light two-wheeled gig of a *cisium* which was fast (Cicero once covered fifty-four miles in ten hours in one) or a choice of heavier, slower, four-wheeled carriages.

A *currus dormitoria*, that mobile sleeping-compartment, was unnecessary. The Gallic *petorritum* was cool because it was open but it was unpleasant in rain and cold. If Catullus arrived at the gates of Rome stylishly it was probably in a Celtic *raeda*, a covered vehicle capable of completing the long journey in a fortnight. Such carriages and teams could be exchanged at the frequent posting-stations at towns along the way.[47]

Near these staging-posts were inns but no one of rank stayed in them. They were far below modern five-star, even run-down boarding-house standards, they were dirty, the food unappetizing, the sour wine well-watered, and the cramped sleeping quarters frequently shared with other travellers, often in the same bed and with only a basin for personal relief during the uncomfortable night. At Pompeii a message had been scrawled on the bedroom wall:

I'm sorry, host. I wet your bed.
And yet, though sad, my face ain't red,
because you stupidly forgot
to give the bedroom one piss-pot.[48]

When away from home the custom for someone of Catullus' social class was to stay with friends, relatives or local governors, with everything arranged in advance. Convenient and congenial, with attentive hosts happy to oblige old friends or important acquaintances, there was no urgency. Even the accommodation in Rome was prepared and of some quality. In several novels about Catullus it has been argued that he was poor when compared with the plutocrats of the Roman upper classes. If so, the poverty was relative.

Catullus was never a Thomas Chatterton starving to death in a garret. He did laughingly write of his purse being filled with cobwebs but they must have been webs flecked with gold-dust. He kept a house in Rome and a place in the country, whether it was a working farm in the Sabine Hills, according to his critics or what his friends praised as a villa in the fashionable resort of Tivoli. He also had a yacht.[49]

Catullus, it seems, had funds. In three poems [23, 24, 26] he warned Juventius, his fickle boy-lover, not to be lured away from him by the penniless charms of Furius Bibaculus, a poet in debt, who owed over 15,000 *sestertii*, English 'Sesterces', on his home, possessed no slave and no cash, the implication being that Catullus had both.

> ...still you must admit to me
> he has neither money-box nor slave.
>
> [24]
> (Lindsay, 1929)

It is probable that Catullus did have slaves. At that time anyone with money had up to ten to maintain appearances. The rich owned hundreds of slaves to maintain their houses in Rome and their country estates. Slaves, like furniture, kitchen utensils and horses, were essential possessions.[50] There is no need to imagine a needy poet in shabby sandals and a threadbare tunic. Poverty would not have attracted Juventius.

That Catullus should have had a homosexual relationship with an adolescent would neither have surprised nor disgusted his contemporaries. 'Like the Greeks, the Romans saw nothing wrong with recreational sex of either type.' Man and boy were willing partners. Although he was the passive companion the youngster was not demeaned. On the contrary he would be flattered by the attentions and desires of the adult. He would be respected; a spiritual and physical association between man and boy was aptly described as 'pedagogical pederasty'. Catullus was explicit about such children's acceptance of homosexuality and how, often, they actively encouraged it:

> If you see an auctioneer parading with some luscious kid
> you can bet the lad's announcing, 'I'm up for the highest bid!'
>
> [106]

Early in the second century BC, Cato the Elder, 'the censor', was shocked to learn that a good-looking boy could be valued at a gold talent, the price of a well-run farm.

In the *Satyricon*, Titus Petronius Arbiter described how they could excite their partner. 'Dimly as through a thick fog I caught sight of Giton standing at the corner of an alley and I raced over... At last I was free to make love to Giton without restraint, and wrapping the boy in the closest of embraces, I took my fill of a bliss even happy lovers might envy. Nor had I done when Ascyltos stole to the door and, springing the bolt, found us at leapfrog.'

Catullus and Juventius would have been no different and few people in Rome, men or women, patricians or plebeians, would have condemned their behaviour. 'Throughout antiquity homoerotic love was considered normal and appropriate. Nor did it preclude heterosexual activity (including marriage)... The ancients considered bisexuality the norm.' The hypocritical moralist, Sallust, deplored the current depravity of both sexes. 'Men prostituted themselves like women, and women sold their chastity to all comers.'[51]

Juventius, however, was just one of the pleasant expenses that Catullus jokingly complained had left him in unlikely poverty. His 'cobweb' poem was one more indication of the respect he had for Philodemus. That poet had invited his patron, Piso, to dinner in Herculaneum:

It's true we have no vintage wine
or tender meat on which to dine
yet if you do but laugh with me
our meal a banquet has to be.

Catullus wrote in a similar manner to one of his friends:

If the gods are kind, Fabullus, we'll dine well
...
as long as it's understood that you bring everything,
the feast and, of course, a pretty girl,
the wine, the salt and the laughter,
that's the bargain. You provide the dinner
and we'll sup like princes. These days Catullus
has a purse that's full of spider's webs.

[13][52]

But that was when he was settled in Rome, long after the tedious miles from Verona.

3

A Day in Rome – 61 BC

At the end of the long journey from Verona Catullus arrived at Rome's Fontinal Gate, one of many entrances through the towering, thick walls of the city, six and a half miles of defence so strong that even Hannibal had not tried to breach it.

Carts brought produce to Rome but carriages were not allowed into the centre of the city. Men walked and slaves carried their burdens. Litters were hired for women, taking their discreetly screened passengers to the heart of Rome and its low-lying Forum between the Palatine and Capitoline Hills. 'Hill' is misleading. The fabulous seven hills of Rome were not of astonishing heights. Even the Palatine rose no more than 140 feet [43 m] above the Tiber. But it was steep. Only 300 yards [275 m] from the Forum it inflicted a breathless trudge to reach the top. From there one could look up and see the splendid houses of the rich along the Clivus Victoriae. Metellus Celer lived there near the Temple of Castor & Pollux.

Opposite, across the valley of the Forum, was the sheer-sided Capitoline Hill with its impressive temples, the most magnificent being the Temple of Jupiter Optimus Maximus, already more than four centuries old when Catullus arrived in Rome. A hundred steep steps climbed from the Forum up to its massive doors of bronze. Immediately below the temple at the south-west corner of the hill was a precipice, high as two tall churches, the Tarpeian Rock from which criminals were hurled to their deaths. From the Forum spectators could watch the executions.

Legend had it that Tarpeia was buried at the foot of the cliff. She was, it was said, a Vestal Virgin of the mid-eighth century, living at the time of the infamous rape of the Sabine women, who had been abducted on the orders of Romulus, founder of Rome, to become the wives of the men of his new town on the Palatine. Sabine warriors besieged it but it was guarded by the slopes of the Capitoline.

Tarpeia had gone down the hill for water and noticed that Tatius, king of the Sabines, had a gorgeous bracelet of gold on his left arm. Seeing her covetous glance the king vowed that if she would open the gate that night he would give her what was on that arm. This turned out to be not the ornament but his heavy war-shield – that struck her to death. Romulus had to wait until Tatius died before he could return to Rome.[1]

Rome was a city of uncritical belief in the powers of the 'other world'. There were temples and statues of gods and goddesses everywhere: gods like Apollo, Jupiter, Mars, Mercury and Vulcan; and goddesses, Juno, Minerva, Venus, Vesta of the sacred flame and Cybele the Great Mother with her wildly dancing priests. It was a city of sacrifices and predictions – goats, sheep, pigs and doves were offered to the gods. The future was foretold through the shape of clouds, the flight of birds, the flashes of lightning. It was a city of spirits, the *lares* who guarded homes and at whose domestic altar, the *Lararium*, a family placed gifts every day. *Manes* were the spirits of ancestors, benevolent spirits of the dead. Offerings were left at their graves.

Not all spirits were generous, however. Worst of them were the *lemures*, vampire-like ghosts of resentful forebears who had died unnaturally, and who emerged from the underworld in the month of May. During this month temples were closed, it was unlucky to marry and in every house there was a nocturnal rite to drive off 'the wandering and terrifying shades of men who died before their time'.

The owner of a house left his bed at midnight, washed his hands, and one by one spat nine black beans from his mouth, each time crying 'with these I ransom me and mine'. The invisible, malevolent spectres ate them. Keeping his back turned the man washed his hands once more, then beat a gong nine times very loudly. 'Ancestral ghosts, depart!' For three nights, 9, 11 and 13 May, the ritual was performed against what the poet Persius described as the 'demons in the dark' and Horace as 'dreams and the terrors of magic, miracles, ghosts at night-time'.[2]

For a newcomer to Rome there were sights to be seen: the Forum with its awesome buildings, basilicas, law courts, the Treasury, the markets for cattle, fish and vegetables, the hills and their suburbs to be explored, two miles from north to south, a mile across, a jostle of crowds and carts in narrow streets. But before these investigations there were social obligations.

There were friends to be met in the unknown city, men who would take Catullus to other friends and poets. Being admitted to literary Rome and its social circles was probably made easier by letters of introduction from Publius Valerius Cato, the respected teacher and poet in Verona, who was already known to young poets like Ticidas, Gaius Cinna and Furius Bibaculus. Meanwhile there were a bewilderment of courtesies, meetings, names quickly forgotten, houses taken to but never to be found again without a guide. For Catullus it must have been an exciting time, daunting but exhilarating.

Even more important socially there were formal letters to be presented early in the morning to the janitor of a great house, the slave at the door

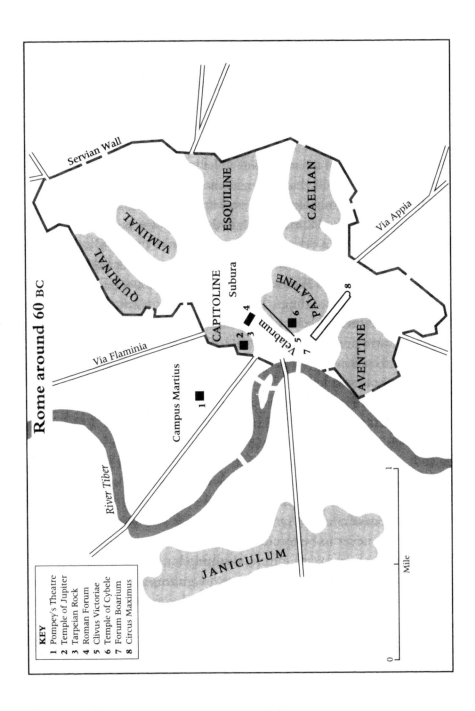

Rome around 60 bc

Servian Wall

ESQUILINE

CAELIAN

Via Appia

VIMINAL

QUIRINAL

CAPITOLINE

Subura

PALATINE

Velabrum

AVENTINE

Via Flaminia

Campus Martius

River Tiber

JANICULUM

Mile

KEY
1 Pompey's Theatre
2 Temple of Jupiter
3 Tarpeian Rock
4 Roman Forum
5 Clivus Victoriae
6 Temple of Cybele
7 Forum Boarium
8 Circus Maximus

who expected, and received, considerable tips, and who would admit him to the *atrium* and the restless gathering of other expectant clients. In privacy, the master of the house would consider the recommendation and whether to welcome the young man so neatly dressed in his toga to his study. There could, instead, be a humiliating rejection to a person of no significance. On the other hand, if the letter had been from Quintus Metellus Celer, ex-praetor, successful soldier, governor of Cisalpine Gaul, man of wealth and distinction, living in the most aristocratic part of Rome, many doors would have been opened to Catullus.

It was admittance to a small, select and intense social circle in which learning and snobbery intermixed, a society in which upper-class women had become emancipated. This was a world of wealth and exclusion but one which was creative, 'leisured but not idle, privileged but also self-critical, capable of stimulating the songs of poets and of tolerating their lampoons'.[3] It was a world very aware of itself and its advantages. For a young man from provincial Verona it was a world of imagination turned into reality.

There were sights best seen during summer days. Unlike the present age, Roman hours were not standardized but varied according to the time of year. There were twenty-four to a day, twelve of daylight, twelve of the night, but in the summer the average hour was seventy-five minutes long, in winter thirty minutes shorter. And the working day differed, in summer from 0430 to 1930, in the dark winter from 0730 to 1630. The first hour of the day was always the one after dawn, midday was always the sixth hour, and the twelfth the one before sunset. Bedtime began with darkness. For illumination at night there were only candles and oil-lamps with their feeble, wavering light and greasy, smoky vapours that injured the eyesight. Roman literature is full of complaints about troubled eyes.[4]

The Roman day began at dawn and because men and women slept in their underclothes getting up was an uncomplicated process. For Catullus there would be a quick wash in warm water brought by a slave who might also shave him and bring him a fresh, clean tunic. Breakfast was light, perhaps bread and cheese or wheat biscuits, a choice of honey, dates or olives, and a drink of water or diluted wine. Then the day could start. There might be the necessity of an early social call or, for the newcomer to the city, districts to be explored in the company of well-informed friends.

There were sights to be seen. The imposing Forum, which was the civic centre of Rome with its temples, law courts, banks, public buildings and shops. The raised Rostra, boastfully adorned with the destructive rams of captured ships, and where orators addressed the people, stood there. The Senate House was at its north. Behind it was the prison. The Temple of Saturn and the Sate Treasury were at the north-west point. At the other end of the Forum was the Temple of Vesta and the Temple of Castor & Pollux, the twins known as the Dioscuri.

The rectangular Forum was not large. From the foot of the Capitoline Hill at the north-west to the House of the Vestal Virgins at the south-east was hardly 200 yards (180m). From Basilica Aemilia and its shops across to the Basilica Sempronia was no more than sixty yards (55m). The Capitoline Hill overshadowed it north-westwards, the Palatine to the east. But it was the heart of Rome.

From his poems it is obvious that Catullus met friends there and knew the neighbourhood well. He knew that Metellus Celer lived not far from the Temple of Castor & Pollux. He knew the public baths of the city and the thieves wandering slyly through their crowded rooms. He had explored Rome's streets and alleyways and watched fires burning down shabby blocks in the slums.

The city was a tinderbox waiting for a flint. The opportunistic Crassus became rich with his bands of trained fire-fighting slaves but there was no public fire service until the emperor Augustus instituted one after a blaze in AD 6. Accidental fires were commonplace and there may have been as many as a hundred minor blazes on any day. Far more damagingly over the centuries there were at least half-a-dozen serious conflagrations in the city.

Too many buildings were incipient bonfires. There were no chimneys in the high, timber framed flats but there were thousands of oil-lamps and wood-burning braziers. Even Augustus' 7,000 men, *vigiles*, were little more than cosmetic as a fire-fighting force. Equipped with feeble hand-pumps whose hoses could hardly wet the first floor of a four- or five-storey block, men armed with grappling-hooks tried to tear down walls, using vinegar-soaked blankets and mattresses to deaden the suicidal leaps ofpeople hurling themselves out of the flames. The most useful member of the team was the doctor.

A fire in the second century AD destroyed 340 dwellings in a day. Nero's infamous fire of AD 64 spread uncontrolled from some wooden booths near the Circus Maximus, reached the Palatine, Esquiline and Aventine Hills and burnt down two-thirds of Rome. Christian Jews were blamed and recent research has provided evidence that the disaffected men may indeed have been arsonists, hating the 'whore of Babylon' on her scarlet beast with its seven heads that God's fire would devour. Whether Christians or others were incendiaries, they were certainly assisted by inadequate defences and the abundance of flammable materials: dry wood, oil and fabrics in the homes, papyrus rolls in the booksellers.[5]

It has been claimed that there were no bookshops in Rome at that time but this is not true. Catullus visited some near the Forum. He wrote in poem [14A] of getting up at dawn to go *ad librariorum*, to the booksellers, to buy

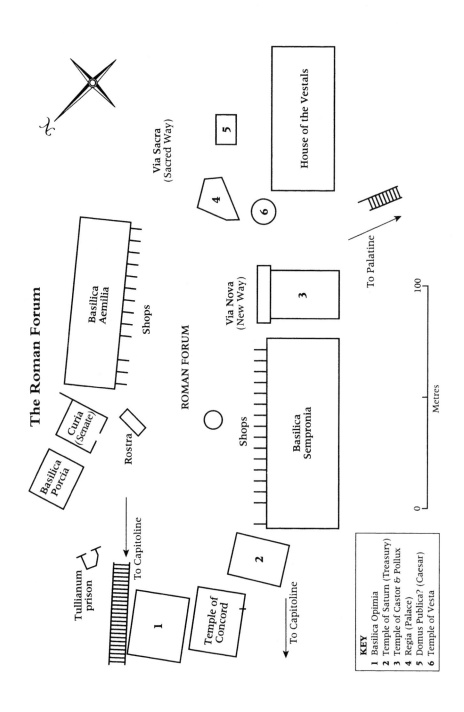

The Roman Forum

some really bad verse to repay Calvus, his friend, who had humorously given him a collection of unreadable poetry. In another poem [55] he had searched all the small book-stalls, *omnibus libellis*, looking for someone who was hiding from him.

Such 'shops' were not emporia filled with shelf after shelf of scrolls. More probably they were booths open to the street, many of them with only single copies of the works of the best-known Greek poets and playwrights and Roman historians. To buy one was to have it copied by the bookseller's slave, sometimes an incompetent and careless scribe who could mutilate great verse into near-incomprehensibility. But Catullus could have purchased books.[6]

What Catullus could not do was use a public library in Rome. There weren't any. In 47 BC the dictator Julius Caesar asked the scholar Marcus Varro, author of the treatise 'On Libraries' 'to build for public use a library of Greek books and one of Latin books, both as large as possible'. But Varro procrastinated and in March 44 BC Caesar was assassinated and the project abandoned.

It was not until the mid-30s BC that Gaius Asinius Pollio, enriched with plunder he had accumulated in Illyria, did have a library built near the Forum. Its two sections for Greek and Roman writers contained statues of many of them, including one of the still-living Varro.[7] Years earlier Catullus had known and respected Pollio, a man 'full of wit and charm'. He also knew his brother, Marrucinus, but had little respect for him. At a dinner when Catullus and his guests were enjoying wine and conversation Marrucinus stole one of the poet's finest linen napkins. Romans, even educated ones, ate with their fingers and guests brought their own napkins, often of excellent material. Catullus was not amused. 'Marrucinus Asinius', he wrote:

> Stop feeling and stealing with your sly left mitt.
> While we're dining, wining, enjoying wit,
> Nicking napkins from the unalert,
> And think it's smart, you piece of dirt...
> ...My thunderous verses could bring you grief,
> Return my napkin, incompetent thief
>
> [12]

In a society as small as Rome's it was a serious threat. A hundred years later napkins were still objects of dishonourable desire. In an epigram Martial called one of the thieves, Hermogenes, a master of sleight of hand:

> Keep your eyes on his right hand, pinion his left,
> and he'll still bring off a theft.
>
> ...

[He] never brings a napkin when he's asked to dine
But he always takes one home – yours or mine.

Satire XII, 8

Martial sold his epigrams through a bookseller, Atrectus, whose door-posts near the Forum were 'plastered with advertisements from top to bottom'.[8]

Although there were no public libraries to provide a rare copy of a Greek or Egyptian work, if Catullus had entrée to the houses of the rich he would have had access to another source of elusive literature, the private collections of well-to-do and cultivated men. Cicero had a library, so did his friend and correspondent, Titus Pomponius Atticus, who sent two assistants to help Cicero's librarian Tyrannio erect shelving and add labelled tags to the rolls. Marcus Terentius Varro, antiquarian and prolific writer, veteran of Pompey's wars, later tribune and then praetor, possessed one that was even more extensive. All these acquisitions needed highly trained slaves as copyists and organizers of subject-catalogues by which the works of a poet or a historian could be located amongst the shelves and pigeon-holes of lacks in which the rolls were stored like the contents of a wallpaper shop.

Greatest and most generous of these bibliophiles was the multi-millionaire, Lucius Licinius Lucullus. He purchased everything he could but did not hide anything away. His library of manuscripts was open to everyone, the rooms and their scrolls, the colonnades where the papyrus rolls could be studied, not silently but, as the custom was, read aloud. There were even lounges where the scholars could meet and discuss the arcane problems presented by some allusive poem.[9]

Lucullus was a remarkable but potentially frustrated man. As a soldier for eight years from 74 to 66 BC he had very successfully commanded legions in the Third Mithridatic War in Bithynia, but two men resented his victories. Pompey wanted to replace him and win the glory and deviously persuaded the Senate to recall his rival. In 68 BC he was helped by a disaffected member of Lucullus' staff, the general's own brother-in-law, Publius Clodius Pulcher, who three years later would prosecute Catiline in a farcical trial and then in 62 BC disgrace himself in the Bona Dea affair. Resenting his lack of military advancement under Lucullus, Pulcher incited the troops to mutiny. Lucullus was summoned to Rome and despite his achievements was permitted only the meanest of triumphs.

Lucullus was allowed no more than 1,600 legionaries in the procession along the Triumphal Way, but he created his own triumph. Spectators gaped at the scores of prows of captured ships, the six-foot-high golden statue of Mithridates with its shield coruscating with precious stones, the twenty wagons laden with objects of silver, thirty-two more with gold, silver ingots gleaming in the Roman sunlight, and on the backs of mules golden couches, chests heavy with almost three million silver coins.

Then he retired to enjoy ten years of luxury in his sumptuous house with the finest gardens in the whole of Rome. He had so many villas in the countryside that he sometimes forgot where he was staying. 'Lucullan' became synonymous with 'unbelievable generosity'. Asked to lend a hundred cloaks for a play, he offered 5,000. Once, dining on his own, his steward, the *promus*, served him courses of ordinary fare. He was rebuked. 'Tonight Lucullus is to dine with Lucullus.'[10]

He had married the youngest sister of Publius Clodius Pulcher, Clodia, 'a woman of most dissolute habits, whom he was also accused of debauching'. Lucullus divorced her and married Servilia, who was just as licentious. His first wife had two sisters. They too were named Clodia, a fact that has caused confusion and uncertainty amongst students of Catullus.

Roman names were complicated. Men usually had three beginning with the forename, the *praenomen*, a personal name of which there were only about fourteen. They were usually abbreviated so Lucius became L. and Titus, T. Only intimates used this name. The important name was the middle one, the family or clan name, the *nomen gentilicum*, a name inherited from the father and commonly ending in -ius as in Gaius [G.] Jul*ius* Caesar of the Julian family. It was the name that women were given so that the daughter of Caesar was known as Julia, and the sisters of Publius Clodius, Clodia. The third name or surname, the *cognomen*, was a kind of nickname indicating some personal trait, likeness or profession. Catullus may have been called 'puppy or cub' from *catulus*. Cicero meant 'chick pea', and Rufus, 'redhead'. Even the most staid and pompous of Romans took no offence when they were addressed as Strabo, 'squint-eye', or Brutus, 'stupid'. Slaves had just one name. If they were freed they adopted their master's *prae*-and *nomen gentilicum*, so that Tiro, the slave of Marcus Tullius Cicero, became M. Tullius Tiro.[11]

For the leisured Roman, G. Valerius Catullus, there were many morning attractions. Browsing at bookstalls or visiting private libraries was for the serious. Men less dedicated might go to the Public Hunt, *Venatio*, one of the bloodthirsty entertainments for which the Romans have become notorious. Infrequent because of the cost, and held originally in the cattle market, the Forum Boarium, later in the central Forum, these were vicious fights held before midday between condemned men and ferocious wild beasts. 'A substantial hors d'oeuvres,' Auguet termed them, a first course before the gladiatorial contests of the afternoon.[12] Catullus seldom referred to the Games, the Hunt, the chariot-races or *quadrigae* in the Circus Maximus, the gladiators. He was probably more interested in the city where he was living.

Catullus knew the Forum and its shops. He also knew Rome and its hills. To the south of the Capitoline and Palatine was the steep-sided Aventine. Like the others it was inside the city walls but unlike the others it was outside the official city boundary. There were few well-to-do properties on it; essentially it was plebeian territory, a 'stronghold of the proletariat'.

Half a mile to the north-east was the Caelian Hill with its oak groves. The Lateran palace stands there today. Beyond the hill was the large but macabre Esquiline Hill, in effect two hills merged into one. Birds of prey hovered there, waiting to feast on the criminals put to death on its slopes. On the hill were mortuaries and crematoria whose chimneys smoked blackly every hour of day and night. Yet it was on this site of mortality that Pliny the Younger chose to have his mansion with its ornamental, fragrant gardens.

Catullus used a graveyard as the setting in a poem [59] for an insulting joke, deriding a vulgar woman from the provinces who put on airs as though she were a proper lady. He made sure that everyone would recognize her. He wrote her name, Rufa, the name of her husband, Menenius, even the town they came from, Bononia (Bologna) on the Via Aemilia. He accused her of being a thief, stealing food from the graves of the dead. He claimed that she had been buggered by a recaptured slave as she stooped to pick up fallen food. She was also sexually warped.

It may not be a coincidence that there is another Rufa in the collection of scribblings and graffiti known as the *Corpus Inscriptionum Latinarum*. It reads: '*Rufa ita vale: quare bene fellas*', 'Farewell, Rufa, how well you give head'. Knowing the line may have prompted Catullus to add fellatio to the other imaginary depravities of the real woman, a form of guilt by association. It was hilarious but cruel, and as the poem circulated through society it must have humiliated the luckless upstart. It read like graffiti on a Pompeian wall.

Rufa comes from Bononian town,
Menenius' wife, but she kneels down
To suck his cock as Rufulus wishes.
In the cemetery she nabs
whatever's handy – funeral dishes
from the pyre. Greedy-eyed she grabs
A loaf that's fallen on the dirt.
Bending there she doesn't mind
The half-shaved slave who lifts her skirt
And shafts her thump-thump from behind.

[59][13]

The vindictiveness of Catullus is unexplained. Rather than the unfortunate Rufa and her unwanted immortality, his real target may have been 'Rufulus', one-time friend but later enemy, Marcus Caelius Rufus.

To the north of the Esquiline with its cemeteries was the smallest of Rome's hills, the Viminal, a cramped and neglected fifty-nine acres of few monuments. Traffic bypassed it; willows grew there, the *salix Viminalis*, whose long, pliable shoots were perfect for basketry. Sprawling to its south, surrounded by the Esquiline, the Capitoline and the Palatine, was the filthy, wet valley of the Subura, the rowdy and disreputable slums of criminals, spongers, the numberless unemployed, and the many tradesmen – cobblers, blacksmiths and shopkeepers.

There were also enticing foodstalls steaming with bacon, fish, smoked sausages and salted sardines, but the Subura was dangerous with its tottering four-and five-storey tenements, badly built, leaning together like hands at prayer, sometimes perilously wedged apart by decaying timbers, frequently collapsing. Cicero wrote that two of his properties had fallen down 'and the rest are developing cracks. Not only the tenants but even the mice have cleared out.'

There were other dangers in the streets, things thrown from upper floors and a total absence of street-lighting. The satirist Juvenal warned about the hazard. 'Anyone who goes out to dinner without making a will is a fool...You can suffer as many deaths as there are windows to pass under. So send up a prayer that people will be content with just emptying out their slop bowls.'

They were emptied on to filth. A hundred years after Catullus, Juvenal grumbled about the noise, the threats of wagons in the narrow, winding streets and the dirt. 'My legs are caked with mud,' he complained. And the city reeked. Without lavatories in the poorer dwellings inhabitants carried their refuse to the nearest pit. 'More than one alley stank with the pestilential odour of a cess-trench.' Nor did the public lavatories, *foricae*, sweeten the air. They were truly public, long wooden or stone benches, perforated regularly with round holes on which people squatted, chatting to each other, asking friends to supper, cleansing themselves with a common sponge and rinsing their hands in the water of a gutter opposite the bench. Privacy was an unconsidered privilege. Ancient Rome was a communal society. Over a century later, and in an imperial palace, the *Domus Transitoria* of Nero, there was a lavatory with sixty adjacent seats.

Places were not easy to find in such a haphazard city. There were no numbered addresses and few street-names. On a dog-collar was written, if the finder could read, 'Return me to the house of Elpidus on the Caelian Hill'. Going anywhere could be a nightmare. Without street lamps, even candles, a moonless night was another of Rome's challenges. In his *Satyricon* Petronius described how a group left the well-lubricated feast of Trimalchio late at night, tottering tipsily through the blackness, meeting no passer-by at that dead hour, staggering in erratic circles, sandalled feet bleeding from the clutter of sharp stones and shattered pots, recognizing no landmark, helpless until luck brought them to their inn.[14] Catullus may have known the taverns, gaming-dens and brothels of the Subura but it is unlikely that he ever went there on his own, and never by himself at night.

Less interesting but undoubtedly safer was the northernmost of Rome's hills, the *Quirinal*. It was respectably wealthy, with many temples and street after street of side-by-side but impressive dwellings, Pompeian in style because of the limited space. Of necessity the houses were close together but remained private because only a door, no windows, opened on to the road. Like the more prosperous homes in Pompeii they occupied a rectangular plot, the door opening on to a vestibule and then the columned *atrium*, the centre of its roof open to the sky. Small bedrooms and stores lay to left and right. Beyond the atrium was the *triclinium*, a dining-room decorated with frescoes and mosaics, and beyond that was a spacious *peristylum*, a pillared garden with pool, covered verandas, fountains and an abundance of shrubs and flowers. At the far end of the house were pantries, larders and kitchens, and a back-door for tradesmen.

Contrasted with the claustrophobic hovels of the Subura, the houses were luxurious, but the luxury was limited. In winter the inhabitants froze if the shutters were open. If they were shut, then with makeshift kitchens and no lavatories, most families using commodes, the houses stank.

A characteristic protection for the home was the stone or pottery replica of an erect phallus jutting from the walls, a safeguard against the evil eye. Children had rings and brooches, *fascina*, with a phallus as protection against witchcraft. *Hic habitat felicitas*, 'here is happiness', was their message. 'The custom of placing the sign of the phallus on houses to avert evil spirits continued into medieval times, and examples have been found on the walls of churches.'[15]

Even more characteristic of Roman Italy were the finely executed murals of explicit sexual activities, usually a man with a woman, sometimes two men together, occasionally a woman with a woman. Such art was commonplace in Pompeii not only in the brothels, the *lupanari* (with their graffiti – 'Here I had Felicia', 'Goodbye, Victor, you gave me a good time', 'if he wants a girl, look for Attice, charge 16 denarii, a high-class girl') but also in many villas and houses of the town: the House of the Vettii, the Cryptoporticus, the home of the poet Menander among them. The Romans had few inhibitions about sex. It was recreational and the scenes were less pornography than entertainment.

Plan of a Pompeian house

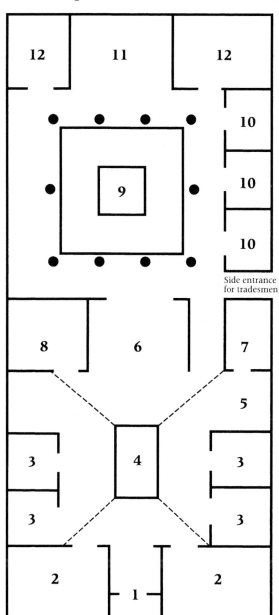

KEY

1 **Vestibulum.** Entrance.
2 **Cellae.** Rooms.
  Sometimes shops.
3 **Cubicula.** Bedrooms.
4 **Atrium.** Central room
  with open roof.
5 **Alae.** Store rooms.
6 **Tablinum.** Room for
  ancestral statues and
  family archives.
7 **Culina.** Kitchen.
8 **Triclinium.** Dining-room.
9 **Peristylum.** Open colonnaded
  garden with central
  pool (Impluvium).
10 **Cubicula** etc. Bedrooms,
  bathroom and lavatory.
11 **Exedra.** Room for
  private conversation.
12 **Oeci.** Reception rooms.

Side entrance
for tradesmen

In Rome now most of the art has gone. Fires, the demolition of pagan sites to make room for Christian edifices, the rebuilding as Rome grew, the continuous changes have destroyed almost all the buildings that Catullus knew. Few frescoes and murals survive. There are some scenes in the recently discovered Villa of Farnesina, one of them an improved copy of a mosaic in the Villa of Centrocelle just outside the city walls.[16]

Even in down-to-earth Pompeii, with its inns, taverns and brothels, not every mural was erotic. There were brightly painted landscapes like those in the house of M. Lucretius Frontone, a man that graffiti recommended for election. A famous painting of Vesuvius decorated the House of the Centenary. There were hunting scenes, scenes from mythological stories, a struggle between pygmies and monsters from the Nile. There was every day life, a mosaic at the entrance to the House of the Tragic Poet showing a snarling mastiff tugging at its chain, *Cave Canem*, 'beware of the dog'. There were portraits, a fine one of Terentius Neo and his wife, she with a stylus and tablet, he, a law-student, with a scroll.

Then there were murals of markets and shops. Near the bakery of Popidius Priscus there was a drawing of a baker's stall with loaves and rolls and hungry customers. In the large, almost opulent residence of Julia Spuria Felix, the forum market was shown with sellers of pans and clothes and cooked foods, stews and sauces. In another room there was a mural of shelves of food, a platter of eggs, four unplucked thrushes hooked on the wall, a wine jug. Not far from Pompeii at the palace of Oplontis there was a beautiful, almost three-dimensional painting of a glass bowl with apples, pears, apricots and pomegranates, just the sort of refreshment preferred for lunch.[17] That, like breakfast, was a simple meal, bread, fruit, cheese, diluted wine, or maybe the leftovers from last night's supper. It was sustenance enough for the afternoon, with the prospect of going to the public baths or enjoying some casual hours in the company of friends. There were also the Games.

Rome was a riot waiting to happen before the white cloth that signalled the start of a race. Only bribery saved the crowded city from violence. To placate its unemployed and penniless men in their squalor Rome satisfied empty stomachs with free grain. To enliven the dangerously idle hours Rome consoled the malcontents with the prospect of games that were free and would satisfy their blood-lust. By the late first century BC no fewer than sixty-six days of the year were dedicated to the Games.

Duas tantum res anxias optat,	The discontented want only two things,
Panem et circenses.	Bread and circuses.

Juvenal, *Satire X*

Of those Games, chariot-races, the *ludi circenses*, with their excitement of speed and spills, were the most popular. They were held at the end of festivals in the lengthy Circus Maximus, south of the Palatine, an arena that could hold almost a quarter of a million spectators. Benches were filled. Streets were deserted. Guards protected the empty houses. Seated sweatingly together, both men and women loved the spectacle, the *quadrigae*, four-horse chariots, the triple teams of Blues, Greens, Reds and Whites, the twelve starting-boxes, the seven-lap race of long straight stretches and sudden tight bends, five thrilling miles, all over in fifteen minutes but there were twenty-four races at a meeting going on well into the evening.

It was an hysterical atmosphere with rowdy fans, fights, betting so heavy that some backers buried *defixiones*, curse-tablets of lead, on the course, stating exactly which driver or horse they wanted hurt, specifying the precise injuries to be inflicted. Diocles, a champion charioteer, famous for his opening sprint, retired with a fortune of 35,000,000 *sestertii*. He was skilful, ruthless and lucky. Many youths and ageing veterans were crippled, even killed during the races. There was little protection for them, a flimsy, lightweight chariot, padded legs, a leather band for the chest, a tunic of the team's colours, nothing more before the suicidally tight-packed rush to the first bend, legs astride for balance, rein-hands close together, hooves of forty-eight charging horses hurling up eye-scraping sprays of sand, teams swerving, wheels grazing, whips lashing in that most dangerous, often deadly first lap. The charioteers never heard the screams and shouts of the crowds.

To avoid boredom in between the races there were shows of wild beasts and public executions.[18] Gladiatorial shows were less frequent and could be boringly repetitive, with similarly armoured men fighting with similar weapons. But there was a poignancy in the certainty of death. An ambitious politician could win thousands of votes if he staged an outstanding event. Julius Caesar knew that.

In 65 BC Caesar had been elected a *curule aedile* with a colleague, M. Calpurnius Bibulus. As well as being responsible for safety in the streets, for the markets, public baths and brothels, and the distribution of grain, they also had to organize the *munera*, public shows that were theoretically paid for by the state but which the *aediles* were expected to enhance by contributions from their own purse. Both Caesar and Bibulus paid but Caesar drew deeply on the willing coffers of his equally ambitious ally, Crassus. Caesar had no money and no power but much ambition; Crassus had wealth but no political power. Only Pompey had both fame and power. In time Caesar and Crassus intended to emulate, perhaps diminish him. Caesar began with a gladiatorial display in the Forum that was talked about for years.

Reputation was very important for a man. Paying for a lavish gladiatorial display could incur enormous debts and ruin a person for years. Yet a memorable performance could help him become a quaestor and then a praetor. That would bring the reward of uncountable riches as the governor of a province.

Caesar was ruthless. Despite the contributions of Bibulus, his partner, he took all credit for the incredible show. His uncharismatic colleague grumbled, 'The Temple of the Heavenly Twins in the Forum is always simply called "Castor's"; and I always play Pollux to Caesar's Castor when we give a public entertainment together.'

As a display of prodigality it was an astonishment. Ferocious animals such as lions were set against criminals armed with genuine silver weapons. After that the bloodshed continued with more than 300 pairs of gladiators fighting with long rectangular shields, greaves, straight swords and crested helmets. The sheer number of the fighters alarmed Caesar's enemies. As a precaution it was decided to limit the number of gladiators a citizen could have. But it was too late.

Caesar gained widespread and enduring popularity. Plutarch wrote: 'By his liberality and expenditure on the theatrical exhibitions, the processions, and the public entertainments, he completely drowned all previous displays and put the people in such a humour, that every man was seeking for new offices and new honours to requite him with.'[19]

Yet despite their popularity Catullus hardly mentions the Games. Presumably he had little interest in them. In his entire work of almost 3,000 lines there is just one allusion to the blood-sports. It occurs in what is arguably his finest poem, *Attis*, in which a man grieves that he is so far from

patria, bonis, amicis, genitoribus abero?	homeland, possessions, friends, parents,
abero foro, palaestra, stadio et gymnasiis.	forum, wrestling-ground, race-course and gymnasia.
	[63], lines 59-60

It is a passing reference suggesting that there were more immediate and satisfying personal concerns to the poet than the vicarious spectacle of danger, accident and death.

In 55 BC Cicero attended the Games put on by Pompey to celebrate the dedication of his new theatre. The orator did not enjoy them. At the end there were wild beast shows, two a day for five days. 'Magnificent – nobody says otherwise. But what pleasure can a cultivated person get out of seeing a weak human being torn to shreds by a powerful animal, or a splendid animal transfixed by a hunting spear?...The last day was for the elephants. The groundlings showed much astonishment thereat, but no enjoyment. There was even an impulse of compassion, a feeling that the monsters had something of human about them.' Pliny the Elder wrote that the spectators cursed Pompey as they listened to the trumpeting of the terrified beasts.

Cicero's reaction was not unique. Others also disapproved. 'On such days, the cultured Roman shut himself up at home or took refuge in the countryside and devoted himself to meditation or leisured study; and could scarcely avoid congratulating himself on devoting to such fruitful pastimes the hours which others were losing watching the tedious manoeuvres of two swordsmen.'[20]

It is known how Catullus did spend one such afternoon because he wrote a poem [50] about the laughing hours that he and his close friend, the orator Gaius Licinius Macer Calvus, 'the bald', spent improvizing sharp epigrams in increasingly difficult metres. Other poets had experienced such contests. The self-important stoic, Crispinus, challenged Horace to bring his wax jotter, name a time, place and umpire and 'then we shall see which of us can write the more'. As Crispinus was a past master of tedious verbosity he may have out-written Horace in quantity but Horace dismissed him as 'blood-shot' and an 'ass'. In quality of writing there would have been no contest.[21]

What rivalry there was between Catullus and the eloquent Calvus was between good friends and Catullus was to write a sad, lovely poem [96] comforting Calvus on the death of his mistress, Quintilia.

There was no sadness about their poetic duel, no fierceness, just merriment, grace, elegance and wit, two sensitive and clever young men struggling to outdo the other.

> Yesterday, Licinius, was a day of pleasure and leisure,
> amusing ourselves jotting on your tablets.
> We agreed to be light-hearted, rather naughty,
> first you and then me composing playful verses,
> experimenting in this metre, then another,
> challengingly each other, joking, wining,
> until I left, so fired with your brilliant ripostes
> that food gave no relief to my disturbed state,
> nor sleep brougnt any quiet to my eyes. (p. 230)
>
>   [50]

Such afternoons, which were more serious to poets than the frivolous tone suggests, were more important to Catullus than the spectacles of death in the arena. He may have watched them only seldom, unlike the population of Rome – including the women – who attended them enthusiastically.

He may not have gone to the Games but women certainly did. By the first century BC the role of women in Rome was changing. With the assimilation of

Greek customs and refinements sexual freedom became licensed and amorous escapades were almost the norm. Not many years before matrons had shown only their faces in public, wearing a long *stola* that completely covered their bodies. It was a white dress, pleated and girdled with a coloured border around the neck and a hemline embroidered or jewelled. The stola was held by decorative clasps at the shoulders and covered by a rectangular mantle, the *palla*.

'With a married lady,' sighed Horace, 'you can't see a thing except her face, the rest is covered by her long dress,' but then added, 'unless she's a Catia' whose

> ...Coan silk allows you
> to see her virtually naked, there's no chance of concealing
> bad legs or ugly feet; you can check her profile. [22]

Silk imported from the fertile Greek island of Kos was almost transparent, an early 'see-through' sensuous material provocatively chosen by Catia, 'an immoderate woman'.

By 60 BC such ostentation had become the fashion and nowhere more obviously than at the Circus Maximus where men and women were allowed to mix. Assignations were made. Adultery was committed. Catia made love to a tribune, Valerius Asciculus, in Pompey's theatre. There was ambivalence in Rome about the punishment for such immorality. Legally, the man's sin was considered negligible, although an outraged husband might react differently. But for the wife, property of her spouse, she was sullied by her immorality, the marriage defiled and she could be dealt with as the husband decided, even by death. [23]

In spite of the perils the period developed into one of furtive love-making. The willingness of allegedly respectable women at that time to take lovers was widely accepted. Some of the matrons were innocent amateurs enjoying the physical pleasures of an attractive man. Others, like the Sempronia that Sallust vilified, were experienced huntresses. 'Her appetite for sex', scowled the historian, 'was such that she took the initiative with a man more often than they with her.' Other well-born but needy wives were no more than harlots. As will be seen in the trial of Clodius Pulcher they were quite prepared to copulate in return for cash.

It was not only the unknown and the insignificant that enjoyed these illicit couplings. Catullus had a patrician mistress. Caesar was a philanderer whose successes were the envy of Rome. 'All agree that he greatly loved pleasure, spent much money in order to gratify his passions, and seduced very many ladies of quality.' They included the queen of Mauritania, Eunoë, and Cleopatra of

Egypt. At home his conquests read like a Debrett's 'Peerage of adultery', lovely woman after woman of high station, most of them married: Postumia, wife of Servius Sulpicius, erudite jurist and one of Cicero's correspondents; Lollia, wife of Aulus Gabinius, corrupt politician who for a bribe placed the boy-pharaoh Ptolemy on the throne of Egypt; Tertulla, an amiable fifty-year-old and the wife of Caesar's own colleague, Crassus; Mucia, the to-be-divorced wife of Pompey.

Above all Caesar was enamoured of Servilia, wife of Marcus Brutus and mother of Brutus, his assassin-to-be. Rumour had it that the boy was his own son, so strong was their physical likeness. It was Servilia's billet-doux to Caesar that, to his chagrin, her half-brother Cato had demanded in the Senate'.

In 59 BC, when Caesar was elected a consul, he gave Servilia a pearl valued at six million *sestertii* in addition to estates he bought at auctions. People remarked at the expense. Cicero made a derisive pun about it. 'The cost was less than you think, Atticus, because it had been reduced by a third.' The pun was on 'third', *tertia*. Tertia was Servilia's daughter. 'Servilia, you see, was also suspected at the time of having prostituted her daughter to Caesar.'[24]

Many of these women were known to Catullus who met them in their homes or as visitors in the grand houses to which he had admittance. He mentioned two by name. Postumia he converted into an impossible *Arbiter Bibendi*. 'The Judge of Drink' at a dinner was always a man, never a female. He decided how much water should be in the wine. Poem [27] is a cheerful drinking epigram, a wine, woman and song poem, with Postumia lapping it up with the men as the adjective *ebriosioris* implies. 'Drunker than a drunken grape,' translated Sir Richard Burton. She was the opposite of Caesar who for all his indulgences was noted for his alcoholic abstinence.

Catullus also had a quiet laugh at Pompey's wife Mucia or 'Maecilia' as a diminutive, whose exploits during the long absences of her husband were noteworthy even by Rome's dissolute standards. Pompey had been consul in 70 BC and then again in 55 BC. During those fifteen years, even after her divorce in 62 BC, Mucia excelled herself

> When Pompey first was consul Mucia, his wife,
> had a cautious lover then another in her house. And
> Now in his second she's reformed her bedroom life,
> jig-a-jogging with two thousand. (p. 248)
>
>   [113][25]

With Caesar's numerous amatory interests, his drawn-out political manoeuvrings and the organizing of the gladiatorial extravaganza it is questionable whether he was much involved with another duty of a *curule aedile* – the condition of the public baths. Perhaps he left that chore to his more conscientious and unimaginative colleague, M. Calpurnius Bibulus. Yet the baths were essential to Rome's social life.

There were well over a hundred of them in the city. In 33 BC another *curule aedile*, Agrippa, not only checked the heating systems, the cleanliness and the proper supervision of the establishments but also made a census, counting 170 *balneae* (baths) in Rome. Many of them were on the Campus Martius, once a spacious tract of land between the Capitoline and Quirinal Hills to the east and the great bend of the Tiber to the west. That there were so many baths is not surprising. Most homes lacked not only a kitchen and a lavatory but anything more elaborate than a pitcher of cold water for washing.

Numerous the balneae may have been but the majority were old and shabby, offering little more than a room to leave clothes, a warm bath, a hot bath and a cold plunge. In contrast, others were almost as palatial as the *thermae*, 'warm baths', of imperial times to come with gardens to stroll in, a pool for swimming, a gymnasium, shops, exercise courts for ball-games and wrestling, stalls selling food and drink (cakes, sausages, lettuce, eggs, lizard-fish). A good *balneum* provided all these facilities as well as the basic requirements of a public bath. 'To visit the baths was to step into the arms of *voluptas*, to enjoy pleasing and comfortable surroundings.'[26]

Mixed bathing did occur but in general men and women were kept separate, women attending in the morning, men early in the afternoon around the ninth hour, after lunch had been digested and the effects of the watered wine had faded. Entrance fees were minimal, half an *as* for women, a quarter for men. (There were four bronze *asses* to one *sestertius*, the commonest of the coins, and sixteen *asses* to the *denarius*. Least of all was the *quadrans*, a fourth of an *as*. At the top of the scale were the scarce gold *staters*, *aureii*.) 'Pay the bathman his fee, take the change' would be a man's order to his slave. Then they could go in.

To enter the baths was a process and an occasion. The process was to take exercise, to cleanse the body. The occasion was to meet friends and acquaintances, to gossip, to talk earnestly, to do business, to invite colleagues to dinner, to wheedle an invitation to dinner that evening. A visit to the baths could take far longer than an hour. Everyone went. Men from the highest class mixed with commoners. Farmers shaved and bathed on market days.

If a man was wealthy, slaves accompanied him, one of them a trained masseur carrying his master's flask of oil, his strigil or scraper, a comb, and a pocket-sized set of utensils on a ring: nail-clippers, tweezers and ear-scoop. Other slaves brought his towels. After entering the *apodyterium*, the changing-room, the man undressed, leaving his outdoor clothes on a shelf or in a wooden container to be guarded by one of the slaves. Wearing only a towel he could then begin the 'process'.

There was no set programme. Pliny the Elder recommended some vigorous exercise with a medicine ball or swimming several lengths of the pool. Lazier people preferred to gamble with dice. Then one went to the warm *tepidarium* placed some distance from the fires of the hypocaust that circulated the underfloor hot air. Once relaxed, there was then a choice of going to the steam-filled *laconium* with its central tub of boiling water, or the drier, just as hot *caldarium* with its pool, then back to the *tepidarium*, and finally the shock of the *frigidarium* with its chilly plunge – all this before the anointing with oil and the scraping away of the sweat and dirt and the pummelling massage.

It could be unpleasant if instead of a skilled masseur the uncertain attentions of a bath-attendant, the *sordidus unctor*, was paid for. An unfortunate in the *Satyricon* of Petronius complained, 'Having a bath is like sending your body to a cleaner. The bathman pulls you to pieces. So I don't bathe every day.' A Latin proverb had a rather similar sentiment. *Balnea, vina, Venus corrumpunt corpora nostra sed vitam faciunt* – 'Baths, wine, women corrupt our bodies – but they make life itself'.[27]

Going to the baths was an enjoyment and could be profitable unless one's clothes had been stolen. It was always a risk even if they had been carefully stored. At the recently discovered Suburban Baths just outside Pompeii a ground-floor room had a mural of sixteen clothes-boxes placed on a deep shelf 'Each box is numbered and accompanied by an erotic vignette...representing sexual acts of an increasing complexity, dexterity and imagination,' 'the most audacious ancient erotic paintings found to date'.[28] The murals are unequivocally erogenous but the lidded boxes, the legs and lockers also show the concern that people had for their clothes.

The baths were crowded and stealing was easy. The satirical Martial claimed to have paid a one-eyed woman to watch over his garments. Inside the baths themselves a slave known as a *capsarius*, 'box-watcher', could be hired if one could trust him. Not everybody bothered and there were skilful thieves as Catullus was well aware.

At the baths the grossest crooks
Are old Vibennius and his son who's queer;
The father's hands are quick-grab hooks,
The son's backside's on offer here.
Clear off, the pair, and go to Hell!
Vibennius is a thieving menace.
As for his son, he'll never sell
His hairy arse for more than pennies. (pp. 226-7)

[33][29]

There were other nuisances at the baths, like pests trying to cadge dinner from reluctant hosts. One of them, Menogenes, infuriated Martial by accosting him while the poet was exercising, praising the cleanliness of the poet's rather grubby towels, bringing him a drink, mopping his brow until, exasperated, 'Oh, come to dinner then'.

Even at his most intimate moments a man was not safe, Martial snarled:

> For hours, for a whole day, he'll sit
> On the public lavatory seat,
> Not because he needs a shit.
> He wants to be asked out to eat.[30]

To be invited to dinner in a great house was an honour and invitations were formal, expressed very conventionally. Catullus actually began a poem with the accepted wording. *Cenabis bene...diebus*, 'the gods permitting [name], you will dine well with me in a few days' time'.[31] It was rude, sometimes imprudent, to refuse but all right to be unpunctual. In an age of inexact time-keeping a guest arriving an hour late was not rebuked.

Removing his outdoor footwear, the guest's feet were bathed by a slave and then, putting on slippers, he reached the dining-room in which he would eat bare-footed. The *triclinium* was 'the room of three sloping couches' whose upper ends were slightly higher than the square, central food-table. The room was spacious, but it needed to be. The couches were not divans. They were larger than king-sized beds, long enough for a man to stretch out at full length, wide enough for the three diners to lie alongside each other, and with sufficient space between them for their cutlery: ladle, spoon, small pointed implement for eggs and shellfish. There were no forks.

The layout of the furniture was socially graded. Opposite the door through which slaves would carry the food and wine was the main couch, *lectus medius*, 'middle', set across the room with the two others at right angles to it at either end. The most distinguished guest occupied the left end of the middle one. In front of him, just overlapping the end of his couch, was the 'bottom' one, *lectus imus*. At its head was the host, who could most easily converse with the main guest. At the other end of the middle couch was the *lectus summus*, the 'top' one, so-called because it abutted the right-hand end of the top couch.

Pictures of diners in togas are misleading. There were accepted forms of 'dinner wear', including the popular synthesis, a 'mixed dress' of brightly coloured tunic and equally vivid short cloak.

The arrangement of the three couches of the *triclinium*

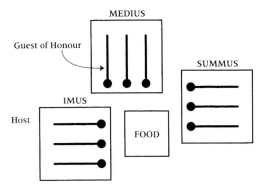

Meals were rarely simple and never brief. It was known, however, for mean-minded hosts to reserve the finest dishes for themselves and a few guests, giving other diners inferior fare. Juvenal suffered from this: he had been given 'wine which a sponge would feel sick to mop up' while 'His Lordship' supped vintage Falernian. Futhermore he was served by an insolent slave 'whom you would not wish to meet in the middle of the night', who handed him a loaf 'so hard it threatened your teeth' while his master enjoyed bread 'soft and snowy-white, kneaded from the finest flour'. That man was given a lobster, Juvenal a prawn and half an egg, the host an imported fish, the poet a blotchy bass from the sewers of the Tiber. But the invitation was gratefully received.[32]

More generous men provided three or more courses, first an hors d'oeuvres of salads, radishes, mushrooms, oysters and shellfish, sardines, eggs, all delicately prepared by one of the most prized of slaves, a master-chef. The course ended with *mulsum*, wine blended with honey. Then came the main course, the dinner itself, a feast of as many as seven dishes for the guests to select: pheasants, geese, peacock, boar with truffles and mushrooms, lamprey, Chian wine from Greece, Italian Alban, Setian, Nomentanum. Extravagant even for Lucullus was wine cooled by snow brought from distant mountains.

When the diners had sated themselves slaves went around with perfumed water and towels to wash hands, others refilled goblets with fastidiously diluted wine, removed the table and replaced it with a second laden with fruit, stuffed dates, honey, nuts. But this was not necessarily the end. An elaborate banquet could begin all over again, sometimes with men becoming drunk and vomiting. It did not matter. Slaves would clean up just as they would clear the floor of lobster claws, snail-shells, broken eggs, fruit stones, apple cores that had been casually discarded during the meal.[33]

Some dinners verged on the farcical. In the *Satyricon* the rich and ostentatiously vulgar host, Trimalchio, obese, self-indulgent and ignorant, boasted about the sealed bottles of fine wine for his guests: '*Falernum Opinianum annorum centum*'.

> Genuine Falernian Wine
> Guaranteed One Hundred Years
> Old!
> Bottled
> In The Consulship
> Of
> Opimius.

Everything was wrong. Opimius had been a consul in 121 BC. Trimalchio held his dinner some time during the reign of Nero, AD 54-68, so that the wine was almost two hundred years old and undrinkable. Falernian deteriorated after twenty years.[34]

Other dinners degenerated into orgies. In 52 BC the tribune Gemellus, 'a man of good blood but coarsened by servile duties', arranged a meal for the consul, Q. Caecilius Metellus Piso Scipio. Debauchery followed. Two noblewomen, Fulvia and Mucia, and a well-born youngster, Saturninus, freely prostituted themselves. Fulvia, the daughter of Sempronia, was notorious for her profligacy and Mucia was infamous for her infidelities.

Scipio was a supporter of Pompey. With Mucia the roles were reversed. 'O bodies laid out to ignominy, destined for the fumbling-toys of lecherous drunkards. O banquet which consuls and tribunes should have visited with strokes of wrath, not of lust.'[35] In 46 BC Scipio was defeated in battle by Caesar and killed himself

Most fine meals, however, were decorous affairs of appetizing food with palatable, somewhat diluted wine of excellent quality and, after the *triclinium* had been cleared of its litter and the *mensa secunda*, the second food-table, had been removed, the host provided entertainment. It was well-performed and serious. There was music on flutes and lyres, there were singers and dancers. Frequently guests heard tales told by a trained story-teller. There could be, rather daringly, actors and actresses, although the comedies and farces were often of doubtful taste.

One of the most attractive of these pleasures was a poetry recital. Whether after a dinner or in an afternoon salon, poetry was sought after and appreciated and in this Catullus excelled. His repertoire was wide – lyrical, classical, provocative, musical or abusive. He could be tenderly reminiscent about his young lover, Juventius:

Juvencius, thy fair sweet Eyes,
If to my fill that I may kisse,
Three hundred thousand times I'de kisse,
Nor future age should cloy this Blisse;
No not if thicker than ripe ears,
The harvest of our kisses bears.

[48]

The verse was one of thirteen poems by Catullus translated by the cavalier poet Richard Lovelace, 'the handsomest man of his time', and an admirer of the poet.

Almost 300 years later a Cornish poet, Arthur Symons, who had lodged with Yeats and read Catullus to him, made a similar translation, showing how faithful to the original Lovelace had been:

Your honeyed eyes, Juventius,
If you would let one kiss,
Three hundred thousand would to us
Seem nothing much amiss:
Could all earth's ears of corn eclipse
That heavenly harvest of the lips?[36]

Catullus could write gently and evocatively of the huntress and deity, Diana, an ancient Italian divinity of the woodlands, protectress of wild things and a fertility goddess. Poem [34] was translated by the American poetess, Mary Stewart. The third of its six verses reads:

Born to be untouched and free,
Mistress of the wild-wood tree,
Goddess of the mountains,
Spirit, too, of light and shade,
Sunny slope and dusky glade,
Spirit of laughing fountains.[37] (pp. 171)

For a different, more flippant gathering Catullus could provide sarcastic criticism like that directed at Quintus Arrius, an ambitious but ill-educated orator who spoke in a 'refined' style but regrettably dropping his aitches. In the Latin of the late first century the aspirate was weak so that 'Helen of Troy' was spoken almost as 'Ellen'. Pompous speakers, however, added incorrect aitches so that Oedipus became Hoedipus. They even introduced it with comical effects. Clodius Pulcher, usually pronounced 'pulker' was transformed into 'pulkHer'. Catullus and his listeners laughed at Arrius.

Whenever H'arrius tried to sound
an H, his 'ope was unavailing;
He always spoke of 'orse and'ound,
His family had that failing.
Then he was gone. He quit his home;
Yet someone murmured wittily –
H'arrius in his years at Rome
H'enjoyed his 'oliday in Hitaly.

[84]

Arrius had left Rome to accompany his patron Crassus to Parthia, crossing the Ionian Sea on his way. G. A. Williamson has suggested that Catullus likened the discordant mispronunciation of Arrius with the roughness of that sea. 'After murdering the Latin language Arrius was now murdering the far more delicate and refined Greek – a ghastly crime to the ears of a cultured Roman.'[38] The unaspirated speaker may have died in the futility of the Parthian War. At dinners in the public baths, people chuckled about him, discussed current overseas affairs, argued over the rights and wrongs of the plebeians, asked if anyone had heard the latest epigram by Catullus.

Late in 62 BC Pompey returned from his victorious campaigns in Bithynia, Armenia, Syria and Palestine, where Jerusalem had been sacked. He was accompanied by almost 40,000 devoted troops. To Catullus the matter was of little importance. To him, any concern about Pompey was limited to laughing (in poem [113]) about the wanton misbehaviour of his soon-to-be-divorced wife, Mucia. But in that year the main topic of conversation was the forthcoming trial of Publius Clodius Pulcher for his blasphemy at the festival of Bona Dea.

4

POETRY AND PASSION – 62-60 BC

The trial no doubt aroused the curiosity of Catullus. Being acquainted with Metellus Celer he would have known his brother-in-law, the controversial, rising politician, Clodius Pulcher, 'the lovely one'. In consequence, the poet may have been one of the hundreds who went to the Forum that morning in May 61 BC.

The trial was the talk of Rome. It was also an innovation, an experiment and a farce. There was no precedent for it. What Clodius had been accused of was not listed as a crime. But it was, the Senate agreed, a sin against religion, an offence made worse by the accused having deliberately disguised himself as a girl musician to avoid recognition – by donning a veil, even wearing a *strophium*, the Roman brassiere. Even more serious, the crime occurred in the *domus publica* of the Pontifex Maximus, Julius Caesar. The gods had been offended. The charge was *incestus*, a pollution, and Clodius Pulcher was denounced for it by Aurelia, mother of Caesar, describing the accused as 'the most elegant and most dissolute character in Rome'.[1]

No existing Roman court was appropriate. The Senate ordered a special one, a *Quaestio extraordinaria*, and to ensure a verdict of 'guilty' the praetor in charge was to handpick the jury. This was high-handed and too much. The Claudii were an ancient, patrician family and Clodius had considerable friends, allies and political supporters in Rome. The biased decree was vetoed only for Quintus Hortensius Hortalus to reintroduce it with the proviso that the jury should be chosen by traditional means.[2]

Hortensius, a friend of Catullus, was a celebrated, gifted but affected orator whose exaggerated mannerisms gained him the nickname of 'Dionysia', a stage-dancer. He was rich: at his death in 50 BC some 10,000 casks of Arvisium wine were discovered in his cellars. He was also one of the 'new poets' although a generation older than most. Catullus was sufficiently fond of him to send him a promised poem even while mourning the death of his own brother. It was not original verse, he explained, but a translation of Callimachus.

But even in my deep sadness, Hortalus,
I send you these verses of Callimachus,

In case you thought your words were lost in the wind,

Forgotten by my grieving mind. (pp. 243-4)

[65], lines 15-18.[3]

In 61 BC Hortensius' recommendation for a fairer jury was accepted and the trial began. Impartiality was not its hallmark. Opponents of Clodius were determined to 'eliminate a formidable political opponent'. Supporters like Crassus were equally intent on reducing the power of the diehards.[4]

The 'trial' was thus a devious affair, filled with underhand manoeuvres in which Cicero had an equivocal part, perhaps engaged in a plot to bring down Caesar, who was steadily increasing his popularity and influence. Elected a praetor in 62 BC, the next year, the year of the trial, he was awarded the governorship of western Spain. Debts detained him in Rome during the trial.

The Forum was packed with onlookers. In front of the high Rostra, decked with the rams of enemy ships were the tiered chairs of the jurors. On either side of the square, facing each other, were the benches for the prosecution and defence. In front of them, held back by guards, were the spectators looking towards the Rostra and the Senate House alongside it. Conspicuous in a threadbare, shabby toga, hair unkempt, tearful, was the figure of the obviously innocent prisoner. With well-connected prosecutors accusing him and with damning evidence against him, it was generally accepted that Clodius would be condemned.

During the trial Cicero was a reluctant prosecution witness. Plutarch said that the orator was bullied by his nagging wife, Terentia, 'for Terentia had a grudge against Clodius on account of his sister', wife of Metellus Celer, 'who was supposed to wish to marry Cicero… As Terentia was of a sour temper and governed Cicero she urged him to join in the attack on Clodius and give evidence against him.' In passing, if any approaches were made between the patrician Clodia and the upstart Cicero they surely came from the man.[5]

With Cicero waiting to give evidence, Clodius claimed in defence that his was a case of mistaken identity. On the night of the Bona Dea festival he had only just returned from Sicily and was in the coastal town of Interamnia (Termoli), a full ninety miles east of Rome. It was a miracle, laughed Cicero. He himself had seen Clodius in Rome only three hours before the desecration. To have travelled so far in so short a time the accused must have borrowed the winged sandals of Mercury. Justice shrugged. Clodius was acquitted by thirty-one votes to twenty-five.[6]

Cicero was depressed. He had seen the jurors. After the trial he wrote to Atticus, complaining about the 'jury of paupers'. 'A more raffish assemblage never sat in a low-grade music hall. Fly-blown senators, beggar knights and Paymaster Tribunes who might better have been called "Paytakers".' There were a few honest men but 'Bald-head the millionaire', his term of contempt for Crassus, had corrupted the majority. An ex-gladiator had been sent to juror after juror, inviting them to go to Crassus, and Crassus in turn made promises, paid bills, handed out cash and, even more contemptibly, 'some jurors actually received a bonus in the form of assignations with certain ladies and introductions to youths of noble families', 'nights with whom cost enormous sums'.[7] Crassus did not mind.

Having concluded his term as praetor Julius Caesar was impatient to take up his new command as governor of southern Spain, but creditors had impounded his carriages and were demanding payment of his incredible debts estimated at 25 million *sestertii*. Crassus saved him, giving him 830 talents, sufficient to settle four-fifths of the money he owed.

Caesar was free to leave Rome but before that he was questioned by the court who asked what he knew of the scandalous accusations against his wife, Pompeia. Caesar replied that 'he had no knowledge of the actions imputed to the accused'. If so, why had he so quickly repudiated his wife. The historian Dio Cassius explained. Caesar replied that 'A virtuous woman should not only be free from any fault, she should not even be touched by a shameful suspicion.'[8]

Angry at the ordeal of the trial, brought about by the Senate and their lackey, Cicero, Clodius joined forces with Crassus and Caesar. Both those ambitious men could see the advantage of enrolling a daring and ruthless patrician with his huge and volatile following amongst the masses.

During the trial the apprehensive jury had asked for guards to protect them against the supporters of Clodius. After the verdict the cynical old aristocrat, Catulus, asked one, 'Why did you ask for a guard? Were you afraid of being robbed of the money?'[9]

Later in the Senate Clodius mocked Cicero. 'They didn't credit you on oath,' he said. To the contrary, quipped Cicero, 'Twenty-five jurors gave *me* credit and thirty-one gave you none – they got their money in advance.' Senators bellowed with laughter but the joke was indiscreet.[10]

Cicero, meanwhile, was putting himself in a precarious position. He was already vulnerable because of his constant bragging about his part in defeating the Catiline conspiracy and his heroic role in the affair. Clodius jeered at him, saying that he was acting like Jupiter, most powerful of the gods, with Minerva, goddess of wisdom, as his sister. Unwisely, Cicero replied: 'If so, at least I picked a virgin sister. Your sister isn't one, thanks to you. Perhaps you should use the name Jupiter yourself'. This was a nasty retort because Jupiter had married his own sister, Hera – 'you really *can* say your sister is your wife'.

It was perilously tactless. In his work, *Of Oratory*, Cicero had warned against impetuosity. 'Unless a man is well-trained in rhetoric what he says in public can get out of control like leaves blown in the wind'. Atticus reproved him for the indiscretion and he agreed. 'A jest, you will say, unbecoming a former consul. I confess it, but I detest the woman.' The 'woman' was Clodia, wife of Metellus Celer, beautiful, rich, proud and arrogant, whom Terentia suspected was tempting her husband Cicero. Clodia and her two sisters, both named Clodia, were all rumoured to have slept with Clodius Pulcher, their 'beautiful' brother, but in broadcasting the calumny Cicero made an unforgiving and influential enemy. And just as his impulsive riposte had imperilled him, so the acquittal made Clodius more popular and an even greater threat.[11]

The matter provides an interesting glimpse into Roman social attitudes. Cicero's career, even his life, were at risk after his insult. Yet it was with carefree impunity that the upper-class Catullus could be just as rude to Clodius, calling him 'Lesbius' and Clodia 'Lesbia'.

> Lesbius is pretty. He really is! Why Lesbia much prefers
> him to you, Catullus, and your whole group!
> So we'll permit 'Pretty' to sell us as slaves – if he can find just three
> men of good standing to kiss him in public.
>
> [79]

A handshake was not the greeting when men met. A kiss was. The insinuation of an incestuous relationship with Clodia and the libellous accusation that respectable citizens would publicly snub Clodius clearly did not bother Catullus as his insolent epigram received the approving nods of Rome's high society.

Wandering through the city, scribbling thoughts on jotters, arguing about techniques and metres with friends, Calvus, Cinna, Cornificius, theirs was an existence that they termed *otium* – not idleness but leisure that afforded the time and means to write. They were not a 'School' with rules, themes and membership, they were young men experimenting in forms of verse that Romans had rarely come across and, in the beginning, were unsure whether to accept as poetry.[12]

Successors frequently termed Catullus 'doctus', not because he was more learned than his contemporaries but because of his good taste – as one of the first generation to be influenced by the Greek poets of the third century BC and their belief in succinct writing. 'A big book is a big evil', pronounced Callimachus, the most eminent of those Alexandrians.

To Roman writers of didactic epics Callimachus was an irrelevance. Almost 200 years later in early first-century Rome Naevius was an isolated disciple and his light, erotic verses in ordinary speech were filled with metaphors that bewildered most of his readers. As F. O. Copley has commented, like Gerard Manley Hopkins in late Victorian Britain, he was born a generation too early. It was not until the chance arrival in Rome of a group of young lyrical writers from the north of Italy that there were sufficient 'new poets' for their 'new writing' to become widely known and slowly accepted.[13]

Like children toying with the keyboard and pedals of an organ, they played with esoteric metres so delicately that their work, with its idioms, strange words and playfulness, seemed more Gallic than Latin.

Much of it is lost. Except for Catullus there are only fragments, a line or two left of his fellows writers. 'Nothing at all has survived of Cato except his reputation for having been very influential as a poet and critic, while Cornificius is reduced to bits and tatters, and Furius Bibaculus has been spared total oblivion to the extent of two not very interesting poems.' Caecilius is known only because Catullus wrote a poem to him.[14]

It is the more regrettable because many of them were very talented. Ovid stated that in comparison with Catullus 'Calvus too sang as finely and as lewdly – a little fellow but libidinous' and there was also Ticidas, Memmius, Cornificius, Hortensius and 'Cato just as bad'. The poet Propertius also praised Calvus, 'Your pardon, Calvus – by your leave, Catullus', placing them together as equals. Lindsay quoted Calvus about the death of his mistress, Quintilia:

When I am soon a red smudge of ash...
perhaps her ghost of dust will thrill at this.

Licinius Calvus, two years younger than Catullus, was a fine poet and also, though small, a fine orator. Catullus remembered the guffaw of a spectator at the trial of Publius Vatinius as Calvus caustically denounced him for his malpractices.

The man
Held up his hands admiringly, exclaiming,
'Ye gods, what a slick-talking mannikin!'
[53]

Yet despite his eloquence Calvus lost. Cicero gained an acquittal for his corrupt client but Vatinius never forgave Calvus for humiliating him. 'Was I to be evicted,' he complained, 'just because that devil can speak so well?'

When his diminutive friend sent Catullus a mock gift of an anthology of doggerel and drivel the poet replied:

Thee did I not more dearly prize
Most pleasant Calvus, than mine eyes,
I'd hate thee with Vatinian hate.
[14]
(Sir Theodore Martin, 1816-1909)[15]

It was the use of ordinary speech that distinguished Catullus. It had a personal touch. Of all the poets — Horace, Tibullus, Propertius, Ovid – 'none is quite so expressive of personal feeling as he'. And he wrote of down-to-earth matters that had never been considered worthy of poetry – wine, friends, enemies, every day events. He had the talent to create excitingly fresh verse: lyrical elegies, stately epics and epigrams that ridiculed, teased and demeaned their targets. His poetry had immediacy, vitality, pathos and nobility but was expressed as though murmuring new truths in the reader's ear like Christopher Marlowe's, 'Who ever loved that loved not at first sight?' or François Villon's, 'Two we were but heart just one'.[16]

It is the language and vivacity of the Roman street that the reader hears in the poems and this is what makes Catullus so easy to enjoy whether he is being charming, sarcastic or virulent. 'The simplicity and naturalness of his language... are in great contrast to the later artificial Latin style...However difficult the metre in which he writes, however subtle the thought he would convey, he is never intricate and never obscure...His language in the epigrams, lyrics and elegiacs, is little removed from ordinary speech. He is full of familiar phrases...He uses the tongue of the wits of the town, the lips of the lover of real life.'[17]

Catullus' poetry is so carefully and fastidiously crafted that it always sounds spontaneous whatever its mood. He could rebuke Alfenus Varus, a cobbler from the poet's home town, who had let Catullus down by failing to keep his promises:

Nor Words, nor Deeds, retracted longer bind,
Your Words retracted, and your Deeds, are Wind.
[30]
(Thomas Cooke, 1703-56)

He could also joke. In poem [97], a 'savage, if genially exuberant, attack on an unknown Don Juan', Aemilius, Catullus deplored that 'He hasn't brains enough to walk a miller's donkey' at a time when such donkeys were yoked to a pivoted millstone, plodding the path of an unending circle that required no steering.[18]

He was often gross. G. Lee calculated that seven out of ten of the poems contained obscenities of some kind. They were explicit, attacking an unlucky person's bodily cleanliness, lavatorial habits, their sexual preferences. The impoverished Aurelius was warned not to pursue Juventius:

It's you I fear – you and that penis of yours
Trying to turn boys, good or bad, into whores.
[15]

If he seduced the boy Catullus would inflict the Roman punishment for adultery upon him, as described by Richard Burton: 'The victim being securely tied, a mullet was thrust up his fundament and withdrawn, the sharp gills of the fish causing excruciating torment to the sufferer during the process of its withdrawal, and grievously lacerating the bowels. Sometimes an enormous radish was substituted for the mullet.'[19]

Such unexpurgated glimpses of ancient Rome caused Fordyce to censor his edition for students. 'A few poems which do not lend themselves to comment in English have been omitted', which in turn led to an anonymous review by one of the professor's own students. '*Tropic of Cancer* has been published in vain. Lady Chatterley has tiptoed naked through the bluebells to no avail.'[20]

Catullus could be vituperative. He cursed Publius Cominius from Spoletum (Spoleto), an upstart whose prosecution of a popular tribune earned him the hatred of Rome:

First your tongue, abuser of honest men, will be sliced off
And chucked to the greedy vulture, your eyes gouged out
And gulped down the black throat of a raven,
Your guts gobbled by dogs, the rest torn and tugged by wolves...

[108]

Other lines were more lyrical.

As virgin Vine her Elme doth wed,
His Oake the Ivie over-spread,
So chaste desire thou joynst in one,
That disunited were undone.
Io Hymen Hymenaeus.

[61]
(Henry Peacham, 1576?-1643?)

and

... which before, with constant mind
He cherish'd, now from Theseus' memory fled,
Like mists from airy ridge of snowy Alp.

[64], lines 260-2
(Charles Abraham Elton, 1778-1853)

And there was sadness, too. The poet mourned the death of his lover's pet sparrow, a bird that had hopped, here, there, chirping happily. Suddenly the poem's tip-tapping quick words were confronted with a polysyllabic monstrosity:

Qui nunc it per iter tenebriscosum   now hopped into a
                                     crepuscular impenetrability
                                     from which no thing returns.

[3]

A deeper sadness affected Catullus when he visited the grave of his brother:

Never shall I heare thee speake, speake with thee?
Thee brother than life dearer never see?
Yet shalt thou ever be belov'd of me.

[65]
(Mathew Gwinne, 1558?-1627)

And there was crude personal abuse in some poems. Catullus snarlingly inflicted imaginary afflictions on his faithless woman and her new lover:

Agonized by gout as his ulcers putrefy
he brings his reeking torment to her bed.
Restlessly they sweat naked thigh by thigh,
she sickened by his odours, he with gout half-dead.

[71]

However, Rome was rather more accustomed to the heroic lines of Homer in his epic of Odysseus, whom the Romans called Ulysses. When that hero returned from the long war at Troy to his island of Ithaca, lying 'low, farthest up the sea-line towards the darkness', the wanderer was shocked to find his loyal but despairing wife, Penelope, besieged by arrogantly insistent suitors. Disguised as a beggar he killed their leader, Antinous, with his great bow that none of his rivals could draw:

...The arrow in his throat took full his fall,
And thrust his head far through the other side.
Down fell his cup, down he, down all his pride
Straight from his nostrils gusht the human gore.

Then with his sword Ulysses slaughtered the others. Eurymachus resisted and:

... with a table flew
In on Ulysses, with a terrible throat
His fierce charge urging. But Ulysses smote
The board, and cleft it through from end to end

Borne at his breast, and made his shaft extend
His sharp head to his liver, his broad breast
Pierc'd at his nipple; when his hand releast
Forthwith his sword, that fell and kist the ground...
Homer, Odyssey, XXII, 104-14 [21]

It was a saga of courage, defence of honour, the protection of home and family that was both familiar and comfortable to high-minded Romans. It was very different from the street-talk of Catullus as in such lines about a man, Furius, who had:

a father and a stepmother, whose teeth
can chew even flint

[23]

and

Aren't we to think a girl who touches him capable
of licking the arse of a hangman with dysentery?

[97]

It was not only Fordyce who recoiled from such lines. Ever since Catullus became known to educated English-speaking readers there had been censorship, resulting frequently in ambiguity. Early in the nineteenth century there was an almost complete translation of the works by George Lamb (1784-1834), an illegitimate son of the Prince of Wales. In his *The Poems of Caius Valerius Catullus* (1821), he left out twenty repellent pieces but 'not one that can be regretted' – yet inconsistently included the obscene poem [32] in which the sex-stirred poet urges a woman, Ipsitilla, whom Lamb called 'Hypsithilla', to join him for *novem continuus fututiones*.

Goold accurately translated that as 'nine consecutive copulations'. Myers decided that 'nine successive screws' was more poignant. The Hungarian poet, Sandor Rakos, translated the Latin into his native tongue. Friends turned his lines into English. The amusing result remained obscene:

My spear's piercing my tunic.
I want you so badly

(Rakos, p. 15)

George Lamb fastidiously ignored the tent-poled tunic and both the *novem* and the *fututiones*, a word not to be found in Latin school dictionaries, writing:

Close thy gate to all beside.
Let no idle wish to roam
Steal thy thought from joys at home;
But prepare thy charms to aid
Every frolic love e'er played.

As though Catullus were flirtatiously inviting a lady to afternoon tea and buttered scones. Lamb explained, 'a literal translation could not be tolerated'. Merritt agreed, 'Contents execrable'. Ipsitilla was expunged by both men.[22]

There is an uncertainty about her and her unusual name. Quinn thought she may have been a daughter of Catiline. Garrison a superior courtesan, Michie a 'tart'.

It is unlikely that Ipsitilla was a harlot wenching in taverns, baths and brothels. Such women were almost literally two a penny. Within a century of Catullus, when currency had been stable for years, the rates for whores in Pompeii varied from one to sixteen bronze asses, the norm for their services being the pittance of two asses, no more than the cost of a mug of nondescript wine.

Roman coinage progressed in fours: four copper *quadrans* to the bronze *as* that was *as* broad and thick as the button of an overcoat, and four *asses* to the similarly heavy *sestertius*. Four *sestertii* made a tiny silver *denarius*. At the top of the scale was the scarce *aureus*, a gold *stater*. With yearly wages of between 1,000 and 1,500 sestertii, a day's pay for a working man was no more than sixteen asses. 'He had agreed with the labourers for a penny, (a *denarius*), a day' Matthew 20:2.[23] A girl costing sixteen asses was exorbitantly expensive. But some men paid. Scribbled on a wall of Faustus' eating-house in Pompeii a satisfied client advised other diners: 'If he wants to have a girl, look for Attice, charge 16 *asses*, a high-class girl'; and 'Arphocas had a fine time with Druca for a *denarius*'.

Such extravagance was not for everyone. More typical was the reckoning scratched on the wall of an inn at Aesernia, modern Isernia, on the Via Numicia.

'The bill, landlord!'
'Let's see. An *as* for the bed;
five for the wine, one for bread, two for porridge,
eight for the girl,
two for hay for the mule.'
'That damned mule will be the ruin of me! '[24]

Garrison's suggestion that Ipsitilla was, 'a hetaera with her own house where she entertains male visitors as she pleases. Many such women moved freely in high society and were much sought after' is more plausible. That explanation could also explain the apparent 'name' which may come from a corrupt text. Catullus may have written *ipsitilla* rather than 'Ipsitilla', an affectionate diminutive of *ipsa*, 'matron', 'the dainty mistress of the household', a cheerful reference to the delights provided by her costly entertainment.

Catullus was very much a man of his time. He was a poet whose sensitive imagination reacted to events and distilled them into intensity. He was not social litmus paper. He was an emotional alchemist sifting his world, transmuting the dross. His only reticence was a refusal to detail the physical pleasures of making love. For all other things he wrote with passion.

His life had many parallels with a poet who lived fifteen hundred years after his death, François Villon of medieval France. Both were virtuosos of musical eloquence in their writing, both endured an unhappy love affair, the output of each man was small, hardly 3,000 lines by Villon, just over 2,000 by Catullus. Nor were their corpora casually assembled. On the contrary, the works of both poets were so artistically arranged that verse flowed into verse as though without artifice. It was an illusion. It was craftsmanship. And both men were masters of brevity. Catullus' *Odi et amo* ('I hate and love') [85] was matched by Villon's *Je ris en pleurs* ('I laugh in tears').

Almost teasingly, each of them derided the woman he loved by mocking her nose. In poem [41] Catullus wrote: *'ista turpiculo puella naso'*, 'that girl with the ugly nose'; and in his *Testament*, [93], Villon almost repeated it with *'ma demoiselle au nez tortu'*, 'my bent-nosed baggage' as though there were some truth in reincarnation.

The similarities do not stop there. The work of both poets survived almost by chance. Both men died in their thirties in unknown circumstances, yet even their supposed ends are contentious. Even histrionic. There are unorthodox suggestions that after his final exile from Paris Villon retired to write and produce a Passion Play in St-Maixent l'École. In a similar conflict with scholarly opinion, Catullus may have lived for some years after 54 BC, turning from poetry to the writing of mimes and plays. Finally and by complete chronological coincidence their books were published within a few years of each other, Catullus' at Verona in 1472, Villon's at Paris in 1489.[25]

Catullus died young but like other youthful poets he had lived intensely. Two words could serve as his epitaph: *vixi*, 'I have lived' and *amavi*, 'I have loved'. He was the epitome of Montaigne's, 'Every man is a complete set of contradictions', and in his work 'the emphasis was on lightness, sophistication, elegance, wit, humour, intermingled with coarseness and vilification'. 'He wrote the most passionate lyrics in the Latin tongue. Their utterance soon stopped for he died when he was about thirty, like a flame going out, so intense and youthful seems his poetry. So died Keats of disease when he was twenty-six...and Shelley drowned at sea when he was thirty.'[26] Keats wrote his own epitaph, 'here lies one whose name was writ in water', words as sad as those of Catullus who had discovered that his mistress's earnest promises to her lover were not constant.

> She sayes so; but what women say to kind
> Lovers, we write in rapid streams and wind.
>
> [70]
> (Richard Lovelace, 1618-57)

Some time after the death of Catullus his poems were published in three *libri*, 'books', whose arrangement, and their poems, was a blend of choice and compulsion: choice in the freedom to select poems which rested most comfortably together, and compulsion in the fact that a manageable roll of papyrus was limited in length and could not hold all the poems.

In the marshes of Egypt papyrus reeds could grow ten feet (3 m) high. To make a papyrus roll the rind was peeled and the core cut into sheets measuring about twelve inches (30 cm) by eight (20 cm). Two were stuck together by the plant's naturally glutinous cells. About twenty sheets could make a roll up to twelve feet (3.5 m) long. With a central shaft of ivory and a parchment cover the roll was about three inches (8 cm) thick, comfortable to hold.[27] Such a roll, up to twelve feet (3.5 m) long, could contain between 750 and 1,000 lines of verse. Hence the three 'books' of Catullus. The roll of each of them, *Liber I* with 848 lines, *Liber II* with 795 and *Liber III* with 646, could accommodate their poems easily. To combine them in one roll would have made it too heavy to hold and too clumsy to unwind.

Without question the books were edited for sense and sequence. *Liber I*, poems [1] to [60], has quite short personal pieces in a variety of metres. Numbers [19] and [20] and usually [18] are omitted as spurious and not part of the Catullan canon. This apocrypha is composed of some priapea, verses to the phallic god, Priapus, attributed to Catullus by Renaissance editors such as Vettori and Muret, a quatrain proposed by Terentianus Maurus, and two single lines suggested independently by Nonius and Porphyrion. They are not included in the three *Libri*.

Liber II, of four long poems [61] to [64], is different. Two of its poems, [61] and [62, are epithalamia celebrating marriage. Many critics consider [63], *Attis*, to be the finest of all Catullus' poems. Poem [64], the mini-epic of Peleus *and Thetis* (see Appendix I) is a masterwork of symmetry. These more 'normal', classically polished works may have circulated individually after prolonged revision.

Liber III is controversial. It is a mixture of elegiac couplets and epigrams, all of them short, the longest, [76], having only twenty-six lines. The poems vary in quality and many are obscene. There is an impression of things almost haphazardly ordered, scraps and oddments assembled by an editor who knew what Catullus had intended.

The arrangement is lucid but the poems are not in chronological order. Poem [1] is one of the last. Yet everything was fastidiously assembled. It is unlikely that anything was written later to fill gaps. Probably the pieces were composed over several years, some revised and updated to be meticulously placed in the books.

The result is not a diary. It is an emotional biography. 'He devoted the most careful thought to the arrangement of his book of poems: if there's anybody who can't see that, "tant pis pour lui".'[28]

There was nothing haphazard about the arrangement. In the three books the poems were not casually set. Nor were they presented in written order like Wordsworth's 'Poems of 1798', 'of 1799' down to the last of '1847'. Neither were they organized in themes like Donne's 'Songs and Sonnets', 'Epigrams', 'Elegies', ending with his 'Holy Sonnets'.

Occasionally editors did arrange Catullus in themes: Lindsay with 'Lesbia', 'Friends', 'Troubles', 'Caesar' etc. Williamson, his selection made simpler by the exclusion of 'unseemly' verses, reclassified the acceptable into 'Friends', 'Poets', 'Brother', 'Lesbia' and so on. But none of it was relevant.

There is an intended balance throughout from poem [1] to [116]. Each of the *Libri, I, II, III* contains echoes of the others, a form of contrast by inversion. There was an intentional arrangement to the poems but it had nothing to do with time or topic. It was contrapuntal, setting off one poem against another to form contrasts. Poems were positioned to create a tension so that the meaning of one was counter-balanced by another. This technique is known as chiasmus, as in Goldsmith's 'to stop too fearful, and too faint to go'.

The entire corpus was teasingly subtle.[29] An elegant example, glowing with classical allusions, is [64], the little epic of *Peleus and Thetis*. Its erudite, perfectly crafted arrangement is discussed in Appendix I.

Once aware of this construction it is like walking through poetical swing-doors to read the poems, entering only to re-emerge, into and out of a series of reversals that has to be studied to be realized. Only the questionable sequence in *Liber III* with its apparent lapses affects the result.

In Rome Catullus was probably admired and respected in the salons and polite dinner-parties for the long and elegant classical poems of *Liber II*, the marriage songs, and *Peleus and Thetis*, very much to Roman taste. Over the succeeding centuries after his rediscovery, the reaction to his unconventional work varied. Early in the nineteenth century, Byron stated that:

Catullus scarcely has a decent poem,
I don't think Sappho's Ode a good example.
Don Juan, Canto I, XLII

And despite Tennyson's late-nineteenth-century admiration of the 'tenderest of Roman poets', not every critic agreed. In his mid-twentieth-century diary Harold Nicolson fumed, 'It passes my comprehension why Tennyson could have called him "tender". He is vindictive, venomous, and full of obscene malice. He is only tender about his brother and Lesbia, and in the end she gets it hot as well.'[30]

Given such reactions it is not surprising that it was not only Fordyce who decided that for students certain poems, even if left untranslated, were unprintable. Yet Williamson felt, 'There is no Latin author more suitable for Sixth Form study than Catullus'. Other editors – Arnold, Aronson and Lawalls – observed that 'Catullus has proved to be a potent resource against boredom for those students who otherwise may think of Roman authors as old fuddy-duddies.' Ironically the very poems that might most appeal to today's student are those excluded (fifty by Williamson, seventy-one by Arnold and his colleagues, whose title of *Love and Betrayal. A Catullan Reader* contained more betrayal than love in it).[31]

Fashions vary. Today it is probably *Liber I* with the beauty of its love poems that captivates readers of Catullus. Yet despite Havelock's 'the first lyric voice of Rome' and 'Catullus is all emotion', the poet was much more than a singer of lyrics. He was a genius of poetry.[32]

It was not just the individual poem. It was all of them put together like separate individual notes that blended into a melody, everything so artistically assembled that the construction itself causes admiration. Poem [55], and its two neighbours, is one of many intriguing instances of meanings within meanings and of themes and jokes that smoothly reveal themselves once the code is understood.

In poem [55] Catullus took his readers on an apparently uncomplicated guided tour of central Rome. In reality it was a medley of imagination, classical mythology, a cipher and what may be a personal revelation. In that frivolous poem Catullus described how he had searched for an elusive person, Camerius, amongst the hills and buildings of the city, wondering where his quarry was hiding and whether he had some secret lover. Despairingly the poet searched everywhere from the 'minor Campus', probably the open stretch of land at the north-east corner of the 600 acres (240 ha) of the Campus Martius. From there he hurried to the Circus Maximus, then into all the booksellers, found nothing, and ran off to pant up the steep Capitoline Hill to the Temple of Jupiter. Finally the frustrated poet rushed across to Pompey's theatre, whose shady archways, according to Ovid, offered the best places to pick up women.[33]

The quest was long and futile, a fatiguing, breathtaking exploration of three miles, all covered at breakneck speed. Catullus gave up. He would never have found his prey even if he had been some mythical being famed for its speed.

> If I became the giant guarding Crete,
> or Ladas, or Perseus with wing-sandalled feet,
> or fast as Pegasus at his flying pace
> or hurtling like the racing steeds of Thrace
>
> [58B]

They were all noted for rapidity. Talos was a gigantic bronze robot who rushed around Crete each day watching for invaders. The Spartan, Ladas, was an Olympic champion who died at the end of a 200-yard sprint. Perseus had magic sandals given to him to find the dreaded Gorgons. Pegasus was a winged horse; and the racing steeds were the famous snow-white horses of Rhesus, king of Thrace, stolen from him by Ulysses. The mortal Catullus despaired. 'You wretch, Camerius! Even if I'd been harnessed to the winds, I'd still be worn out in this hopeless pursuit.'

Poem [55] teases. Camerius is not mentioned until line 10. The reader is never told who he was nor how old. He is unknown, perhaps a boy longed-for by Catullus or a pet of his mistress, maybe a friend enjoying a girl in an inconspicuous hideout.

The poem is typically complicated and reveals Catullus at his most playful. He makes an arcane pun on the name of Camerius.

> Distracted now, I scan the street,
> And seize all Females that I meet,
> 'Where's my Friend?', aloud I cry,
> 'Naughty Camerius, speak or die'.
> One making bare her saucy Breasts,
> Cry'd, 'Seek no further, here he rests'.
>
> [55]
> (Nahum Tate, 1652-1715)

It was a play on two words, 'Camerius' and the Greek for brassiere, καμαριον 'kameriou', in Latin, camerium. The Roman was 'strophium', a narrow band across the breasts, tied at the back. Camerius could not have concealed himself in such a desirable if confined, space but to Romans the pun was erudite and amusing. Pliny the Elder's essay on 'Brassiere', recommended men with headaches to fold one around the head for relief.[34]

The poem encapsulates the reasons why Catullus is popular with his readers, and why editors puzzle and despair over him. It is not one poem but two. Poem [55] is about the search for Camerius. Poem [58B] describes the mythical creatures. Its lines are often thought to have been uneasily inserted into the middle of the first like a joke that had been thrown on to the cutting-room floor only to be replaced.

That is the usual interpretation. It is arguable, however, that [58B] is one more example of *chiasmus* – a poem artistically positioned to look backwards and forwards to its neighbours. If so, then [58B] was part of poem [55], that was extracted to be placed behind [56, 57 and 58] to make [55] and [58B] a 'bridge' of innocence between three poems of sexual sin. Only Catullus could make such a choice. Few editors would have the effrontery to cannibalize poem [55] and shift it three poems away. To the contrary, such Catullan excisions and interpolations are frequent and always constructive.

It was a light-hearted Catullus who wrote the poems. Camerius is mentioned in both [55] and [58B], separated by [56], [57] and [58]. Knowing that Catullus' poems were fastidiously arranged, with poem flowing into poem like the chapters of a book, the juxtaposition of three poems between them suggests a connection and there is one. Sexual depravity. Poem [58] concerns the shameless appetite of a debauched woman on the streets of Rome. In poem [57] Caesar was accused of homosexuality with his military engineer, Mamurra. Poem [56] is also about sodomy but not about two men. It concerns Catullus and a boy, perhaps linking him by association with Juventius and Camerius. It is short but shocking.

Cato, it was funny, really silly
and you will guffaw willy-nilly.
If you love Catullus feel delight
that I took such advantage of the sight.
A little boy, bare-bottomed, sex-mad mite,
was at it with a girl – so – quite right, Venus,
between his cheeks I shoved my rigid penis. (p. 232)

[56]

Although sexual relations between a man and a boy was normal practice, Roman attitudes to relations between adult men were more ambivalent. The aggressor was regarded with something like approval, the recipient with something like contempt – but it was still acceptable.

That poem [55] should be found immediately before two concerned with homosexuality makes it likely that the poem similarly associates Camerius with a latter-day Juventius, mischievously running off with another man to the only half-earnest distress of Catullus. Camerius may have been a similar object of Catullus' desires, which would explain the chase around Rome for the missing boy.[35]

It was an idyllic time for a young man of genius. The politics of the Roman Republic were of little interest. Pompey's army near Rome and the anticipated return of Caesar may have caused apprehension in the Senate. But there is no mention of these momentous matters in the poetry of the Neoterics.

Despite the indifference of the poets to politics, however, 61 BC was a fateful year for the Republic of Rome. By the end of the year the Senate had contrived to antagonize every one of its most dangerous enemies: the *equites* on whom they relied for support; and Crassus, Pompey and Caesar.

A syndicate of businessmen, the *equites*, had contracted to collect taxes from the newly conquered Asian territories that Pompey had taken but quickly realized that they had offered too much for the privilege. Led by Crassus, they asked for a reduction. It was refused by the short-sighted Senate, thus depriving them of the backing of many influential men; and the resentful Crassus began scheming for retribution.

After years of successful campaigning Pompey returned to Rome. Fearful that a military commander with legions of loyal troops might become a second Sulla, the Senate humbled him. Although he was accorded a splendid Triumph his two modest requests were vetoed: that the treaties and agreements he had made overseas should be endorsed, and that his veterans be awarded land and means for their retirement. Nor would the Senate permit him to stand for the second time as consul. The vain and tactless Pompey, who had so spitefully humiliated Lucullus over Bithynia, was left without strength. He looked for allies.

Julius Caesar had proved to be a very capable soldier and general in Spain. Returning to Rome he also asked to be nominated as consul. Perceived as an increasing threat to the comfortable status quo, the Senate complacently refused to accept him as a candidate. Crassus was embittered at the loss of revenue from tax-collecting. Pompey was resentful of his declining popularity. Caesar had received neither a military triumphal parade nor backing for his ambition to become a consul.

This period marked the onset of an unstable but ominous alliance between the three men, the 'First Triumvirate' of 60 BC, seemingly strengthened by the marriage of the divorced Pompey to Caesar's daughter, Julia. It was the start of the final years of the Republic and it would end in civil war.[36]

It was also the time of one of the world's most famous love affairs.

5

CLODIA – 60-57 BC

Catullus called her Lesbia. Her real name was Clodia Metelli, wife of Quintus Caecilius Metellus Celer, a cousin on her mother's side.

Celer's was an old but not aristocratic family, whose members, in Lindsay's cruel phrase, provided Rome with a succession of 'stupidly efficient officers'. In the middle of the third century BC Lucius Caecilius Metellus defeated the Carthaginians in Sicily during the First Punic War. At the end of the first century his descendant, Quintus, was nick-named 'Numidicus' because of his successes against Jugurtha, king of Numidia. A jealous Marius took most of the credit.

There were two blemishes to the Metellan name. Immediately after the Roman disaster at Cannae in 216 BC Marcus Caecilius panicked, thinking that Hannibal would conquer Italy. While planning to desert the young tribune was arrested.

In Rome a few years later the poet Gnaeus Naevius, who had written an epic about the first of the Punic Wars, rashly insulted the family in one of his stage-plays.

> Either: by destiny the Metelli are consuls at Rome;
> Or: to the ruin of Rome the Metelli are consuls.

The Metelli retorted that they would give him a beating and, according to his fellow playwright, Plautus, they had him imprisoned and then exiled to north Africa where he died in 201 BC.

Those were the ancestors of Caecilius Metellus, known as Celer, 'the swift', husband of Clodia, the man who led legions against Catiline and who in 62 BC was governor of Cisalpine Gaul. He lacked humour but not pomposity. On 12 January of that year he sent a letter to Cicero complaining that the orator had impugned the honour of his brother. Cicero, also not lacking pomposity, protested. The brother had tried to demean him, refusing him the honoured custom of being permitted to address the Senate on his last day as consul. Cicero, 'the Consul and saviour of the commonwealth', had appealed to the wife of Metellus, 'the lady Claudia', and to Metellus' sister, Mucia, Pompey's wife, hoping they could persuade Pompey to help him. It was petty but not to such self-important personalities. But Cicero had the final word, describing Metellus Celer, a man who had been elected a consul in 60 BC, as 'a barren seashore and a void of space and utter desolation'. That was the person that Clodia had married, bearing him a daughter, Metella.[1]

Clodia was the eldest of three sisters, all by custom called Clodia. She also had three brothers: Appius, Gaius and the youngest, Publius Clodius Pulcher, whose grand-daughter, Claudia, gained reflected ignominy by marrying the consul, Publius Quinctilius Varus. His three legions were ambushed in a German forest in AD 9 and slaughtered. 'Quinctilius Varus! Give me back my legions,' grieved Augustus.[2]

The Claudians were a patrician family of many generations and they behaved with the arrogance of people who throughout their history had casually disregarded the laws of Rome. Clodia Metelli was no exception. Her house was on the Palatine's Clivus Victoriae, the oldest, most exclusive street in Rome, some of whose cobbled paving survives today. There were two well-used ways of reaching it. One was from the marshy Velabrum in the south-west, busy with the market traffic of foodstuffs, oils, wines and cheeses. The *clivus*, 'slope', climbed steeply along the edge of the cliff past the Temple of the Great Mother on its right, constantly noisy with the wild songs of Cybele's eunuch priests, their shrieks and clashing cymbals audible to every house on the road.

The preferred approach to the Palatine was from the north near the Temple of Castor & Pollux. Clodia lived nine pillars or doors from it, stated Catullus in poem [37]. At the hilltop the Clivus Victoriae extended southwards along the brow of the Palatine, its great houses overlooking the muddy valley and the Capitoline Hill beyond. Only the most privileged citizens had homes on the street. Catulus the aristocrat and conservative senator lived there. Aemilius Scaurus, praetor, builder of a magnificent temple and an enriched governor of Sardinia, was his next-door neighbour.

These were not ordinary houses, not even those of the ordinary rich. They were mini-palaces tended by large households, with domestic quarters and poky cells for slaves, with airy reception rooms, wine-cellars, everything supervised by a *mater familias* (housekeeper) and *promus* (butler/steward). To be admitted, even as a guest, to such luxury was a privilege. Cicero wanted the prestige of such an address and finally through nefarious bribes and favours, acquired a property at a cost of 3.5 million *sestertii*. An impression of the size of the dwellings comes from the fact that Clodius Pulcher had a house on the Clivus 'that he tried in 58 BC to extend into a palatial mansion with a 300-foot [90 m] portico'.

Clodia had lustrous eyes – 'Ox-Eyes' Cicero called her admiringly, and likened her to 'Hera the goddess', famed, for her large, brilliant eyes. Clodia was talented, educated, an exquisite dancer, a lover of the arts, particularly poetry. It was said that hers was a beautiful face that gathered light to it. There were many references to her fine looks, and there is an art-gallery world of Roman busts, carvings of attractive women, not just Agrippina, Livia, Matidia, wives of emperors whom sculptors would flatter, but representations of lovely, unknown women in Pompeian murals, or the charming bust of the Tortolian Maiden from Vulci, a girl of 'pristine adolescent beauty'. Roman loveliness was very much in accord with today's taste. Clodia was beautiful.[3]

But she was also imperious, insistent on respect, never to be taken for granted. '*In triclinio Coa, in cubiculo nola*', wrote a former lover, 'in the dining-room an island of silken delight, in the bedroom the Fortress Unassailable'.

One man, Vettius, after a luckless night with her, stupidly sent a few worthless, *quadrans*, as payment. The jibe circulated. Men sniggered in private, jeeringly referring to her as *Quadrantaria*, 'Yours for a few farthings'. Vettius was brutally buggered by two of her followers, Marcus Camurtius and Marcus Caesernius, to make the expense of his punishment balance the cheapness of his gift.[4]

It was dangerous to cross such women. In his *Satyricon* Petronius tells of the vengeance that Circe inflicted on a hoped-for conquest after his two unsuccessful attempts at love-making. She was not the mythical enchahtress of the *Odyssey* but a fictional temptress corrupted by a yearning for low life, which she hoped to satisfy by coupling with the low-born Encolpius, 'the crotch'. His sexual reputation was high but his performance was not. Although wanting the woman he was impotent. Receiving a second invitation he took the precautions of avoiding his boy-friend and paying for physical stimulation and aphrodisiacs from a witch. Despite his preparations he failed again. 'Stung by these public rebuffs and frantic for revenge' Circe had him flogged by slaves, spat on by her women and kicked out of doors.

Clodia had a similar temperament. The case of Vettius proves that real life could be just as cruel as fiction.[5] Clodia did as she wished. Even in an age of promiscuous well-born women her reputation was shocking. Adultery did not shock and discreet affairs were almost approved, certainly accepted – but incest was not.

To Romans such intimacy was not criminal but 'contrary to divine laws and was punished under the *ius gentium*', the family laws of all mankind. In AD 33, during the reign of Tiberius, Sextus Marius, the wealthiest man in Spain, was hurled from the Tarpeian Rock for having seduced his daughter. Yet it was widely believed that Clodia, as well as her two sisters, had slept with their brother, Clodius. Cicero was to describe her lifestyle as a depraved existence of 'orgies, love-affairs, adulteries, jaunts to Baiae, beach-parties, dinner-parties, revels, musical entertainments and boating picnics...[and] her river-side gardens, a fashionable place for young men to swim and for Clodia to pick up young men'.

Little of this would have horrified her contemporaries, but for Cicero to liken her to Hera, sister and 'wife' to Zeus, was to proclaim her unnatural vice. In June 60 BC he wrote to Atticus about the bawdy joke he had made while he was walking with Clodius. 'He asked me whether I used to give the Sicilians seats at the gladiatorial shows? I said, "No". "Well," said he, "now I am their new patron, I intend to begin the practice, although my sister who as the consul's wife has taken so much space that she will not allow me a single foot." "Oh, don't haggle about a mere foot with your sister," I answered, "you can get between the pair of them whenever you wish."[6]

Clodia may have been careless about her good name but she would never have been casual about her fine looks. The daily toilet of a fashionable Roman lady was long-drawn out and elaborate, a period of some apprehension for her slaves. It began with a fragrant bath of just the right temperature. Maids could be whipped for carelessness. On a carved slab from Neumagen in Germany there is a scene of four women in long-sleeved tunics, hair pinned up in buns, one holding a mirror, attending their mistress, who sits in a high-backed basketwork chair. It is a scene of quiet composure, but this may not have been typical.

The bedroom, door bolted against men's eyes, was a miniature beauty salon containing pots, jars, flagons of liniments, unguents, pomades and cosmetics, of scissors, pins, nail-files and looking-glasses, everything required to prepare the lady for the outside world. Hands, ears, teeth cleaned, body washed, the toiletry could begin. Face foundation was evenly, gently applied, a ground-up paste of barley, peeled narcissi bulbs, Tuscan seeds, honey from Greece, lupins – a thin cream to be delicately smoothed into the skin. The slight scratch of a fingernail was to be avoided. Even more carefully any unwanted hair was extracted.

Then it was time for the *ornatrix*, the hairdresser, a slave expertly trained to arrange anyone of the many complex styles of the day. Such women were prized artists but they must have dreaded the days when their mistress was in a hurry. One tress, one lock out of place and the girl would

> ...have to submit
> to having her hair torn, her shoulders and breasts uncovered.
> 'why is this curl sticking up!?' And at once the strap of bull-hide
> comes down to punish the heinous crime of the errant ringlet.
>
> Juvenal, *Satire* VI, 490-3[7]

The coiffure was the midway stage through the hour or so of painstaking and sometimes pain-provoking preparation. Additional make-up followed, a choice of chalk, white lead, pale vermilion, rouge, whatever the lady wished, even subtle shades of red, carmine, or more exotically an extract of crocodile. There was eye-shadow of ash, powdered antimony, saffron or black lead, toxic ingredients that no modern woman would use.

Finally it was time to dress, the simple underclothes of a loincloth and the breastbands of either *strophium* or *mamillare* and then the long white *stola*, drawn in at the waist and prettily ornamented at neck and hem, or a tunic in a choice of fabrics – wool, cotton, silk – the lightness and thinness selected for elegance as were the colours: sea-green, azure blue, Tyrian purple, all simple but expensive and sophisticated. Shoes were of supple white leather.

Now only the jewellery was to be selected. Since Pompey's eastern campaigns Rome glittered with luxurious stones, the popular emerald for pendants, opals and aquamarines to adorn the dress and hands and, best of all, pellucid pearls for earrings. For attaching to robes or decorating shoes, pearls on joined-together pendants hanging from the neck, clicking as they tapped against each other, everything set off with gold, the serpent bracelet, the rings, the brooches. Only diamonds were missing. The art of cutting those stones was still a mystery.

For the rich it was an age of extravagance. Antonia, widow of the general, Drusus, attached earrings to fish in her ponds so that she could watch the bright flickerings as they swam through the waters. Lollia Paulina, briefly one of Caligula's wives, once wore 'the revenue of an entire province' at what was only a modest betrothal feast.[8]

Bathed, face made up, hair done, dressed, bejewelled, Clodia was ready for the late morning light of Rome.

It has been argued that Clodia was not Clodia Metelli, and which of the three Claudian sisters enchanted Catullus has been a question of tediously unnecessary debate. The woman was certainly married but all three of them were: one to Metellus Celer; another to Marcius Rex, consul in 68 BC, the third to Licinius Lucullus, the millionaire and bibliophile. If nothing more were known then the identification of 'Lesbia' would remain one of Havelock's *'it could have been'*.

Even Ovid did not know who she was, just that she had existed.

Often did salacious Catullus sing
about his lover, hiding her as Lesbia.
Their private love was not enough. He advertised it
all the time, proclaiming his adultery.

Ovid, *Tristia* 2, 427-30

There are facts, however. The erstwhile friend of Catullus, Caelius Rufus, had replaced the poet in the favours of a Clodia as the first lines of [58] reveal, 'Caelius, our Lesbia, that Lesbia, the Lesbia that Catullus once loved ...' And that particular Clodia was specifically and unpleasantly named by Cicero in the trial of Rufus in 56 BC as the wife of Caecilius Metellus, Clodia Metelli. And unlike her sisters she became a widow, which encouraged Catullus to beg her to marry him [70]. It was that Clodia who inspired some of the finest poetry of love in the world. It was ingenuous to claim that 'few would now claim that the Lesbia poems reflect the history of a real love affair'. If they do not then in Shakespeare's words:

> If this be error, and upon me prov'd,
> I never writ, nor no man ever lov'd.
> >   Sonnet, CXVI [9]

It has seldom been suggested that that playwright's collection of 154 sonnets was a random bunch of unconnected technical conceits rather than poems about two emotional friendships, one with a man, the other with a woman. The language is too personal, too truthful In the poems, wrote Peter Levi, 'there are tones that are impossible to fake: that of Villon, that of Archilochos, that of Catullus'.

Villon has already been mentioned. Archilochos was an early seventh-century Greek poet from Paros, much admired for his direct speech. He writes of his lost shield and that some barbarian must be strutting with it.

> It's nothing, I saved my skin, so let it go.
> A new one will be as good.
> >   *Elegiac Fragment 5*

Philodemus thought little of him as a poet.[10]

There have been arguments about the chronological order of Shakespeare's sonnets, as there have about the *Libri* of Catullus. In the sonnets, however, there has been no consensus about the identities of the two people involved: whether 'Mr. W. H.' was a back-to-front Henry Wriothesley, Earl of Southampton, or William Hall, an insignificant printer who chanced to 'procure' the sonnets for publication; whether the 'Dark Lady' was Emilia Lanier or one of several other women such as the prostitute, 'Black Luce'.[11]

No such uncertainties surround Clodia Metelli and no doubts need diminish the sincerity of the poems concerning her. In them can be found the surprise, fascination and delight at the beginning of the romance, the deepening, wondering love, the first worries, the reconciliations, the dreads and self-loathing, the resigned acceptance that the promise of an eternal ecstasy had drained into an everlasting nothingness. There is even, the sarcastic 'thank you' to Cicero for fouling her name like streaks of mud throughout the streets and slums of Rome in poem [49]. The poems are the history of a real love between two real people.

Where, when and how Catullus and Clodia first met will remain a mystery, but it is a mystery of little importance. Of the few likely possibilities, the most reasonable is that it was at one of the many dinner parties in Rome and an occasion when the poet was invited to offer his audience one of his newly written poems. Perhaps this was the lilting wedding of poem [45], a conversation between two lovers, Acme and Septimius, of which this is the final verse:

Favour'd thus by heav'n above,
Their lives are one return of love;
For he, poor fellow, so possess'd,
Is richer than with East and West,
And she, in her enamour'd boy,
Finds all that she can frame of joy.
Now, who has seen in Love's subjection,
Two more blest in their connection,
Or a more entire affection?
(Leigh Hunt, 1784-1859)

It was light, well written and inoffensive, exactly the kind of verse that would have pleased his well-brought-up and polite audience. It was decorous. It was not the poetry that Catullus would give Clodia. To protect a married woman from scandal and himself from rough treatment by her husband he disguised her behind the clever and very complimentary false name of 'Lesbia'.

Laughingly Catullus adroitly sang and
Made Lesbia better known than Helen of Troy.
Propertius, *II*, 34, 85-94

'Lesbia' remained anonymous until she was recognised as a Clodia by the north African writer, Lucius Apuleius, the second-century author of *The Golden Ass*, the only Latin novel to survive in its entirety.

Apuleius, married to a rich widow Aemilia Pudentilla, was accused by her depraved family of bewitching her and of changing proper names in his works to avoid the risk of libel. In his *Apologia, 10*, a record of his trial at Sabratha in AD 157, Apuleius defended himself skilfully and humorously. There were many precedents, he said. 'They might as well charge Catullus with using the name Lesbia for Clodia; likewise Ticidas for writing Perilla when the girl was Metella, and Propertius, who speaks of Cynthia to conceal the identity of Hostia, and Tibullus for having Plania in mind when he puts Delia in his verse.'

Probably Apuleius found the information in the now lost section about Catullus in Suetonius' *De Poetis*, the historian in turn obtaining the information from Julius Hyginus, the librarian of Rome's Palatine Library in the reign of Augustus. It was not until the sixteenth century AD, however, that the humanist Petrus Victorius wrote that the Clodia of the Catullan poems was the wife of Metullus Celer.

An accepted rule seemed to be that the assumed names had to be metrically interchangeable: Lesbia and Clodia, Cynthia and Hostia. Metella, perhaps the wayward daughter of Clodia, becoming 'Perilla'. Even Ovid played the same poetical game. His 'Corinna' seems to hide the forgotten name of his first, young and briefly married wife, whom he ungallantly described as 'neither worthy nor useful'. Yet it is feasible that she herself was the enigmatic 'Corinna'. Poets enjoy riddles.[12]

Catullus set several of them, typically a melange of the obvious, the puzzling and the almost insoluble. He was the first to use a pseudonym yet there was no obvious need for it. He could have left his lover in safe anonymity. Instead, he invented 'Lesbia'. There were reasons, one obvious, the other a private compliment.

There were other safeguards against discovery. Intentionally, Clodia criticized Catullus to Metellus Celer.

Before her husband LESBIA calls me names,
And at the lewdness of the town exclaims;
This tickles the poor Cuckold to the life
And he thanks heav'n for such a virtuous Wife
Contented Fool!

[83]
(Nicholas Amhurst, 1697-1742)

By using a false name he protected a married woman from the scandal of adultery. This is the obvious reason but it is insufficient. The name could have been any that fitted metrically: Julia, Livia, Marcia, Tullia, all would have sufficed as a shield. Unlike them, however, 'Lesbia' had a significance that would delight the educated Clodia. Literally meaning 'from Lesbos' it evoked associations with that legendary island, 'the great seat of lyric inspiration in antiquity', a place of music, poetry, lovely women, of beauty contests, of a landscape of quiet inlets and wild flowers. Sappho sang of her lovely birthplace:

> And in it cold water makes a clear sound through
> apple branches and with roses the whole place
> is shadowed and down from radiant-shaking leaves
> sleep comes dropping.
>
> [Fragment 2][13]

To choose 'Lesbia' was to flatter Clodia. It compared her with Sappho, famous for the erotic refinement of her verse, praise all the more appealing because Clodia was noted for her own poems. Even Cicero, who despised her, referred to her as 'a poetess who has many such works to her credit'.[14]

In the poems of Catullus the pseudonym first appears in poem [51], a translation of Sappho, but with characteristic Catullan deceit that link with Sappho is withheld until late in *Liber I*. The first mention of Lesbia occurs over forty poems earlier in poem [5] in which Sappho does not appear. The poem is about kisses, love and money as if referring to a courtesan from Lesbos. The obvious in Catullus is often an illusion.

The invented name also subtly freed Clodia from the tyranny of being a possession of her husband. As Lesbia she was independent, but as poems to her were composed and read, people speculated and discovered the truth. In Martin's apt observation, 'More like a negligée than a suit of armour the pseudonym revealed and flattered in a number of ways the figure it pretended to conceal.'

Though the gradual discovery may have caused apprehension, it was nevertheless unique. 'Catullus is the first ancient poet to treat a love-affair with one commanding lover in depth, in a related collection of mutually deepening poems. This had simply not happened before.'[15] It had begun with a silent infatuation for the woman who sat by her husband, admiring her, delighting in the music of her voice, wondering how to attract her attention and become close to her. The dilemma prompted the creation of yet another device, the seemingly innocent recital of a translation of Sappho, a rendering that was almost faithful but containing secretive undertones of desire. It was a declaration of love that was close to the original, but one that contained hints. If Clodia understood and approved then it was a success. If not, then it was just a good translation cleverly written in exactly the same difficult metre.

There is an irony. In her sad poem of longing, Fragment 31, 'He seems to me to live with the gods', Sappho was not talking to a man. She, a female, was speaking to a desirable young woman that she could not have because that girl was already promised to the man.

Sappho's was a lesbian poem. And from the early Middle Ages to Victorian times such 'unnatural' sex was tastefully altered. The speaker became a man talking to a man-friend. In Reynolds' phrase 'Sappho was gradually becoming fit only for the boudoir'.

Quite differently, long before that homogenised Christian expurgation, Catullus also converted the admired poem, not for any sexual propriety but to use it as a personal statement of his own very masculine love for a very adorable feminie woman.

SAPPHO [Fragment 31V]

He seems to me to live with the
gods, the man that sits in front of
you, and so close, can hear
your voice

and your laughter. The sound
makes my heart tremble, go away,
for as I look at you I cannot speak
a word.

In silence my tongue dies,
a fire flames through me,
my eyes see nothing, my ears
ring.

CATULLUS [51]

He seems to me the equal of a god,
and if gods allow, better than the
gods, the man before you, and again
and again seeing you and hearing you

laugh, something steals from me
I am helpless, senses gone when I
look at you, Lesbia, not one word
remaining on my lips.

my tongue is silent, a fire
burns through me, sounds deafen
my ears, my eyes see only
darkness.[16]

Then, abruptly, the literal translation was abandoned:

SAPPHO

I sweat, trembling
through my body, soaked as grass,
I near the last phases
of death.

CATULLUS

Idleness, Catullus, is your disaster,
idleness delights you, entices you,
idleness has led to the ruin of kings
and of long-established cities. [16]

[51, 51B]

Critics have interpreted Catullus' four lines as a meaningless addition, or a blunder by Renaissance scribes, even a later qualification by Catullus who tacked it on to the end of [51] to wreck the meaning of his once-lovely poem. It was none of these. It depends on the interpretation of the word *otium*, which can mean 'leisure', or 'idleness' but which also has the more significant meaning of 'doing nothing'.

It is arguable that Catullus was rebuking himself for wanting a woman but lacking the nerve to do something about his desire. The four lines could then be read as; 'doing nothing, Catullus, is your downfall, doing nothing is easy, timidity gives you an excuse if your hopes do not succeed. But doing nothing has been the calamity of once vigorous kingdoms and idle mercantile cities.'[17]

He must have done something. Or perhaps Clodia sensed his longing, was attracted to a sensitive and charming young poet, ten or more years her junior, who wrote amusingly delicate poems about her and her possessions, and befriended him.

At first they may have met decorously in her home in the company of others, he hurrying up the hill with another of his whimsically domestic verses, one of his two 'sparrow' poems that have enchanted poets from Martial to the present day.

Sparrow! Lesbia's lively guest,
Cherish'd ever in her breast!
Whom with tantalizing jokes
Oft to peck her she provokes:
Thus in pretty playful wiles
Love and absence she beguiles.

                          [2]
(Walter Savage Landor, 1775-1864)

The poem was a doubly attractive gift because it provided one more link with Sappho. In her poem, 'Ode to Aphrodite', the only complete one to survive, the chariot of the goddess of love was drawn by sparrows, a bird that the Greeks associated with fertility. Some translators have changed them into blue thrushes, chaffinches and swans but it was sparrows that Sappho wrote of:

Deathless Aphrodite: ... And fine birds brought you,
quick sparrows over the black earth
whipping their wings down the sky
through midair –

                          [Poem 1]

In his second sparrow poem [7] Catullus could charm even when describing death. The Tudor satirist, poet laureate and enemy of Cardinal Wolsey, John Skelton, imitated it in *Phillip Sparow*, about the death of a schoolgirl's sparrow killed by a 'foule cat':

CATULLUS	SKELTON
Grieve, Venuses and Cupids	Reportynge the vertues all
And all you lovers:	Of my sparow royall.
My girl's sparrow is dead,	For it wolde come and go
Sparrow, my beloved's pet,	And fly so to and fro;
Whom she loved more than her eyes.	And on me it wolde lepe
For honey-sweet he was and knew his	Whan I was aslepe,
Mistress as well as a girl knows her mother,	And his fethers shake,
Nor would he ever go from her lap	Wherewith he wolde make
But hopping, now here, now there,	Me often for to wake,
Kept chirping to his mistress	And for to take him in
Until he teetered into that crepuscular chasm	Upon my naked skyn;
From which no thing returns.	God wot, we thought no syn.[18]

[3]

There was no sin, only delight and wonder. For a man whose emotions always shaped his life, it was a time of joyous disbelief as he was charmed by her gracefulness, the flowing, shining folds of her silk gowns, felt her fingertips brushing his hand. She was beyond perfection. He heard late summer in her voice, trees losing leaves, the gradual darkness; a day without her was a day without ending; a day with her was an hour, a minute, a transformation of time. He inhabited two worlds – her world, and another existence of almost emptiness. It was not only her body, her beauty, it was everything – body, voice, elegance, laughter and understanding.

Later he was to remember those days and nights, a time that had passed but which would never be forgotten:

...As glorious a love as that
Brought to me by my light, my love, who came into my arms.
...
She came with Cupid dancing, his golden scarves circling behind her.

(Gregory, [68B], p. 249)

He thought of nothing but her. Outside her there was only the next time that they would meet.

In the outside world these were unusually quiet years for politics in Rome. Caesar was leading his conquering legions in southern Gaul. Pompey brooded, wondering where his power and popularity had gone. Crassus increased his fortunes, purchasing tenements threatened by fire. Cicero preened himself as the man who had saved the Republic from Catiline even though that had been two years ago. Clodius plotted, gathered a rabble

Right: Bust of Catullus in
Sirmione. 87 BC is three years
too early

Below: Airport car parking
sign, Verona

Arena (Colosseum) in Verona

Villa of Catullus (Sirmione) with Lake Garda beyond

Above: Roman wall in Verona

Right: Statue of Can Grande above the church, Verona

Left: Tablet listing executions in Tullianum prison

Below: The condemned cell, Tullianum

Paul Getty's replica of Piso's villa, Herculaneum. View from the main peristyle pool garden

Across Basilica Sempronia to the three pillars of the Temple of Castor & Pollux. Palatine Hill in the background

Temple of Vesta, Rome

Drawing 'Death of a sparrow/Clodia's sparrow'

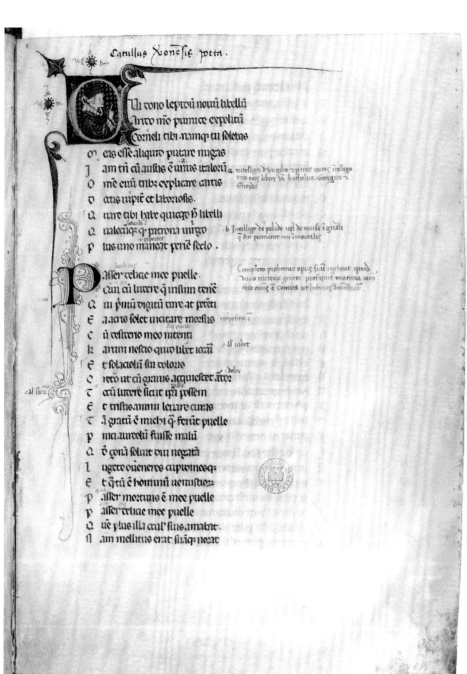

First page of Codex 'O'

of ruffians, waited for the moment to destroy Cicero, the man who had betrayed him at his trial.

Meanwhile Clodia and Catullus lived in a private world of growing love and kisses, living for the moment.

> Let us live, my Lesbia, let us love,
> Ignore old prudes who disapprove,
> Give not one farthing for disdain.
> Suns going down will rise again,
> But ours is one brief day, one brief light
> Before the long, last, everlasting night.
> Kiss me a thousand kisses, then a hundred,
> A second thousand and a hundred,
> Yet one more thousand kisses, one more hundred,
> Again a thousand and again a hundred... (p. 223)
>
> [5]

Until, with all those kisses computed on an abacus and stacked in pillars of coins, they would knock them over, hide them, tell the world that they were bankrupt, concealing their rich and private love. It was a conceit but it was their private conceit.

Catullus played with words, juggling them in clever contrasts so that their similarities of sound clashed with their different meanings, using *lux* at the end of one line in [5] with *nox* at the beginning of the next. For once the English is even better with 'light' opposed to 'night'. He could exaggerate the number of kisses as uncountable coins or the millions of grains of sand in a desert or stars in the limitless sky. It was intellectual love-making.

Well over a thousand years later the kiss' poem in its original Latin, '*Vivamus mea Lesbia, atque amemus*', was well-known to Elizabethan poets. Three of them, Thomas Campion, Samuel Daniel and Ben Johnson composed their own English versions of it. [19]

The first 'kiss' poem, [5], is the famous one. The second, [7], although seeming laboured today, is as good. It was a literary joke.

> You ask, Lesbia, how many of your kisses
> will be enough to satisfy my desire?
> As many as the countless sands of Libya
> filled with the resinous weeds of Cyrene,
> from the sweltering oasis of Jupiter-Ammon's temple
> to the tomb of ancient Battus,

as many as the sky has stars that icily look down
on the fond caresses of secretive lovers. (pp. 168-9)

                                                              [7]

The poem appears strained. In reality it was delightful erudition. Catullus did not use the Latin *osculum* for a kiss but the unknown *basia*, a soft Celtic word from his native tongue. It was a novelty so pleasingly intimate that it became part of European languages: in Italian 'il bacio', in French 'le baiser', even in English 'buss', although that has been almost forgotten.

Laughingly, 'Lesbia has asked Catullus a straightforward question to which the poem is going to be the answer. Or is it? It may be an answer but it is anything but straightforward. The signal is given with the word *basiationes* for which the English "kisses" is a woefully pale shadow...[sounding] as odd in Latin as the corresponding English phrase, "basiations of you".' But that was only because the Catullan equivalent, 'buss', had gone out of fashion. Shakespeare had used it.

> Come, grin on me; and I will thinke thou smil'st
> And busse thee as thy wife.
>   Shakespeare, *King John III*, iv, 34-5

In *Hesperides* Robert Herrick explained why the word lapsed into disrepute.

> Kissing and bussing differ both in this,
> We busse our wantons, but our wives we kisse.

And by the mid-nineteenth century 'buss' had become an archaism used only by poets such as Browning, Meredith and Tennyson with his 'nor buss'd the milking maid'.

'*Basia*' was one subtlety of poem [7]. The geography was another, teasing and challenging Clodia with its levity. 'The Lesbias [of Rome] were not only beautiful, they were intelligent, well-read and witty, and one courted them on all counts.' It was humorous courtship and erudite seduction.

'Cyrene' was not just the capital city of Cyrenaica. It was the birthplace of Callimachus, the poetical model for the new poets. Battus was its legendary founder. He was so revered that Callimachus called himself 'Battiades', the son of Battus. The temple and the tomb were not close together but 300 miles apart, the land between covered with health-giving plants, a metaphor for the goodness of their own love. The foul-smelling silphium weed, asafoetida, was so needed for medicines and herbal remedies that at the onset of the Civil War in Italy Caesar found two-thirds of a ton of it stored in the State Treasury.

So far from being an aridity of classical references, the poem invited Clodia to recognize the allusions and understand how personal they were to a poet like Catullus. It was light-hearted but it was also arcane learning. Despite its superficially contrived images the poem contained ciphers that would have intrigued, impressed and pleased an educated Roman. And it ended simply with a contrast between the erotic bodily heat of the desert and the remote eyes of the stars gazing coldly down on the world's adulteries. How many kisses would satisfy Catullus? They would be

> Too many for foul prying eyes ever to compute,
> and sufficient to bewilder the evil babblings of men's tongues.
>
> [7]

They made love. A hiding-place had been found by a friend of Catullus, Lucius Manlius Torquatus. A few years older than the poet and a patrician he had gone against convention and married Junia of the Aurunculeia plebeian clan. That romantic impulse may have made him sympathetic to the romantic predicament of Catullus.

The refuge had to be well away from the house of Metellus Celer and in a neighbourhood where the arrival of a curtained sedan would be an ordinary event to the well-brought-up ladies of the neighbourhood, perhaps somewhere amongst the dwellings on the respectable Quirinal Hill. Slaves carrying the chair would skirt the unsavoury Subura, plod up the stones of the Alta Semita, past the Temple of Quirinus, one of the oldest in Rome with a lucky myrtle tree outside its portals, enter the street, stop outside the house into which the slave-janitor would admit the visitor.

> ...my radiant goddess entered,
> trod on the worn threshold, sandal tapping
> as she paused...
>
> [68B], 70-2

There were long afternoons and evenings, talking in the shaded garden, reading poems, making love:

> in that house fragrant with the scents of Assyria,
> during that wondrous night she gave me pleasures
> filched from the lap of her token husband.
>
> [68B], 144-6

There is a reticence about the writing despite its warmth. There is deep pleasure and ecstasy in it yet there is no physical description, no embracing arms, no breasts, no bodies, a sensitive restraint in which nothing is lost of the love. But everything is wrong about the poem.

There are, in fact, two poems, [68A] and [68B], a contradiction not unknown in the rather untidy *Liber III*. The first, [68A], is a letter to Manlius who has requested the gift of a poem which Catullus is unable to write. He was in Verona, grieving the death of his brother. The letter is succeeded by [68B] dedicated to the misnamed 'Allius' (Manlius), probably composed after 57 BC when Catullus had returned from a year's service as a staff officer in the province of Bithynia.

There is unease in the poem. Despite the delights Catullus had been aware that there had been murmured warnings in that first day of love-making.

> ... my radiant goddess entered,
> trod on the worn threshold ...

Romans were superstitious about entering a house. It always had to be done with the right foot crossing the sill first, never touching the stone, and such a ritual was obligatory for brides.

'By resting her foot on the threshold, Lesbia commits an unlucky act ... Unlike the bride, ducking her head and lifting her feet carefully over the threshold to avoid bad luck, Lesbia places her foot on the threshold of the borrowed, sensuous and unsanctified house.' Brides were usually carried over the entrance stone. 'In Roman ceremony, the bride must be carried across the sacred *limen* so that she doesn't tread on it.'[20]

Clodia arrived like a surreptitious bride but with the arrogant indifference of the Claudii she offended tradition. Catullus was to see it as an omen and a warning. In love he tried to ignore the portents even though he already had reservations about the woman he loved.

> And though she is not content with Catullus alone
> yet shall I put up with the rare lapses of my discreet
> mistress, lest I be a nuisance like stupid men.
>   [68B] lines 135-6

What neither he nor Clodia could ignore was the sudden and unexpected death of Metellus Celer in January, 59 BC. That date settles one more controversy. The poet's association with Clodia must have begun before then because Catullus stated that Clodia had made fun of him to her husband. Attempts to delay the affair until 56 BC are historically meaningless.

The death was so unexpected that there were rumours of poison and Clodia, though never directly accused, was suspected. In Rome, poison, its taste disguised in heavily flavoured food, was the favoured means of overcoming personal inconveniences.

Cicero raged against the death. 'While he was still in the prime of life, enjoying excellent health and full bodily vigour, only two days after he had been seen at the height of his powers in the Senate, the law courts, and all the political affairs of our city, his life was snatched away from our midst.' He snarled viciously at Clodia. 'Now shall the woman that comes from such a house have the audacity to start discussions about the speeds with which poisons take effect. Ought that dwelling not, rather, to inspire her heart with terror, in case it shrieks forth the tale of her guilt? Will she not recoil in dread from the walls which know her secret, and shudder at the memory of that fatal, miserable night?'[21]

In a contest for Europe's most successful poisoners the Borgias, when contrasted against their Roman predecessors, would have been flattered to compete. For skill, ingenuity and ruthlessness the classical world was unmatched. Aware of the possibility of having to commit suicide, Cleopatra experimented with snakes, using condemned criminals as test-tubes. Trials proved that fast-acting venom left their victims in agony. Slower toxins brought gradual numbness, drowsiness and oblivion. She selected the Levantine asp.

Agrippina, wife of the emperor Claudius, killed him by having his favourite dish of harmless mushrooms coated with the sauce of a deadly variety. Nero eliminated his young rival Britannicus with cunning. At a banquet the apprehensive lad's drink was poisoned. The slave wine-taster sipped and fell dead. Another flagon was brought. The second wine-taster survived but the drink was intentionally very hot. Cold but poisoned water was poured into it. Britannicus drank, reeled, slumped to the floor. Nero ignored him. Just one of his epileptic fits he reassured his guests. Slaves removed the distasteful corpse from the feast. The murderous potions had been prepared by an expert on herbal drugs, Locusta, 'a woman recently sentenced for poisoning, but with a long career of imperial service ahead of her'. It ended when the emperor Galba had her put to death in AD 68.[22]

There were many Locustas in Rome. 'Think of those engaged in preparing and selling poisons,' wrote Juvenal in his *Satire XIII*, 154. Whether Clodia had employed one to free her from the imprisonment of marriage was neither proved nor even investigated. As an unsupervised widow, she could with outwardly sensible observation of the decencies indulge her whims, be less cautious of being seen in public with Catullus, and enjoy her sexual freedom.

First, however, there was the funeral which, as was correct for a former consul, was a formal and elaborate ceremony. Undertakers washed and oiled the body, making it presentable for its lying in state for the days before the burial. Then, on an eight-man litter, covered with flowers, followed by paid mourners and musicians, women wailing dirges, the corpse, lying on its left side as though at a feast, was carried to the Forum. Behind it came the chariots of the relatives, men in the purple-bordered toga of a consul, all with the death-masks of the ancestors as they sat in their thrones. It was an occasion for the family, for brothers, uncles, sons, nephews, the widow, close friends. Catullus would not have been invited.

At the far end of the Forum at the Rostra the corpse on its bier was raised to an upright position so that his mourners could see it during the long eulogy as an orator praised the family of the dead man, his eminent and admired ancestors, his own life and achievements. Encomium followed encomium. These were illustrious forebears: Lucius Caecilius Metellus, who had triumphed in the First Punic War, returning to Rome with thirteen captured generals and over a hundred Carthaginian elephants. Later as Pontifex Maximus he had fearlessly rushed into the flames of the burning Temple of Vesta to rescue the statue of Pallas. The price was the loss of an arm and blindness. In gratitude the State accorded him the singular honour of being transported to the Senate in a chariot.

Another ancestor, Quintus Caecilius Metellus, 'Macedonicus', had made Macedonia a province of Rome. In the city he built the temples of Jupiter Stator and Juno Regina. Another Pontifex Maximus, Lucius Caecilius Metellus had tried three Vestal Virgins in 114 BC for immorality. He acquitted two.

Early in the first century another Quintus Caecilius Metellus was acclaimed 'Numidicus' for his exploits against Jugurtha. Quintus Caecilius Metellus, his son, had been one of Sulla's generals. Amongst these merited tributes there was no mention of the cowardice of one of the family after the battle of Cannae in 216 BC.

Then came the laudation for Quintus Caecilius Metellus himself, a soldier who had fought valiantly in the armies of Pompey, who had led legions against Catiline and who had been consul in 60 BC. Following that honour he was to have been governor of Transalpine Gaul in 59 BC. It is an irony that after the death of Metellus that command was given to Julius Caesar. If Clodia did murder her husband, she may well have changed the history of the western world.

The panegyrics continued for hours until, at last, the time came for the burial. In the mouth of the dead man a bronze coin was placed to pay the aged and shabby ferryman Charon to carry the soul across the River Styx to Hades where the gods would decide whether the ghost merited the pleasures of Elysium or the pains of Tartarus.

After the litany of speeches the corpse was placed on a handcart and dragged by corpse-bearers, the *vespillones*, out of the city to the roadside cemetery where passers-by could see and admire the line of ostentatious tombs. The body was carried inside the stone-built, heavily carved sarcophagus. Food, drink, a platter for libations, a gold ring, perfumes of myrrh and frankincense were left to make the dead man's journey more enjoyable. The tomb was then closed.

It was a long, impressive day. The funeral feast was followed by a second, nine days later, after which all the participants had to be purified before being allowed to rejoin the world of the living. The period of mourning then began – a few days for the men, a year for women. And every year, from the 13th to the 21st of February, there was the festival of Parentalia when temples were shut, magistrates closed their offices and weddings were forbidden. Once again families visited the tombs, left simple offerings there, putting them on broken bits of pot that symbolized the broken life: ears of corn, a garlanded tile, grains of salt, bread soaked in wine, flowers. It ended with a family reunion to worship the Lar Familiaris, the, spirits of their dead ancestors.[23]

How much it meant to Clodia is a guess. Outwardly much, inwardly perhaps a shrug. There followed a year of surreptitious meetings with Catullus as the months of mourning lingered. In his hope and passion Catullus begged her to marry him. She consented – with a caveat: as soon as it became acceptable to society for the wedding to be announced.

> Even in his amazed delight the poet wondered.
> My loved one swears it is only me that she would wed,
> Even if Jupiter himself were to be a suitor.
> What a woman promises to a tearful lover
> Should be written on the wind, engraved on running water.
>
> [70] (p. 184)

With the close of 59 BC came the end of the period of widow's mourning. Winter became spring, spring became early summer and it was time for the annual exodus to Baiae and the celebrations of the living.

By the month of May it was becoming too hot in Rome for the wealthy. Sea breezes were sought after and of all the places Baiae in the Gulf of Pozzuoli west of Naples was the best. Private, luxurious houses and flourishing gardens spread along the sheltered inland side of its little peninsula. There were no hotels for the well-to-do, only one's own homes. Cicero, not notably rich, had six in Italy. Julius Caesar, Mark Antony, Lucullus had properties at Baiae. Hadrian died there. Nero tried to drown his mother in the Gulf of Pozzuoli.

The resort was a spa, no better than Naples but more fashionable. There were sulphur steam baths and warm springs to relax in according to one's preference: nitre, bitumen, alum, salt. There was yachting on Lake Lucrinus, swimming in the nude, and all kinds of pursuits through which to gain a bad reputation. Baiae was commended for its delights and condemned for its depravities. Everything was relaxed, almost uncensored. Even ageing, conservative senators appeared publicly in short tunics that they would hesitate to wear in the privacy of their own gardens in Rome. Seneca the Younger, philosopher and moralist, quitted the town after just one night, disgusted at drunkards staggering along the beach, at the raucous boating parties, the loud music that would not let him sleep. For young people it was expensive bliss, summertime traders typically charged extortionate prices, with cheap local produce going at city prices. Propertius worried how steadfast the morals of Cynthia would be as she carefreely went on holiday to Baiae.

> But you must quickly leave degenerate Baiae.
> Those beaches bring divorce to many,
> Beaches for long the enemy of decent girls.
> A curse on Baiae's waters, love's disgrace.

Martial, who knew the place well, wrote a sardonic epigram about Laevina, a woman traduced by the spa's temptations:

> A good wife, loyal to her husband's penis,
> never wandered from her virtuous path
> until she came to Lake Lucrinus
> and steamed up in a Baian bath.
> With body tenderized and syrupy
> she ran off with a handsome boy.
> Once a pure Penelope,
> Now just Helen, whore of Troy.[24]

Whether Catullus ever visited Baiae is not known. He never mentions it in his poems but then he was not writing a travelogue, and it may have been of little importance to him.

He was busy extolling the praises of Clodia at the expense of another much admired woman.

> In the eyes of many Quintia is beautiful; she is fair, tall
> straight. Yes, I'll readily grant all this;
> but the all-embracing 'beautiful', never! There is
> not a grain of charm, of appeal in that ample body.
> Now Lesbia truly is beautiful: not only is she loveliness, but
> she takes some quality of Venus from every other woman.
>   [86] (pp. 185)

Politically 59 BC was critical and Publius Clodius was central to the crisis. The Senate's insensitive and provocative denial of Pompey's demands, depriving him of power or influence, drove him into a misjudged alliance with Caesar and Crassus. It strengthened them and simultaneously weakened both Pompey and the Senate which became indecisive, easing the path of the single-minded Triumvirate.

A political observer would realize that the 'triumvirate' was in fact a 'duumvirate': Crassus had the money and Caesar had the popularity and acumen. Pompey was just an appendage. An even more astute analyst would have seen that the two men and the third hanger-on was really one leader with two lieutenants, Crassus and the intrusive newcomer Clodius. Pompey was just a name. To ensure his loyalty the divorced general was married to Julia, Caesar's daughter. It proved to be a happy union.

The Senate was split by factions: the patricians were concerned to retain their status, the businessmen were anxious not to lose their incomes, and men like Cato and Cicero futilely endeavoured to maintain the Republic's status quo. Whenever partnerships evolved they broke into fissures as self-interest drove them apart. Senators became like early settlers in the Wild West, nervous at the distant yelping of coyotes, unaware of black widow spiders in the shadows of the log cabin. To extend the metaphor, the cabin itself, the Senate and its laws, was to be blown away by the approaching tornado.

Publius Clodius was more than a sexual pervert. He was a social incendiary. In the past his patrician Claudian family had contained unstable renegades, men that changed sides whenever they saw an advantage but of them he was the most brilliant, callous and ambitious. He had already betrayed Lucullus. He alienated Metellus Celer who, as consul, had vetoed his application to become a tribune because the post was forbidden to patricians. One of the minor 'What ifs?' of those dying Republican years might be: 'If Metellus Celer was indeed murdered, was the crime committed by his wanting-to-be emancipated wife or his frustrated wanting-to-be-tribune brother-in-law?'[25]

In 59 BC Clodius persuaded Crassus and Caesar that if he were a tribune he could be an influential supporter of theirs with the persuasive menace of his street gangs. His patrician status could be changed. It was. Under the auspices of Crassus and Caesar he was adopted into the plebeian Herrenius family, the 'son' of a nineteen-year-old youth, and was popularly elected a tribune in 58 BC.

He was already despised by Rome's respectable citizens, but Catullus especially loathed Clodius for his incestuous desecration of his sister's body:

Lesbius, it's not for me to criticize your filthy morals
If only you keep them for your foul companions.

But your disgusting saliva has dribbled
Into the pure mouth of a decent girl.

[78B]

Tribunes had political strength. As a form of magistrate protecting the rights of the proletariat they could summon assemblies, propose laws, interrupt the proceedings of the Senate, even veto its decrees. Importantly for the vengeful Clodius they could imprison a consul who had acted improperly against the accepted laws of Rome.

Clodius quickly showed himself a schemingly capable demagogue, shaping the mob to his wishes by appealing to theirs. By his first law of January 58 BC he became one of the most popular men in Rome, not with the indignant patricians but among the impoverished, half-fed population. Over 300,000 citizens had been granted the privilege of buying corn very cheaply, Clodius now abolished the payment altogether. To subsidize the enormous cost he confiscated the Egyptian kingdom of Cyprus from its high priest, Ptolemy, brother to pharaoh Ptolemy XII. Powerless to resist, Ptolemy took poison. From his island Clodius extorted 7,000 gold Greek talents, a fortune.

Spitefully he appointed one of his patrician opponents, Cato the Younger, to be responsible for its safe delivery to Rome. Apprehensive of its disastrous, possibly fatal loss at sea, the honest, stubbornly conservative senator packed it in hundreds of vases, each containing just two talents and 500 silver Greek drachmas, a long precautionary cord attached to each pot. It arrived safely.

With the populace behind him Clodius obtained his long-standing revenge on the man who had betrayed him at the Bona Dea trial. He had Cicero banned from Rome. As consul during the time of Catiline's conspiracy the orator had high-handedly put Roman citizens to death – to safeguard the state he had claimed. But it had been illegal and now Clodius attacked him. In late January or early February 58 BC, he passed two bills. The first bought off the consuls. The second successfully prosecuted Cicero for his illegal actions. The man was to be outlawed to Thessalonica 400 miles from Italy. He vainly appealed to the bribed consuls. He appealed to Pompey, who said he was unable to help him. Caesar generously offered him a post on his staff in Gaul, but Cicero refused to be allied with, such an enemy of tradition. He went into voluntary exile to Greece.

In front of a crowd in the Forum Clodius exulted. 'Whereas Marcus Tullius Cicero has put Roman citizens to death unheard and uncondemned; and for that end forged the authority and decree of the Senate; it is ordered that he be interdicted of fire and water; that nobody presume to harbour or receive him on pain of death; and whoever shall move, speak, vote or take any step towards recalling him, shall be treated as a public enemy, unless those should first be recalled to life whom Cicero unlawfully put to death.'

Cicero's property was confiscated. His fine house on the Palatine was destroyed and Clodius maliciously had a temple dedicated to Liberty built there so that the ground became sacred and could never again be used for secular purposes. Two villas at Tusculum (Tusculo) and Forrniae (Mola di Gaeta) were also demolished. Cicero's subsequent appeal of January 57 BC to be allowed to return to Rome was blocked.[26]

These events were taking place on the fringes of Catullus' world. Politics, wars, social disturbance existed but they existed on the periphery of his awareness. His world consisted of emotions, words, transforming a thought into a written image. Clodia was at its heart until the appearance of Marcus Caelius Rufus.

Caelius Rufus was a rival in love, a few years older than the poet, born perhaps on the same day as Catullus' friend, Calvus, 28 May, 82 BC. He came from Interamnia (Terni) some fifty miles north of Rome. His father was an affluent banker and, helped by paternal funds, Caelius Rufus became a promising pupil and friend both of Cicero and Crassus. Fourteen of his letters to Cicero show him to be witty and a penetrating observer of people. He summarized Pompey sharply: 'He is accustomed to think one thing and say another, and yet is not clever enough to conceal his real aims.' Wiseman made another assessment, this one of Caelius Rufus: 'almost the best known minor character in Roman history'.[27]

Tall, good-looking, a capable orator, he was a man about town who mixed comfortably in the literary coterie of Catullus and his friends, a dandy with an extravagant lifestyle. He rapidly became well-known and liked, almost famous after his speech in 59 BC when Antoninus Hybrida, 'mongrel', one-time ally of Catiline, was tried for avarice.

Antoninus had abandoned Catiline when Cicero offered him the province of Macedonia. Even in the corruption of late first century his rapacity there had been so outrageous that he was put on trial, condemned by Caelius Rufus and, despite being defended by Cicero, found guilty.

By 58 BC Caelius Rufus had become a praetor, dealing with Rome's financial affairs at the time when Publius Clodius was building a strong political base for himself The two became colleagues and friends. Clodius had purchased the most palatial of all the mini-palaces on the Palatine at a price, remarked Pliny, 'worthy of the madness of kings', and he leased a nearby house to Caelius at a peppercorn rent so that, according to Cicero, Caelius could be near the Forum and to 'visit us at our houses and to receive visits from his friends'.[28]

Clever, vivacious, a frequent guest at the home of Clodius Pulcher and, by deduction, a visitor to the nearby house of Clodia, nothing in his unprincipled nature prevented him from making love to her. It can, as Havelock might have added, be assumed that she did not resist.

Catullus exclaimed in anger:

Rufus, I trusted you, your vain and faithless friendship.
Vain? It cost me everything of my life.
You wormed inside my trust, deep into my being
And stole my happiness, made it wretched, took all I love.
You raped it, smirched it with your poisonous lust,
You bitter contamination of friendship!

[77]

Bewildered, enraged, in despair and out of his mind with the destructive emotions of disappointment, disbelief, vengeance, self-pity, Catullus now wrote as though words were dead things.

Odi et amo ...　　I loathe her and I love her. 'Can I show
　　　　　　　　how both can be?'
　　　　　　　　I loathe and love, and nothing else I know
　　　　　　　　But agony.

[85]
(Havelock, pp. 58-9)

Next year, 57 BC, with his true friend, Gaius Helvius Cinna, he left Rome to go overseas to join the staff of Gaius Memmius, new governor of Bithynia.

6

BITHYNIA, VERONA, ROME – 57-56 BC

There were many reasons for leaving Rome. Catullus had been betrayed by Clodia. News that his brother had died near Troy reached him from Verona. There was the expectation of liberal gifts as an administrator in a province. Wiseman has connected two seemingly unrelated facts: the familiarity of Catullus with the counting of coins, and the death of his brother in Bithynia, suggesting a possible business connection with the province. The prosperity of the poet's family may have come from a concession to be tax-farmers and exporters from Bithynia. It would explain the poet's knowledge of the language of business and the presence of his brother there.[1]

It was a long voyage. From Brundisium (Brindisi) the ships crossed the Adriatic, sailed around Corinth and veered northwards through the Aegean, to the narrow mouth of the Hellespont. To the east was the tree-covered mountain range of Mount Ida from which the gods had looked down on the siege of Troy.

Once through the strait and the Sea of Marmara the fleet filtered through the constricted Bosphorus, one part so narrow that dogs barking on one side could be heard on the other. Then, after weeks of cramped quarters, 1,500 miles of changing spring weather and currents, the Pontus Euxinus or Black Sea was reached and they came to the port of Heraclea Pontica (Eregli), a third of the way along the 600 miles of the north coast. The new governor could take up his post. Gaius Memmius was a poet, Neoteric, an opportunist and, in Catullus' coarse and cutting phrase, 'a greedy, grasping git' who 'didn't give a fart for his aides'[10]. He had married Fulvia, daughter of Sulla. Calculating the political odds he sided with Pompey against Lucullus, even insultingly debauching Lucullus' wife, Clodia, the youngest sister of the woman that Catullus loved. Cicero disparagingly called Memmius a 'Paris', a man with a scandalous sex life who attempted to seduce Mucia, the immoral wife of Pompey. Yet his own wife was no better, being notorious for her promiscuity.

Cicero also praised him, as a connoisseur of literature, of such standing that the poet Lucretius dedicated his great work, *De Rerum Natura*, to him. Of Memmius' own poetry only one line is known: 'Strive not to climb the steep slopes of fortune.' In Bithynia he ignored the advice.[2]

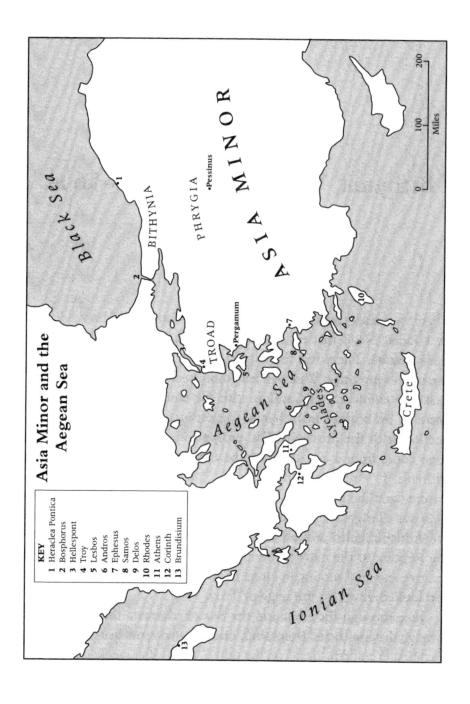

Asia Minor and the Aegean Sea

KEY
1 Heraclea Pontica
2 Bosphorus
3 Hellespont
4 Troy
5 Lesbos
6 Andros
7 Ephesus
8 Samos
9 Delos
10 Rhodes
11 Athens
12 Corinth
13 Brundisium

The province to which Paphlagonia and Pontus had been added was a vast 600,000 square miles of northern Asia Minor, with the Black Sea as its northern frontier, Phrygia to the south and the Troad to the west. Nicodemus IV had bequeathed the kingdom to Rome in 74 BC and like a profligate heir it had ever since been enriching the governors and officials of Rome. Extortion 'reached a peak of avarice and ruthlessness in the late Republic ... filling the pockets of Senators, equites and Italians who had settled abroad'.[3]

There was little control over such a remote province. Even a crow would have had to fly a thousand miles from Rome to reach Heraclea. Travel by sea was much longer in distance and time. 'Given good winds a ship in normal conditions might make 120 sea-miles in a day.' But in AD 145 bad weather and turbulent seas caused a 600-mile journey from Crete to Rome to take a fortnight. In effect a governor of remote Bithynia was an independent autocrat, ruling according to his uninhibited desires. There was money enough. He received no salary but had been given a fund for his maintenance and that of his staff and troops. It was neither accountable nor returnable.[4]

Memmius did send reports to Rome, informing the Senate of necessary changes. By the *Lex Republicae* the governor was responsible for the supervision of revenue, for law and order and for public taxes taken by local municipal authorities. He also regulated other taxes on land, on farming rights, cattle, on exports and imports, all of them looked after by tax-collectors who eagerly paid for the lucrative appointments. The family of Catullus may have had such a post. Today the senatorial lack of inspection seems incredible. In the first century BC it was unavoidable and every advantage was taken. Of people living in the province only Roman citizens had the right to appeal against a decision of the governor. An unscrupulous governor simply abused the system. He could sell prisoners of war as slaves. He took bribes. Cities quickly understood how sensible it was to 'reward' the governor for a benefit he had granted. There was corruption everywhere and in everything. Justice could be sold. Loans could be blocked to cities that were in debt unless substantial gifts were provided. The governor could disregard, for a 'consideration', the exorbitant interest rates of money-lenders. He could threaten to billet expensive troops on a town or village unless 'persuaded' that there really was no threat of an invasion.[5]

Yet it is not surprising that no province rebelled against the maladministration. Even with the worst of governors the region was still protected by the power of Rome. Under Memmius there was no protest. His storehouses became treasuries. Catullus received nothing. Some years later his friends Fabullus and Veranius returned from Spain equally penniless after their year under Piso, patron of Philodemus. Catullus had a wry smile at their expense. Now that you've suffered frost and famine with that creep, he asked:

Do your current accounts reveal as much profit
As mine showed loss?

[28]

But he would have appreciated poetic justice. In 54 BC Memmius tried
to become a consul, and was defeated. Two years later he was involved in a
scandal, apparently trying to sell consulships, was accused, condemned and
exiled from Rome. He never returned.

Catullus was aggrieved at the lack of reward for his year's absence from
Rome. It may be, however, that his own funds were reduced by his decision
to visit distant places: to the Troad and the grave of his brother; and long
miles through the mountainous valleys of Phrygia to the temple of the Great
Goddess, Cybele. Only seventy years earlier that ancient realm, birthplace of
the reed pipe with its curved end like a bass clarinet, kingdom of the legendary
Midas, had become part of the province of Asia.

To the poet, Cybele was a siren. Her Phrygian rock-cut sanctuaries, built to
face the rising winter sun, were everywhere. Her castrated priests in their trances
leapt and howled to rhythmic, raucous music of cymbals and drums that was
hypnotically contrapuntal. It was a bedlam performance that both intrigued and
repelled the staid citizens of Rome. The wild dancers were like dervishes, bloody
with self-inflicted wounds, who would kill anyone who stumbled during their rites.

Known as *galli*, the name deriving from the Phrygian river Gallos with its
therapeutic waters, their sexual mutilation was voluntary, using an ancient
stone knife to slice off their genitals. 'There be eunuchs which have made
themselves eunuchs for the kingdom of heaven's sake' (*Matthew*, 19:12). Their
half-naked bodies were tattooed in patterns of vine-leaves, the sacred plant of
Attis, the emasculated, dead companion of Cybele.[6]

Over the centuries the worship of the goddess spread to all parts of the
Roman empire. The probable burial of one of her priests was found in Britain
near Catterick. The slightly built young man in a long-sleeved, belted woman's
gown had a necklace and matching bracelets of jet, a shale armlet and an
expanding anklet of bronze. The late fourth-century AD transvestite was
probably a *gallus*, a follower of Cybele the remains of whose temple or shrine
may lie underneath Bainesse farm near her priest's burial.[7]

Catullus was fascinated by Cybele:

whose ivy-crowned Maenads throw back their heads,
they shriek and celebrate their rituals,
the goddess's dancing celebrants fling themselves around
and we, transported, join the wild whirl of ecstasy.

[63], 23-6

By the time of Catullus Phrygia had been part of the province of Asia for decades and a party of Roman enthusiasts could safely go to Pessinus where local people could tell them about Cybele and the wonders of her religion. Hers was an involved, sometimes contradictory story.

Sleeping at the foot of Mount Dindymus Zeus had spilled some of his seed on the ground and from it was born an odious creature with male and female genitals. In horror the gods castrated it. That was how Cybele, the Great Mother, was born, exposed on a mountainside and suckled by lions and leopards. Her statues were of a heavily built woman, pregnant, sometimes with many breasts as tokens of her fertility.

That was half the account told to the curious Romans. The experiences of Attis, a handsome young man, formed the remainder. Some said he was Cybele's son; others that the goddess loved him but had been rebuffed and in revenge had driven him mad. In contradiction, a third version said that he had desired the unattainable goddess and in despair had castrated himself, bleeding to death in the shadow of a pine tree.[8]

From this tale of love, despair, fear, mutilation and death Catullus was to compose the strangest of all the great Latin poems, *Attis* [63].

Catullus would have known about Cybele long before going to Bithynia. The oriental misfit had a temple on the Palatine Hill amongst the staid Roman pantheon of gods, where it was as out of place as a strip-tease artiste ululating in the home of the Vestal Virgins. The edifice stood above the Clivus Victoriae and the occupants of the Metelli household could hear the shrill wailing and discordant music of her priests. Hannibal caused her to be brought to Rome and a Claudia saved her. The temple was built a century and a half before Catullus went to Bithynia, constructed because Roman superstitions were aroused by the successes of Hannibal. By 204 BC the Carthaginian general had been defeating legions and raiding and ravaging the Italian countryside for fourteen years. In Rome there were bad omens: stones had fallen from the sky, there had been two suns together, daylight came in night-time, there were meteors and lightning. The three Sibylline Books were consulted, those collections of enigmatic prophecies described by Frazer as 'convenient farragos of nonsense', but devoutly trusted by the Romans. In them soothsayers discovered a prediction that an invader would be expelled if the statue of Cybele could be brought to Italy. Confirmation came with envoys from the oracle at Delphi. Every portent had been propitious.

The Senate sent five envoys, one of them yet another of the ubiquitous Metelli – Caecilius – to greet Attalus, friend of Rome and king of Pergamum in Mysia. Thirty years earlier he had driven invaders back to Galatia and had become the master of much of western Asia Minor. Proud of his success he had commemorative statues made of the defeated warriors, one of them the famous 'dying Gaul' that is now in the Capitoline Museum, Rome.

In 215 BC Attalus joined Rome in its struggle against the Macedonians. His city was rich, picturesquely terraced, and with a famous library of 200,000 volumes that was later given to Cleopatra by Mark Antony. The books were written on parchment. Even in those days there could be trade wars and embargoes. The Egyptian pharaoh Ptolemy had forbidden the export of papyrus to Mysia to prevent his rival, Eumenes, from assembling a library equal to that in Alexandria. In retaliation Eumenes used skins of sheep and goat, 'parchment' or *pergamina*, 'writing-material from Pergamum'.[9]

The Romans arriving in five enormous warships, quinqueremes escorting a fleet of cargo vessels 'with persuasive gifts and a request that Attalus assist Rome in its need. The envoys were accompanied by several legions, many of the men hardened in skirmishes against Hannibal's armies.

Rome had no allies in Phrygia and so had to make a tiring journey of over 200 miles to Pessinus (modern Baltisa, south of Ankara) through tortuous ravines and unmarked trails that could prove impassable to strangers, through a tree-dense landscape as gloomy and dispiriting as Dracula's Transylvanian forests. Attalus provided guides and his own troops to defend the invaders against the Galatians on Phrygia's far borders. It was indeed a determined enterprise to capture one small, black and unshaped stone, the meteor by which the goddess had come to earth, but fighting was inevitable. To the natives of Phrygia it was not merely the desecration of the shrine of Cybele at the foot of Mount Dindymus near Ankara, but the rape of the goddess herself, the seizure of her 'body' from her temple. Roman historians were unusually reticent about the sacrilege. Livy wrote no more than Attalus 'escorted them to Pessinus in Phrygia, gave them the sacred stone supposed by the natives to represent the Mother of the Gods, and told them to take it back to Rome'.[10] Ovid added that she was carried in a specially built ship of Phrygian pine.

Whatever the unrecorded indignant but inadequate resistance the stone was removed from its sanctuary and successfully brought to Rome's port of Ostia. Then, on the Tiber there was disaster. The vessel with the sacred object ran aground on a shoal and could not be dislodged even by the heaviest of barges. It seemed an ill-omen. The goddess had been outraged and Rome was doomed to endure more years of Hannibal's devastations.

But once again a member of the Claudian family saved the city. Defying her dubious reputation, Claudia Quinta, ancestress of Catullus' beloved Clodia, ended the crisis. She detached her stola or girdle, tied it to the ship and, proving her immaculate chastity, the boat instantly floated into midstream and was safely brought to Rome.[11]

Claudia subsequently became immortalized in a play.

You whose rape moved dilatory Cybele,
Claudia, rare handmaid of the tower-crowned goddess.
                    Propertius, Poems IV: 11, 51-2

The drama was performed at festivals, especially whenever a Claudian was a consul. The black embodiment of Cybele was temporarily lodged in the Temple of Victory until her intended shrine could be built.

The Sibylline Books were proved correct. The very next year, 203 BC, Hannibal left Italy and never returned. But he left behind one last, mocking gesture. Before leaving the small port of Crotona (Crotone) in the south-eastern heel of Italy he had a huge bronze tablet erected in the Temple of Hera. On it, in Punic and Greek, was recorded the size of the army he had brought over the Alps and all the disastrous defeats he had inflicted on so many Roman armies.

Rome may have laughed last. On its coinage it was forbidden for a citizen to stamp a personal likeness. When Julius Caesar was one of the annual mint-masters he struck a coin with an elephant on its reverse, apparently a reference to Hannibal's fearsome beasts. In fact the Carthaginian word for 'elephant' sounded very like 'Caesar'. Caesar had advertised himself.[12]

Cybele gained her own temple on 11 April, 191 BC. The *Aedes Magna Mater*, 'of the Great Mother', stood on the south-west corner of the Palatine. It had the distinction of being the first to be built of masonry, a mixture of rubble and mortar faced with fine slabs of stone. Inside, the small, rugged meteoric stone was set in a silver statue of the goddess. When the temple caught fire eighty years later, the statue of her saviour, Quinta Claudia, was saved by yet another Metellus. The building survived almost untouched through the worst years of the empire, remaining unharmed until the fifth century AD. Even today, at the south-western corner of the Palatine, amongst the ruins some inscriptions and a broken statue have been recovered, almost certainly the remains of the temple.[13]

Catullus identified with Cybele. To him she was a goddess who had destroyed the manhood of Attis. Attis was a man who had given his manhood to a female divinity to whom he was no more than a moment of amusing mortality. His loss of sex was a triviality. Attis wept. He had become:

... the gods' servant-girl, Cybele's handmaiden,
a Maenad, a half-man, no man.

                    [63], 68-9

Cybele would not release him. Chased by her lions he fled to the forests, hiding from her angry contempt, begging her to leave him in peace, to find others to drive into her destructive madness.

The festival of Cybele, the *Ludi Megalensia*, 'Games of the Great Mother of the Gods', was held from 4 to 9 April and celebrated in front of her temple in its oak grove. It lasted six days with stage performances, especially the drama of Claudia Quinta, chariot-races and hunts of wild animals. The Romans were ambivalent in their attitude to the celebration. Patricians, proud of Trojan ancestry, Troy being on the west coast of Phrygia, welcomed the abandoned cult. Sterner Romans deplored the cavorting eunuchs dancing in public with flutes, drums and cymbals around the cart bearing Cybele's statue as it was drawn through the streets by two lions, with her devotees dancing to tom-toms, cymbals and pipes. They had fasted for a week. Now they lacerated themselves with knives until their arms and shoulders were blood-covered. Some novices became so excited that they castrated themselves in public.

At the festival a pine was brought to her temple shrouded like a corpse and wreathed in violets that were the drops of Attis' blood. His effigy was fastened to the trunk. On the third day of the festival, the Day of Blood, the High Priest cut his arm deeply, offering the blood to his divine Mistress of the Mountains.

Catullus used Cybele as a spiritual counterpart of his mortal goddess, the radiant divinity who had abandoned him to desolation and long, empty silence. Clodia was Cybele made flesh. One short poem, [60], told of his emptiness. Its position was significant. It was the last of *Liber I* before the two happy wedding songs [61], [62], the bleak *Attis* [63] and the worldly cynicism of *Peleus and Thetis* [64] as human beings who have lost their innocence. Poem [60] contained a concealed message.

Num te leaena montibus Lybystinis
aut Scylla latrans infima inguinum parte
tam mente dura procreavit ac taetra
ut supplicis vocem in novissimo casu
contemptam haberes, a nimis fero corde?
Who gave you birth? A lioness from the hills of Libya
or the hideous six-headed Scylla sucking men into her maelstrom?
Which one gave you such humanity with an inhuman mind
so contemptuous of a lover's broken pleading,
leaving him death's desperation, cruel, harsh, heartless?

In it an acrostic was hidden, a succession, of first letters that, deciphered, revealed a sentence. Many poets have used this device. Cicero referred to a Sibylline prophecy that spelled the name of a king. Poets like Abraham Cowley used acrostics. So did Ben Jonson at the beginning of his play, Volpone. In the opening 'Argument' the first letter of the first word in its seven lines read:

Volpone, Offers, Lies, Presents, Other, New, Each, 'Volpone'. More recently the Peak District poet, Leonard Newton, introduced acrostics in the first line of his two verses to spell out the names of the woman he had lost:

Gone is love, lost in a night,
and
Cloud and moon pass.

A genius of the practice was François Villon who advertized his name in no fewer than seven of his poems, all but one of them a perfect acrostic of FRANÇOIS or VILLON. Once, however, ingeniously and quite intentionally, he upset the spelling in the seventh ballade of his Testament (lines 958-64), 'False beauty who has cost me dear', to show how ruinously his own love had been killed by a woman who had thrown him over and condemned him to the shame of being publicly whipped around the street-corners of Paris. The first letters of the lines read: Ung, Jaunir, Je, Lars, Viel, Or, Ne, to make a cleverly heart-broken V I L V O N.[14]

In poem [60,] Catullus devised a different form of acrostic that was almost undecipherable. He used the first letter of the first word in each line downwards and then the last letter of the last word in each line upwards: *Num, aut, tam, ut, / contemptam*, and then corde, casu, / taetra, parte, Lybystinus, to form the sentence: *Natu ceu aes*, 'from birth as unfeeling as bronze'.[15]

While he was in Bithynia no word came from his unfeeling goddess in Rome. What did come was news of rioting, bloodshed and gang warfare. Cicero had been recalled to Italy and an enraged Clodius, who had already plundered his enemy's possessions, incited his mobs to smash, burn and destroy all Cicero's remaining belongings. Recklessly, Clodius had also been provoking enemies amongst the Senate, the patricians and businessmen and doing nothing to placate them.

In retaliation the indignant Senate appointed Pompey to be in charge of the grain's distribution for the next five years. It was the first of a succession of setbacks for Clodius. The second came directly from Pompey. Always wishing to maintain the stability of the Senate against anarchy, the former soldier made a military decision. He financed an experienced rabble-rouser to quell the disorder. Clodius had already antagonized the general by commandeering the wealth his legions had brought to Rome from Asia to pay for the enormous cost of the free corn so ruinously promised to the public. Now he was to be confronted by a savage and relentless opponent.

Titus Annius Milo, the same man who had thrashed the wife-lusting Sallust, came from a rich family. Ambitious, without compunction, he had been elected a tribune at the end of Clodius' year of office, and hated his 'plebeian' rival.

With Pompey's copious funds he quickly attracted and organized ruffians to oppose any action of Clodius that displeased his patron.

As early as January 57 BC there had been a proposal to return Cicero to Italy but it had been blocked by the ferocious, near-murderous activities of rampaging Clodian thugs. Despite overwhelming public sentiment on behalf of the exile, it was not until August that a successful law was put forward to free Cicero from his banishment. This time there was no violence. Milo came to the Campus Martius with a highly paid and daunting band of gladiators and free from danger there was heavy voting in favour of the bill. Cicero landed at Brundisium (Brindisi) and by 4 September was at the outskirts of Rome and being greeted, he complacently reported, by many men of stature and 'by the common people who welcomed me with vociferous applause'.[16]

There was better to come. The College of Pontiffs decided that the charges brought by Clodius against Cicero had been unjustified and illegal. The Senate decreed that public funds should be provided for the restoration of the orator's house in Rome and his two country villas. Two million *sestertii* were allotted for the house. Cicero was content. But only a quarter of that sum was allowed for the villa in Tuscany and just one-eighth for the villa at Formiae on the west coast halfway between Rome and Naples. 'Very ungenerous', he complained.

The years following 57 BC onwards were 'the most anarchic time [for Rome] that had been seen since Catiline's day, and the perpetual riots and affrays stirred up by Clodius and his rival Milo made the city almost uninhabitable'. Cicero wrote melodramatically about the civil chaos. 'The Tiber was full of citizens' corpses, the public sewers were choked with them and the blood that streamed from the Forum had to be mopped up with sponges.' His brother, Quintus, only escaped being fatally stabbed by lying as though dead amongst a clutter of mortally wounded bodies and corpses in the streets.

Cicero himself was imperilled. Workmen rebuilding his house were scared away by the weapons of Clodius' men. Next door the already damaged house of Catulus was torn down. The home of Quintus was bombarded with stones and set on fire. Everybody deplored the mayhem. Nobody did anything. Day by day life deteriorated. On 11 November, walking along the Via Sacra, Cicero was assaulted by a gang shouting, throwing missiles, waving clubs and swords. He fled to the security of a friend's house.

Clodius, out of his mind with the frustration of losing his influence and popularity, insanely stormed Milo's house on the morning of 12 November. A counter-attack killed several of his hoodlums. He hid in Sulla's old home.

Without a police force and with Pompey's legions disbanded and dispersed there was no law, no order, just alternating and unpredictable lulls and onslaughts. The Senate wrung its impotent hands. Only Milo and Clodius had power and they were the hirelings of Pompey and Crassus, theoretical allies in the Triumvirate but enemies in reality. Their third colleague, Julius Caesar, having subdued southern Gaul the previous year, was far away fighting and winning battles against the Belgae in the north. There was to be no relief for Rome.[17]

Reports of those distant incidents might have interested Catullus but they did not cause him concern. What did intrigue him was the recent murder in Rome of an ambassador from Egypt, because the man accused of the crime had been a close acquaintance of the poet.

In 1998, during the excavation of the harbour of Alexandria, a statue of a sphinx was recovered. It had the head of a pharaoh, Ptolemy XII, father of Cleopatra. Depraved, homosexual and a drunkard, he pretentiously entitled himself the New Dionysus. His unimpressed Alexandrian subjects rudely called him 'Nothos the Bastard', and scornfully, Auletes, 'the flute-player'. A dedicated ally of Rome, he had been deposed because of that and in 58 BC he went to Rome, taking the eleven-year-old Cleopatra with him, to plead for his restoration. With the irresistible golden bribe of 6,000 talents he gained the support of the Triumvirate.[18]

Learning of this and alarmed at the prospect of an invasion by Roman legions, an Egyptian delegation was despatched from Alexandria to argue against the pharaoh's return. The mission was unwelcome. Representatives were assaulted. Others discreetly retreated to Egypt. Obstinately their leader, the philosopher Dio, went on to Rome only to be assassinated.

Blame for the murder fell on Marcus Caelius Rufus, one-time friend of Catullus, one-time lover of Clodia, acclaimed orator and ambitious politician. He was accused of plotting sedition in Naples, beating up Egyptian delegates at the port of Puteoli (Pozzuoli), stealing possessions from a woman, Palla, and the killing of Dio. Yet these matters, fearful though they were, became almost trivialities when set against the most serious charge of all. Caelius Rufus was accused of attempting to poison a patrician Roman citizen, Clodia, widow of Metellus Celer.[19]

The trial was arranged for 56 BC. It is another irony of history that in that year, just when Pompey and his soldiers were preparing to escort Ptolemy back to Egypt, a statue of Jupiter in its temple on the Alban Hills near Rome was struck by lightning. The equivocal Sibylline Books were consulted. Obligingly the seers 'discovered' a suitable pronouncement. There could be no reinstatement of an Egyptian ruler if he was accompanied by an army. Ptolemy had to wait until 55 BC and the payment of a further substantial sum to have Aulus Gabinius, Roman governor of Syria, take him back to Egypt and his throne.[20]

Ptolemy died four years later and his eighteen-year-old daughter Cleopatra, 'the glory of her father', became Queen Cleopatra VII of Egypt. Later her young half-brother, whom by custom she had married, became pharaoh Ptolemy XIII and joint ruler with her. It was not to be an enduring alliance.[21] Nor was Caesar's triumvirate.

'By early 56 BC the coalition of Pompey, Crassus and Caesar was a shambles.' With Caesar absent fighting in Gaul the antagonism between his partners resulted in Pompey informing the Senate that Crassus was scheming to have him assassinated. Taking advantage of this, and intending to weaken Caesar's influence, Cicero made a ferocious verbal attack on Clodius, the tool of Crassus and Caesar, hoping through this to lure Pompey away from the others. At the same time a tribune proposed to remove Caesar from his military command.

Caesar did not hesitate. At his winter quarters in Ravenna he consulted Crassus and then invited Pompey to join them at Lucca for a conference to end their disagreements. He suggested that they two become the consuls for 55 BC and the next year each be given an army and a province – Spain to Pompey, Syria to Crassus. It was cynical, calculated and constructive. Even in times of rank ambition, disruptive street-gangs and rampant dishonesty there was still sufficient respect for the laws for a consul to exercise considerable control over events. Pompey and Crassus were nominated as candidates for the coming elections.[22]

In the early spring of 56 BC Catullus ended his financially unprofitable stay in Bithynia. Instead of returning to Rome he ordered a yacht to be built that would take him to Verona. While waiting for its completion and the unpredictable equinoctial weather to calm sufficiently for the voyage he went to his brother's grave in the Troad, that coastal region of western Asia Minor where the ruins of the besieged Troy, rebuilt centuries later as the classical Greek city of Ilium in 700 BC, were still to be seen. The visit led to the composition of one of the loveliest, most serene of his elegies, written in the style of an Hellenistic funeral epigram. It was a dirge, a greeting and a departure, *Ave atque Vale*, sensitively and beautifully translated by Symons.

Wandering many waters and many lands,
I come, my brother, to do sad rites as of old;
See, I bring you the death-gift in my hands,
Hear, I speak to you, speak to the ashes cold.
All that fortune has left me in place of you,
Alas, poor brother, bereft of innocent breath!
Yet, as our sires before us have done, I do,
I bring the same sad gifts, an offering for death.
Take them, that they of a brother's tears may tell;
And now, for all time, brother, hail and farewell.

[101] (p. 185)
(Arthur Symons, p. 67)

Verona, Sirmio and Lake Garda

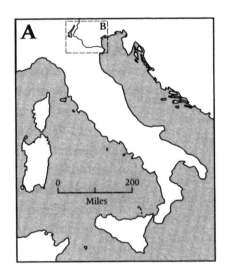

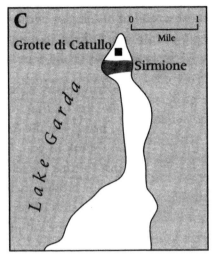

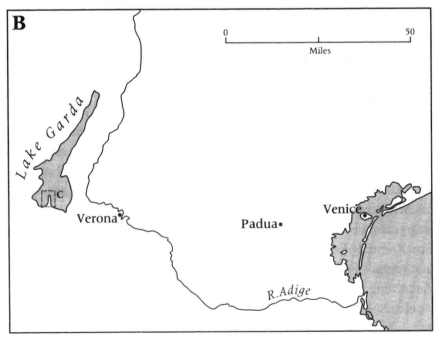

Fitzgerald noticed how its lines were a reverse image of Homer's *Odyssey*. This was not a journey from Troy to home but one from Rome to Troy, not Odysseus coming back to the living joy of his wife Penelope, but Catullus through 'many waters and many lands' reaching the sad death of his brother. It was a journey back to death and also to birth. Troy was where Rome's founder Romulus had been born.[23]

Catullus left Bithynia in his custom-built phaselus, a kidney-bean-shaped pinnace designed for speed. It came from the prestigious shipyards below the hills of Mount Cytorus on the shores of the Black Sea, a densely forested region renowned for its finely grained boxwood, a material also excellent for the making of musical instruments. According to its owner, the vessel 'was the fastest ship there ever was'.

He chose to write about it and his voyage in the very difficult metre of iambic trimeters and succeeded triumphantly. In poem [4], with its succession of sibilants – *silescit, quos simul, aestuosae* and others – one can almost hear the hissing of spray against the ship's sails and the splashing of the waves. (pp. 167-8)

The poem was dedicated to the twin deities of Castor and Pollux, guardians of seafarers. Flashes of their St Elmo's Fire in an electrical storm were guarantees of safety. The poem was composed in the form of an inscription that went with an offering to the gods, reciting a worker's career and retirement, here the final berth of the pinnace on Lake Benacus (Garda) after its long, wearing voyage from Bithynia.

Catullus departed late in March 56 BC, after the stormy weather had abated. His year-long companions who had arrived with him left for Rome. He went to Verona. In poem [46], almost a travelogue, he told how his ship sailed southwards, hugging the coastline of Asia Minor, Homer's 'wine-dark sea' in a leisurely Grand Tour of antiquity very popular with affluent and educated Romans. He sped to 'the famous seashore cities of Asia', Pergamum, Smyrna, Ephesus, with its famous temple of Artemis, one of the seven wonders of the ancient world. On 21 July 356 BC it had been burnt down by an Ephesian, Herostratus, 'so that posterity would remember his name'. The egomaniac has never been forgotten, particularly as legend claimed that his crime was committed on the very night that Alexander the Great was born. The temple was rebuilt within twenty years. Catullus may have wandered around it.

From Bithynia he passed numerous islands: Lesbos where Sappho sang, Samos where Pythagorus was born, down to the beautiful island of Rhodes, famous for its teachers of rhetoric, at whose harbour stood the enormous but earthquake-shattered remains of the bronze statue of the Colossus, whose fragments were sold as scrap-metal a thousand years later. A hundred years after Catullus, Pliny the Elder examined its remains. 'Few men can clasp the thumb in their arms, and its fingers are larger than most statues. As for its broken limbs, their insides look like vast caves.'

From Rhodes the westerly route of the pinnace passed through the Cyclades, 'the circle' of fifty islands around Delos, the birthplace of Apollo, and on to the prosperity of Corinth, across whose miles-long isthmus ships with wealthy masters could be dragged. Before reaching it the waters of Salamis were reminders of the decisive naval battle of 480 BC in which the Greeks had defeated the Persians and broken the power of Xerxes. Beyond the isthmus lay the Ionian Sea, overlooked by Corinth's notorious temple of Aphrodite 'where lascivious women resorted, and sold their pleasures so dearly, that many of their lovers were reduced to poverty'. In 464 BC the athlete Xenophon promised the goddess a hundred girls if he won the Olympics. He paid.

Finally it was a duller sailing northwards up the Adriatic to the mouth and course of the river Adige until, west of Verona, the yacht had to be hauled four miles overland to Lake Garda and the thin peninsula of Sirmio. There, after her lingering voyage, she was semi-retired and turned into an ageing pleasure-boat for the lake, sea-going no longer.[24]

> . . . now she is old,
> in peace and at rest, becoming a dedication to you brothers,
> Castor and the twin of Castor. (pp. 168)
>
> [4], 25-7

It is seldom questioned why it was that Catullus had chosen to go to Verona rather than return to Rome. Tentative guesses hint that he may have been reluctant to be in a city where Clodia still lived, but this is unlikely. A year had passed since his anger about her infidelity and over the months his rage may have mellowed into excuses. Excuses could become exonerations, refusing to believe occasional infidelities could ever endanger an everlasting love. He wrote as much:

> And while she is not content only with Catullus
> I'll bear the few lapses of my discreet woman,
> I will not be a nuisance like other, weaker men.
> Even Juno, greatest of all the goddesses,
> Never raged at her philandering husband.
>
> [68B], 135-9

He may have dreamed that Clodia would come back to him once he was in Rome where she was living. If so, the reason for his being in Verona was not because of the living but because of the dead. Three poems, [68A], [68B] and [31] offer some explanation.

Mourning his brother in [68A] he had written, 'our whole house is buried with you', a line repeated word for word in [68B]. And in [31], as he celebrated his return to his beloved Sirmio, he cried 'Rejoice with your master' as though he had become the senior man of his family. It is known that his brother had died in the Troad. It is plausible from what Catullus wrote that other relatives, including his father, had also died. If so, then Catullus was the eldest survivor and now the master of the house and the business. There would have been many problems to be resolved and decisions made before any thought of travelling to Rome.[25]

In his poem to Manlius he apologized for his absence but explained that it was not a shame for him to be in Verona but a sorrow. Nearly all his books were in Rome, he had just one box with him. Rome was his life but misfortunes were drowning him and he was so overcome that he was unable even to think of those intellectual challenges and delights that had been his entire existence. Then there was a convenient coincidence. Even had he arrived in Italy in time for it, he would certainly have been staying in Verona when the trial of Marcus Caelius Rufus began in April 56 BC.

The trial lasted for two days, starting on the public holiday of the *Ludi Megalenses*. Unlike trials in ordinary courts, those concerning political violence could be heard at such times. In the Forum, within a crowded semicircle of spectators, the magistrate, the praetor Cnaeus Domitius Calvinus, and his panel of judges sat with the speakers for the prosecution and defence on either side of them. There were two separate charges: that Marcus Caelius Rufus had incited public disorders at Naples and Puteoli and had stolen goods from a lady named Palla; and that he was guilty of the murder of Dio, the leader of a delegation from Alexandria in Egypt.

The many temples and buildings around the narrow space at the end of the Forum near the Rostra acted like a sounding-board, making the speeches audible to everyone at the trial. But with the angry protests, brawls and interruptions, it was often difficult for anyone speaking to be clearly heard.

Atratinus, the seventeen-year-old son of Calpurnius Bestia, opened for the prosecution with the usual defamation of character. The accused, he informed the court, was infamous for having mixed with the gangster Catiline, and he had lived so profligately that he was hugely in debt. He was also of brutal disposition and had badly beaten up an innocent senator, Fulfius at the pontifical elections.

A freedman, Publius Clodius – but not the brother of Clodia brought the most damaging evidence with a succession of witnesses. Caelius had intended to kill Dio, but lacking funds had borrowed from Clodia, lying to her, to purchase poison. Aware of the danger Dio had left the safety of the home of Lucius Lucceius, Pompey's friend, and gone to Titus Coponius, a man he had met in Egypt. But this was no safe haven and he was slain there by Caelius and Publius Asicius. Clodia would testify that she had lent Caelius some gold ornaments but discovering what was intended she confronted the would-be assassin who, in turn, had attempted to bribe her slaves to poison her.

Finally for the prosecution, Lucius Herrenius Balbus quietly, reasonably and convincingly revealed how treacherous Caelius Rufus could be. He had supported the candidacy of Calpurnius Bestia as a praetor in 57 BC but by the following year was putting him on trial for electoral bribery and when confounded by an acquittal denounced him yet again, presumably for the same offence at the next year's elections! The problem for the prosecution was that it dared not reveal the affair between Caelius Rufus and Clodia. They could be certain, however, that the defence would have to be equally reticent because truth would prove the accused to be an adulterer.

The first to speak in defence was Marcus Caelius Rufus himself, dishevelled, in torn, grubby robes as convention demanded, tearful in his protestations. Behind the façade he viciously attacked his former lover, reminding his entertained listeners of the nickname that the frustrated Vettius had given her, *Quadrantaria*, 'Yours for four coppers', a 'bargain-basement Clytemnestra' like the queen who had murdered her husband Agamemnon, king of Mycenae, on his return from Troy. It was a hint, quickly understood by everybody, that in the same way Clodia had killed her own husband Metellus Celer on his return from Cisalpine Gaul.

Clodia was, he assured the court, a deceitful wanton, *Cos in triclinium, in cubicula nolam*. 'In the dining room a teasing creature in translucent Coan silks but, in the bedroom, an impregnable fortress.' Nola was a walled town notable for its resistance to Hannibal. The sentence was also a clever play on words. 'Cos' was a pun on coitus. 'Nola' was similar to *nolo*, no sex.

In full view of the court and the audience Rufus ended by brandishing the so-called poison-phial. Was it, he asked, an innocent container for lotions, cosmetics, scents? Instead, he jeered, it could be the jar that Vettius had sent her filled with his unwanted semen.

Crassus followed him, always ready to oppose Pompey. He explained that the accused man had nothing whatsoever to do with the events at Naples and Puteoli. Nor had he ever stolen anything from anyone. Then came Cicero.[26]

It was the second day of the trial. The judges had already endured five long speeches at a time that should have been a holiday. The orator had to be tactful but he intended to demolish Clodia. He hated her brother, Publius Clodius Pulcher, for the hurt inflicted upon him two years earlier and the trial presented an irresistible chance to obtain retribution. The opportunity was all the more enticing because he could damage Clodius through the very vulnerable target of his sister. He did it meticulously and systematically like a sadist peeling strips of skin from a helpless victim.

He offered his sincere sympathy to the judges for their patience dismissing most of the so-called offences as trivialities. Other accusations, he claimed, were untrue. Such arguments were customary and predictable. What was not expected were the two words in his third sentence, *opibus meretriciis*, 'the actions of a strumpet'. The prosecution, he stated shockingly, had been financed by the resources of a whore. Briefly he left the astonished court in suspense.

Quietly he appraised the character of the well-known orator, Marcus Caelius Rufus. This was a young, impressionable and talented man who had indeed been duped by Catiline like so many others, including Cicero himself. But he had never been involved in the criminal conspiracy. As for his debts, what young man new to, Rome had not overspent? These were trifles not worth debating. Just because he had rented a house from Publius Clodius on the Palatine for 30,000 *sestertii* – 10,000 would be nearer the truth – that did not make him a felon. Everything levelled against him had already been disproved by Crassus.

As for the assassination of Dio, every person in the city knew that it had been instigated by Ptolemy, the deposed pharaoh. It is true that Asicius, the companion of Caelius, had been tried for the murder but he had been acquitted. Suggestions that the jury had been traduced were nonsense. Cicero was sure of it. He had been the principal speaker for the defence.

All these charges of extravagance, violence, associating with members of the underworld, were deliberately raised to deflect the court's attention from the real criminal, Clodia, 'the Medea of the Palatine', he said. Medea – queen, sorceress and poisoner – had been rejected by her lover, Jason. In revenge she had killed his wife by sending her a gown impregnated with flesh-searing venom. Thus Clodia, rejected by Caelius, was trying to destroy him.

The crux of this farcical trial was to be found in two things – gold and poison – and they were both introduced by the same person, a woman who must have been very intimate with Caelius Rufus to have lent him gold. Cicero was reluctant to attack a lady but she was so central to the investigation that he could not ignore her. 'Indeed,' he sighed, 'my refutation would be framed in considerably more forcible terms if I did not feel inhibited by the fact that the woman's husband – sorry, I mean brother – I always make that slip – is my enemy.' Waiting for the laughter to die, he added, 'I never imagined I would find myself in a court of law fighting, with a woman – especially this woman, who is said to be the friend of every man she meets.'[27]

It was cruel, masterly, destructive – and it was only the beginning. Cicero addressed the court as though he were Clodia's revered ancestor, Appius Claudius Caecus, censor, consul, builder of Rome's first aqueduct in 296 BC. That great man, declaimed Cicero, had not brought water to the city to wash away her filthy copulations. Even her own brother would wonder why she had brought such a preposterous prosecution and he was a very sensitive, almost timid gentleman. As a little boy it was well known that he had feared the dark and suffered such bad nightmares that he had often gone to the comfort of her bed. More laughter. To poison her Caelius was accused of trying the toxic draught on a slave. Preposterous. And what a ridiculous story about her treacherous slaves collecting the poison in the busy daylight of the public baths. From sarcasm Cicero turned to condemnation. Shall that woman, coming from this house in which her husband died, dare to speak of quick-acting poison? Is she not afraid of the very house itself, lest it should speak? Does she not dread the walls, which know her guilty secret? Does she not shudder at the memory of that fatal and melancholy night?

The truth was obvious. A dissolute and vindictive woman had tried to ruin an honest man, who had been decent and moral enough to reject her unwelcome advances. This was a woman who offered herself to every man, who kept a diary for separate lovers, a lascivious woman living the life of a harlot. She dressed like a strumpet, spoke like a drab, she was depravity itself, 'an unstable, evil-tempered nymphomaniac' .[28]

Even those so-called treacherous slaves of hers were suspect. 'Clodia and her slaves can scarcely be described as normal. In a household like that, headed by a woman who behaves like a prostitute, where abnormal lusts and unheard-of vices are practised on a daily basis, where slaves are invited to share an inordinate amount of intimacy with their superiors – well, those slaves are slaves no longer. They share everything with their mistress, including her secrets. They become her companions in loose living. In a household like that, the people on the bottom are sometimes quite literally on top.'[29]

It was outrageous, hilarious and it was annihilation. Nothing more was required. Marcus Caelius Rufus was almost forgotten. Cicero had to remind the men who would pronounce the verdict that his client was a man of great ability and it was they who might benefit in the future from his efforts. But the orator had disproved nothing. He had asked rhetorical questions and given no time for denial. He had ignored awkward truths and distorted what the prosecutors had claimed. In modern terms it had not been a defence. It had been a performance by an artist, brilliant and effective. Caelius Rufus was acquitted. Clodia was disgraced, humiliated and ostracized by polite society. Promiscuity must have been a gene. Hardly a hundred years later a relative behaved even more scandalously. Clodia's great-great-great niece, Valeria Messalina, wife of the emperor Claudius, had a lover, a 'ballet-dancer who violated the emperor's bedroom'. Failing to satisfy her he was flogged. She prostituted herself indiscriminately with man after man for sheer sexual pleasure, and would continue till morning, still unsatisfied. Once Claudius was drunkenly asleep:

Under an ash-blonde wig, she would make straight for her brothel,
With its odour of stale, warm bed-clothes, its empty reserved cell.
Here she would strip off, showing her gilded nipples and
The belly that once housed a prince of the blood. Her door-sign
Bore a false name, Lycisa, 'The Wolf-girl'. A more than willing
Partner, she took on all comers, for cash, without a break.

Juvenal, Satires 6, 119-24[30]

Narcissus, an imperial slave, informed Claudius of the empress's behaviour. Messalina ran away but was too scared to commit suicide. Soldiers killed her.

That was a century after the trial. Meanwhile, when he heard about Cicero's treatment of the defenceless Clodia, Catullus was bitter. He sent the man an equivocal epigram, sarcastically hateful rather than approving.

Most eloquent of all the sons of Rome
that have ever been, o Marcus Tullius,
or will be in the coming years,
Catullus sends you his most sincere thanks,
he who is the worst of poets,
the very worst of poets in the same degree
as you are the very best of advocates.

[49]

Shortly after the trial the elections for 55 BC should have been held in July, but they were prevented by riots. In August Caesar won a vital sea-battle at the Bay of Morbihan in Brittany against the naval power of the Veneti. A prehistoric mound at Tumiac is still known as the 'Butte de César', the observation point from which he watched the struggle. He needed the seas secured for his intended invasion of Britain. There was no resurgent rebellion and all the counsellors of the Veneti were executed and the remainder of the tribe sold as slaves.[31]

In Rome that November senators assembled in mourning. The elections had been deferred for the second time. The Senate was powerless to end the street-fighting and killings that erupted whenever an election was announced. But not everything was gloom and despair. In the middle of this political turmoil Catullus confessed to an incident of self-inflicted embarrassment.

In a delightfully idiomatic poem [10], full of everyday speech, Catullus chatted about meeting his friend Quincilius Varus in the Forum. He was introduced to the man's latest pick-up, a bit of a trollop but quite an eyeful. He grumbled that he had just come back from Bithynia without a denarius because of that skinflint Memmius. 'Bithynia?' cooed the wench, 'Bet you got some of them famous litter-bearers, didn't you?' Catullus forgot himself 'Oh, sure,' he bragged, 'Bought eight really strong chaps.' 'Catullus, darling, won't you lend me them for the, afternoon? I've got to go across town to the shrine of Serapis.' 'Hold it,' stammered the poet, 'I didn't mean they were really mine. They're my chum's, Gaius Cinna. He lets me use them when I want.'

As they parted he muttered to himself, 'Impudent baggage. Why take everything so literally, take the words out my mouth? A real pain in the neck.' But as he knew, and as all his readers knew, the joke was on him.[32]

It was a joke but he was able to laugh. Perhaps in need of sympathy from someone she could trust after the lacerations of Cicero, perhaps because she had genuinely missed his tenderness and company, perhaps just as a whim, Clodia welcomed Catullus back into her life. Surprised, elated, unmindful of insincerity and hurt, he laughed with unheeding happiness.

> If something wished for but past hope should happen,
> Come unexpectedly to someone in despair then it is here.
> To me it is delight, relief, and richer than gold,
> That you, Lesbia, have come back to me,
> To one who yearned but disbelieved, you return
> And it is the calendar's white day, a day of celebration.
> What man could be happier? What man could say
> That any joy could be lovelier in this life of mine?
>
> [107]

FINAL YEARS – 55 BC?

The year began badly and did not improve. Late in January the elections were at last forced through and by bribery, intimidation and the convenient presence on leave in the city of hundreds of Caesar's legionaries, Crassus and Pompey became consuls. There was fighting on the Campus Martius, a torch-bearer was beaten to death, but the struggle was over. The Senate was no more than a token body. Cicero retired from public life.[1]

In the north of Italy Julius Caesar planned the organization of men and ships for his invasion of Britain, that *terra incognita* across the sea.

In Rome, Publius Clodius Pulcher commandeered the Temple of Castor & Pollux in the comer of the Forum, only a short step from his house on the Clivus Victoriae. His men removed steps, barricaded walls, converted the House of the Heavenly Twins into a fortress. People shrugged. It was just one more profanity in a year of insults, violence and sacrilege. It was a year of anarchy.

There was also private anarchy. Even Catullus in his optimism had doubts about the steadfastness of his reconciled lover. He needed to believe her.

> You promise me, my darling, that our love
> Will be agreeable and will last for ever.
> Great gods, ensure that she is speaking truth
> And makes her assurance from her heart
> So we may keep throughout our lives
> This long alliance of unbroken friendship.
>
> [109]

There is a tragic probability that it was Catullus rather than Clodia who caused the affair to end. She wanted pleasure. He wanted marriage. It was two years since the death of Metellus Celer, her widowhood was past and she had promised to marry him. To the poet it was a vow and he had been brought up in Cisalpine Gaul, a province of old-fashioned morality where the virtues of *pietas*, a sense of duty, *fides*, trust and faith, and *verecundia*, reserve and modesty, were deeply held and observed. 'The poet had grown up in a hard-working, straight-laced, traditional society . . . that took seriously the responsibilities of honest dealing.'² Marriage was honourable and desirable. The attitude of Catullus towards it is displayed in his two beautiful *epithalamia* [61] and [62], that extolled the solemnity, the joy and the gladness of a wedding with its promise of faithfulness and family.

His characteristic use of *chiasmus* in [63] and [65/66] reveal how he considered erotic passion to be both destructive and fulfilling, the destruction of wild emotion unlike the fulfilment given by marriage. Martin contrasted the two states. In [63], 'Attis is the humiliated love-slave of Cybele, the implacable *dominatrix*, while Berenice in poem 66 is the devoted and faithful wife of her royal husband.' Both made sacrifices but whereas that of Attis was sterile, his blood dripping into the dry earth, the shorn tresses of Berenice were 'transformed into a glittering constellation' of eternal stars.³

Catullus longed to marry Clodia. It is unlikely that she shared the wish. Too much had happened to her. Thoughts of their quiet and respectable existence as man and wife were impossible. Catullus dreamed. Clodia was realistic and was, as always, prepared to defy convention. Everywhere in Rome there was talk of her, gossip about a dead husband and a lubricious widow, 'yours for four farthings', casual visitors to her home, whispers and innuendoes that drifted like grimy fog around the streets and alleys of the city.

Perhaps she also shrugged as if to reply, 'If that's what they think I might as well prove them right', and, as the whim moved her, took lovers: Egnatius, Gellius. Mamurra and others in a kind of *nostalgie de la boue*, 'a yearning for the mud' that savaged the heart of the one man that loved her. Constancy was not one of her virtues. On occasion she could be voluptuous in the dining-room then perversely virginal in bed, as the luckless Vettius and maybe Caelius Rufus had found to their frustration.

That was no consolation to Catullus. Their reconciliation was slowly fading, subject to long separations, uncertainties, then doubts and, corrosively, suspicions. As he became sadly convinced of her infidelities he blamed the men, claiming that she was their victim. It was only later that he accepted that the fault was hers, that they were only taking advantage of her available and attractive body. That was later. At first it was the men that received his excoriating satires, jeering at their bodies, their habits, their inadequacies, their sexual abnormalities.

One of her lovers may have been Tanusius Geminus, a third-rate historian from Padua already mentioned in the Introduction. In poems [95] and [36] he is disguised as 'Volusius'. Poem [36] epitomizes Martin's observation that Catullus is an illusionist whose scowling face is often hidden behind a jovial mask. The poet, wrote Martin, is so frequently 'immediately accessible to the reader that we tend to think of him as simple, direct and unaffected ... Most of the time, however, they simply do not apply to Catullus, whose voice and sensibility are more accurately described as complex, duplicitous, artful and ironic.'[4]

It is true of [36] that began:

Annals of Volusius, you shitty sheets
Fulfil a promise that my girl made,
Vowing by Venus and by Cupid
That if I would return to her
And stop writing my biting iambic epigrams
She would give the very best of your verses,
You, the worst of poets, to Vulcan
To be burnt in a blaze of dried-out timber.

[36]

Catullus gives weight to the promise the unnamed woman has made by sending news of it to the well-known shrines of Venus, her sacred grove at Idalium, her temples of Amathus and Golgi on her island of Cyprus, to Cnidus in Asia Minor with its world-famous naked statue of the goddess by Praxiteles. But the poem ends sceptically. He agrees to his girl's terms. He will return to her. But first she must keep her word and burn the *cacata carta*, the soiled lavatory papers of Volusius.

'Fulfil the promise' of *mea puella*, 'my girl'. The two words are evidence that he was addressing Clodia. *Mea puella*, 'my girl', appears in three of the Lesbia poems, [2], [3] and [11] and only to her. Clodia wanted him to stop the bombardment of scurrilous verses that were being recited around Rome. But poem [36], apparent light-hearted banter, was one of the very worst. In it he gave Tanusius Geminus a pseudonym by disguising it, metrically correct, as 'Volusius'. He used *Volu* in which the *u* was interchangeable in Latin with *v*, making it *Volva*. It was a pun and it was vilely crude. *Volva* was not only the female sexual organ, vulva, but also meant 'the womb of a sow'. It was one of the foullest of his insults to Clodia. Catullus despised 'Volusius' for his puerile *Annals* and hated him for ousting the poet from the woman that he loved.[5]

As for her promise Catullus was understandably distrustful. Let her keep her word. Perhaps she did burn some of the detested lines in a ritual destruction and brief reconciliation. If so, the reunion did not last. The half-hearted banter of [36] soured into bitterness. The abuse became particular, naming the corrupters of the woman Catullus loathed and desired. The aspersions were personal because the men were abusing the person that the poet loved. He ripped into their private lives, exposed every frailty. But at the beginning he never named her even when she began an affair with Mamurra.

Mamurra was a military engineer who had fought with Pompey against Mithridates, and with Caesar in Spain and Gaul. From uninhibited plunder and the ruthless sale of defeated tribes as slaves he had made fortunes so fabulous that Cicero referred enviously to his wealth. There was a palatial estate, at Formiae on the west coast seventy miles south of Rome. Around this magnificent villa were fish ponds, game reserves, pastures, fields, woods and lakes. Mamurra was the first millionaire to have pillars of solid marble. The walls were covered with rare and costly coloured marble. Everything was expensive, ostentatious and recklessly ruinous.

In eight scornful and damning poems, [29], [41], [43], [57], [94], [105], [114] and [115] (more than he had written about any other man), Catullus nicknamed him Mentula, 'the prick', and denounced him as a glutton, gambler and spendthrift who would bankrupt himself. He also had ambitions as a poet.

Big Cock wrote doggerel but so ill,
The Muses pitchforked him from their hill.

[105]

By association with that despicable man Caesar was dragged into the calumny, reminding an audience of his own reputation as a homosexual.

What a fairy pair of faggots, what a thorough
Brace of buggers, homo Caesar, gay Mamurra.

[57]

The ninth of that poem's ten lines contained the word, *puellularum*, implying that the two had not only unnatural desires but were also parthenasts on the lookout for little girls. The charges were virulently offensive. 'Yet Caesar, while admitting that these were a permanent blot on his name, accepted Catullus's apology and invited him to dinner that same afternoon.'[6]

In poem [41] Mamurra was apparently consorting with a big-nosed girl usually called Ameana, occasionally Amentina, sometimes unnamed, but coming from Anneianum, a town halfway between Padua and Mantua. In [43] the same woman with a malformed nose, 'mistress of the Formian bankrupt', was compared unfavourably with Lesbia.

It seems straightforward but there is a puzzle. The woman, whatever her name or home town, is mentioned nowhere else in the entire Catullan canon. Nor was 'Ameana' a known Roman name. Yet Catullus chose to write no fewer than eight cruel poems about Mamurra. If the number had been just one or two then his mysterious mistress could have come and gone as ephemerally as

Mucia, Quintia and Rufa, even Camerius or Juventius. That Mamurra should receive eight lampoons suggests that he was of much greater significance to the poet: There may never have been an Ameana from Anneianum. Instead, poems [41] and [43] could link Mamurra with someone who did matter to the poet – Clodia.

The first line of [41] is equivocal. In most translations it reads: *Ameana puella difututa*, 'Ameana, the shagged-out girl'. Sometimes 'Amentina', even Anneianum, is substituted. Neither appears in the earliest versions of [41], which read brokenly: *a me an a*. Editors have struggled. A nineteenth-century proposal was *amens illa puella difututa*, 'that lunatic, much-laid girl', a reference to a girl who was off her head. *Amens*, 'mad', is plausible because the accusation of insanity was repeated six lines later with *non est sana*, 'out of her mind'.

The suggestion has been ignored by later editors but it could be correct. Faced with a badly copied or damaged first word, in which only *ame* and two indistinct letters could be read, a puzzled scribe had to decide whether the two letters were a single 'n' or two 'l's. He decided on *ame na* but the metre demanded an extrasyllable such as 'a' and the solution was Ameana. If that interpretation was mistaken then there was no Ameana only *amens illa*, 'that crazy ...'. Mamurra's promiscuous mistress was, it is implied, the demented and concupiscent Clodia.

There are clues to that identification. In poems such as [11] and [37], which certainly refer to Lesbia, Catullus uses the word, *moecha*, 'adulteress'. In [42], a poem deliberately set between [41] and [43], he wrote *moecha turpis*, 'filthy adulteress', once, and *moecha putida*, 'sickening adulteress', four times. In [11] and [37] he asked the large-nosed 'Ameana' *tecum Lesbia nostra comparatur?*, 'do they compare you with our Lesbia?' They did simply because she was Clodia. Catullus used exactly the same phrase, *Lesbia nostra*, in [58], his poem to Caelius Rufus.

The reason for the accusation of being out of her senses could also lie in [41] and [42] where the 'foul tart' had refused to hand back some wax tablets to the poet unless he paid 10,000 *sestertii* for them. At a time when a Roman legionary was paid a mere 900 *sestertii* for a year's service the demand was outrageous. How exorbitant it was can be judged from Cicero's remark at the trial of Caelius Rufus that it was twelve months' rent for a house on the Clivus Victoriae, the most desirable address in Rome. The tablets presumably contained poems that Catullus had given Clodia and now wanted returned. He did not pay her. The poems were not returned.

He took revenge. Spitefully he distorted her beauty, writing of the huge nose, the clumsy feet, runny eyes, stubby fingers, dribbling lips, affected laugh, foul language, nothing like the Lesbia he had known, afraid to look in a mirror at her ageing face. It was unpleasant but that it was Clodia rather than 'Ameana' that was his target is the likeliest explanation for the 'Ameana' poems [41] to [43]. As Lee remarked of [43], 'presumably we have here a negative picture of Lesbia'.[7]

Mamurra was not the first of her changing lovers, nor was he the last. There was the Spanish poet Egnatius, a rhymester of little merit but a person whose everlasting white-toothed grin dazzled because his teeth had been cleaned with his own urine:

> You the shame of rabbity Spain,
> Egnatius with the uncut hair,
> who owe your dandihood to this,
> a thick beard and teeth washt with piss.
>
>   [37]
>   (Lindsay, 1929)

Egnatius smiled shinily everywhere, in the solemnity of a trial, at the funeral of a child – and it hurt that such a foppish stranger, even the wealthy Mamurra, could become a lover of Clodia. Hurt became like a death blow when Catullus was betrayed by a friend. His life was founded on trust and when that trust was broken by a comrade such as Caelius Rufus there was heartbreak and distress. Now he learned that another friend had betrayed him and wrote about it enigmatically:

> Gellius, I hoped that you would be a true companion
> While I suffered this long calamity of love,
> Not because I thought you trustworthy
> Or capable of restraining your impulses
> But because I knew with certainty that she
> I love was neither your mother nor your sister.
> So, having known you for a long time,
> I assumed that no woman outside your family
> Would interest you. But anything forbidden
> Is clearly irresistible to your crude desires.
>
>   [91]

and in *Liber III* he went on to compose six vicious epigrams about the unsavoury man. No defect was too trivial. Catullus would broadcast all of them, one by malicious one.

Gellius was Lucius Gellius Poplicola, son of a consul, who in the wars against Spartacus had defeated a German army under Crixus in 72 BC.[8] The matrimonial history of the family was like a bedroom farce – marriage, divorce, remarriage, a carnal medley, in and out of beds whatever the sex and whatever the relationship. Catullus punctiliously itemized his victim's misdeeds.

They were well known because of domestic tittle-tattle. Rich households had slaves. Most were confined to the *domus* but some went to the market and the street-stalls, where stories of domestic excitements were whispered: 'Did you hear ...', 'I've just been told ...'. It was an underworld of half-truths, innuendo, gossip and scandal, but like slugs slithering out from dark logs and sliming into the daylight the stories reached the wealthy homes and the outside world. Catullus converted the dross into poetic missiles.

Gellius, he wrote, masturbated constantly, 'munching himself with his head bent' [88]. Twice daily he performed fellatio on 'Victor', perhaps a low-born gladiator making the oral salacity socially degrading:

> ... Can it be certain what rumour recalls
> That you're mouthing his knob and licking his balls?
> It's got to be right! Victor's an emptied-out hunk
> And your lips dribble white with the smears of his spunk.
>
> [80]

Gellius even debased his own family. Of his two married brothers one had a good-looking son, the other a very attractive wife. Gellius 'introduced' the pair:

> Gallus has two brothers, one whose wife's a beauty,
> The other has a handsome son. Gallus sees his duty
> Is to be a pander whose mission will be done
> Once the lovely wife's in bed and underneath the son.
> But Gallus is an uncle too, short-sighted, truth to tell.
> Lustful nephew, nubile wife, can cuckold him as well.
>
> [78][9]

There was worse in that interconnected, interrelated social world of Rome. The father of Gellius had divorced his wife and married Palla, the woman from whom Caelius Rufus had been accused of stealing property. It was no coincidence that enmities developed with rancorous sides being taken by non-participants.

Gellius' father had married Palla but in turn she divorced him and married Marcus Valerius Messalla Rufus, who had a grown daughter, Valeria. Widespread gossip of an incestuous triangle compelled an alarmed Gellius to defend himself in court, accused of the attempted murder of a close relative and of *novercam commissum stuprum*, debauchery with his stepmother. Relatives arranged for the hearing to be held in an informal and compliant council at which Gellius was acquitted.[10]

It did not save him from four more excruciatingly explicit epigrams from Catullus about how the satyr had slept with his mother-in-law, with his 'sister' Valeria, and with his aunt. Poem [88] was unambiguous:

> Gellius, undressed in bed and humping with your mother,
> Then turning to your sister even though you are her brother!
> Does your uncle realize that you're groping with his wife?
> How can you excuse your vile, incestuous life?
> Gellius, understand that neither Tethys nor great Ocean
> Could cleanse away your sins, not with the strongest lotion.
> You could not be more beastly even if you were to duck
> On to your erection and suck and suck and suck!
>
> [88]

The verse circulated around Rome, not only in the luxurious mansions but in the taverns and brothels. It was doubly clever because it not only specified incest with mother and sister but reinforced the accusation by reminding a knowledgeable audience that Oceanus and Tethys, parents of river-gods and nymphs, were themselves brother and sister.

Three more savage poems followed, one [74] repeating that the insatiable Gellius had slept with his aunt simply to mock his prudish uncle, repeating the charge in [88], 'what is to be said of a man who cuckolds his own uncle?'

Even his physique was mocked. With all these family 'commitments' it was not surprising that Gellius was so thin [89], exercising with his aunt and doing physical jerks with an enterprising mother and an energetic sister. That Palla was not Gellius' real mother and that Valeria was not his true sister did not detract from the venom and the wit of the lines. The quartet ended with more classical insults:

> Will Gellius and his mother breed
> An Eastern Wise Man? For it's said
> Only a son's and mother's seed
> Can sprout a seer in their bed.
> Persian Magi choose no others,
> Shagging just their natural mothers.
>
> [90][11]

There were no more epigrams but it was the most protracted invective in the entire Catullan canon: three [74], [78] and [80] close together, four [88],

[89], [90] and [91] following on each other's vitriolic heels, demonstrating how deeply the poet had been hurt by the affair between Gellius and Clodia.

It is surprising, therefore, to find yet another Gellius poem, [116], at the very end of *Liber III*. In the past, it said, Catullus had intended to send some translations of Callimachus to Gellius in the hope that the two men could be reconciled. Understandably Gellius did not respond. The onslaught, therefore, would have to continue. As there was no continuation it is to be wondered whether a well-intended editor had misplaced the poem which would have made more sense after [80] and before the diatribes of [88]-[91]. Modern editors are undecided.[12]

For his part Gellius was untroubled. Savage though the attack had been his career was uninterrupted. In 36 BC he became a consul. He fought in the civil wars, first with Pompey, later with Mark Antony. 'Sticks and stones may break my bones', observed the nineteenth-century proverb, 'but words will never hurt me.' The pachydermatous Gellius, if not the sensitive Catullus, would have agreed.

In the August of 55 BC Julius Caesar invaded Britain. Taking two legions he landed safely on the south coast but late summer gales damaged the shored vessels and prevented cavalry from crossing the channel. Weakened and ferociously attacked by Britons in their war-chariots the Romans retreated to the beaches and retired thankfully to Gaul. Learning from this setback Caesar decided to return the next year with a much stronger force.

In Rome matters between Catullus and Clodia were at their worst. To his tormented, unbalanced mind her home on the Clivus Victoriae had become little more than a red-light bordello and she, beyond redemption and forgiveness, no more than a harlot with several hundred clients.

> Brothel-cum-tavern and you nightly visitors,
> Nine pillars up from the Temple of Castor and Pollux,
> Do you believe you're the only ones with pricks,
> The only ones allowed to screw the girls
> And rest of us just rancid goats?
> ....
> ... I'll daub
> Obscene graffiti on your whore-house wall
> Because the girl who slipped from my embraces,
> Who was more loved by me than anyone was loved,
> For whom I fought and struggled,
> She's the occupant.
>   [37]

Catullus used the filthiest word he could think of, *glubit*, to describe Clodia as in his raving mind she lingered lasciviously on the streets.

> *nam in quadriviis et angiportis*
> *glubit magnanimos Remi nepotes*
>
> [58]

It is one more challenge of converting the Latin into faithful English, to explain exactly what Clodia was accused of with the bountiful heirs of Remus. *Glubere* is 'to peel', 'to skin', to remove the husk from corn. There have been some seemly translations:

> now haunts the street corners and alleys,
> sapping the great-souled descendants of Remus

and more literal ones for *glubit*: 'husk', 'peel', 'rub up', 'suck', 'shuck', 'skin', as well as the more suggestive 'with public lips and hands', and the cruder but not prurient 'ready to toss off, 'milking with cocks' and 'deep-throat for suckers'. Less faithful to the Latin, but perhaps truer to the image of filth that Catullus intended, was Jaro's *glubit*, 'gluts her cunt', as though Clodia were insatiable, demanding the man again and again, never fulfilled, leaving him drained, sore, beyond pleasure.[13]

John Donne knew what could happen:

> And he whose thou art then, being tyr'd before,
> Will, if thou stirre, or pinch to wake him, thinke
> Thou call'st for more,
> And in false sleepe will from thee shrinke.
>
> *The Apparition*, lines 7-10

Perhaps that had been the downfall of an exhausted Vettis, pretending to be asleep to resist Clodia's further demands. Next day, petulantly, he sent the unsatisfied woman his 'gift'. Others learned from his mistake. Better soreness than sodomy.

> Now at crossroads and in alleyways,
> gluts her cunt on the generous sons of Rome.
>
> [58]

Clodia would never have been a street-walker but the poet could see only hell in her and in his disgusted fantasies pictured her thrusting body with man

after man. His repulsion exaggerated the scene, making her the cheapest and
dirtiest of prostitutes. He tried to banish her from his life:

> Let her live and be happy with her lovers,
> three hundred she services together,
> loving none, but hungrily rupturing
> the groins of every one. (pp. 225-6)
>   [11]

It was one of the last poems that he wrote of her and it echoed that lovely
one, [51], that was the first. 'He seems to me to be a god ... again and again
seeing you'. It was written in the same Sapphic metre, the only two poems that
use it, and it repeated the same word, *identidem*, 'again and again', reminding
her of the pleasures and love that they had known together and that she had
wilfully destroyed.

It is sometimes said that he never abused Clodia, his Lesbia, by name, and it is
true as poems [41] to [43] show that at first he condemned her anonymously. Her
association with Gellius changed that. That she should welcome so contaminated
a creature into her bed sickened the poet. Lesbia was then named in four poems:
in [58] as she offered her wares; in [72] as the woman who had promised Catullus
that she was his alone; and in [79], set neatly between two curses at Gellius,
denouncing her incest with her brother. Catullus had lost her but he could not
leave her. Like Attis he was chained to a goddess who had no care for him but who
would never let him go. The fourth of the anti-Lesbia poems [75] said as much:

> I am brought to this, Lesbia, through your treachery,
> My mind in ruins because it was always loyal.
> I can never speak well of you, even if you were perfect, nor
> Ever stop loving you whatever you may do. (p. 245)
>   [75]

She was his devil. And, he, driven away, abandoned, shorn of his manhood
by her withdrawal, had become Attis. It was psychological castration. Almost
hypnotized by the glory of the Great Goddess, Attis had been drawn to her in a
trance and, in thrall to her command, had castrated himself, slicing off his genitals
with a flint knife. He became 'she'. With conciousness returning, in horror and
shame 'she' fled but Cybele sent lions in pursuit and Attis in her fear hid in the
dreary forest, imprisoned, alone, the handmaid of the goddess for eternity.

Catullus had been drawn to Clodia, had given himself fervently in a
devotion unbecoming to a man, had thrown away his freedom and become
her slave for all time.

Technically *Attis* [63] is brilliant but its greatness lies in more than its imagery. It is a tumultuous poem, composed in the demanding galliambic metre often short syllables, always difficult in Latin where longer units of pronunciation were more common, the lines divided into halves, the words rushing and tumbling over themselves. Harrington likened line 21 to the effect of jazz played on drums and cymbals:

> *ubi cymbalum sonat vox, ubi tympana reboant*
> where the cymbal clangs out, where the light drums bellow back

Tennyson experimented, not very satisfactorily, with the metre in *Boadicea*.

Attis is a marvel, a short masterpiece of ninety-three lines with 'a nervous vigour and swing of feeling that are unique in Latin literature'. It has the intensity of a nightmare, a nightmare that Catullus endured through sleepless days.[14]

The intensity of a great artist, a genius, can be self-destructive. Despair at the condition of the world he lived in, affected by a city rabid with lawlessness, greed, lies, lust, deprived of the thing he most wanted, Catullus even thought of suicide. Everything was rancid, even the highest offices of state. In 55 BC there was a nonentity, Marcus Nonius Sufenus, bragging that he would be the next consul. Another windbag, Publius Vatinius, suborned electors with bribes and malpractice to ensure his own success. Why bother to go on living?

> What's stopping you, Catullus? What's wrong with death?
> There's the toad, Nonius, squatting on his aedile's chair,
> And Vatinius proclaiming he is already consul!
> What is it, Catullus? Why put off dying?
>
> [52]

The year 54 BC began with rioting in the streets of Rome between the gangs of Clodius and Milo. Ironically, one of the consuls was Clodius' own brother, Appius Claudius. Consular elections were not held until the following July. Candidates proposed by the Triumvirate were heavily defeated, one of their opponents in 53 BC being Valerius Messalla Rufus, whose daughter, Valeria, was enjoying her nocturnal playmates, Gellius and her mother-in-law, Palla.[15] In the hot summer of 54 BC Julia, the wife of Pompey and daughter of Caesar, died in childbirth. With her death the uneasy association between Pompey and Caesar weakened and deteriorated into antagonism and outright enmity.[16]

Yet for Catullus there were brighter moments that year. He wrote the light-hearted joke about Camerius [55], the boy he had looked for in Pompey's year-old theatre. The poet was also polishing his mini-epic, *Peleus and Thetis*

[64]. In it were eleven phrases from the *De Rerum Natura* of Titus Lucretius Carus, who had died towards the end of 55 BC. In his inaccurate 'history' St Jerome recorded that 'a love potion drove [Lucretius] mad, and he composed, in the intervals of his insanity,' several books which Cicero corrected. He committed suicide aged 43.' His great work, dedicated to Memmius, was posthumously supervised by Cicero, whose brother Quintus read a copy in 54 BC, probably during the months when Catullus was inserting extracts that he admired into *Peleus and Thetis*.

The Triumvirate went their separate ways. Crassus took his legions to Syria, plundering the Temple of Jerusalem before going on to Parthia. Pompey should have left for Spain but, distrusting what Caesar might do in his absence, delegated the responsibility to his staff officers and stayed at his home outside Rome. In July Caesar invaded Britain for the second time but with much larger force: five legions, 2,000 cavalrymen, and 800 ships, the largest fleet in the Channel until the Normandy landings of 1944. Even the Spanish Armada contained barely a sixth of Caesar's number.

Caesar defeated Cassivellaunus of the Catuvellauni tribe, took tribute and hostages in September, then learning of 'sudden commotions in Gaul' went back to the European mainland and stayed watchfully in Arniens until every legion was at its appointed station.[17]

In poem [11] Catullus may have mentioned those events, jokingly telling his friends Aurelius and Furius that he intended to visit places known to Caesar, the Rhine in Gaul, the Britons at the world's end. If he was referring to the invasion of 54 BC the poem must have been written late in that year.

Late 54 BC to May 51 BC is a poorly recorded period of Roman social history with no letters from Cicero to relate scandals and the movements of people. There is a hint that Catullus may have been taken ill. Tuberculosis and consumption were common afflictions and the 'remedies' prescribed by badly trained doctors were rest, warm drinks and, for the prosperous, a voyage to the warm, dry climate of Egypt. By coincidence, Cybele could cause and cure disease.[18]

In poem [44] Catullus pretended that the 'frigid' bombastic style of the orator Sestius had brought on a cold spell, forcing him to retire to the healthy countryside of his farm-cum-villa where 'my persistent cough and villainous cold on tht chest I've cured' and

> ... I was chilled and shivered
> with choking coughs and fevers
> aching my bones until I reached my country home
> and had some nettle-broth and rest.
>   [44]

He slowly recovered.

Unwell and unable to forget Clodia, Catullus may even have turned away from poetry. There are the vaguest of hints that he began writing plays and mimes at this time. It has been claimed that *Attis* was publicly performed by au actor/singer, or even a troupe taking the roles of Cybele's priests, the *galli*.[19]

Tantalizingly, Cicero wrote to a friend who had been in Britain with Caesar, advising him to come to Rome quickly before there were stories of misdemeanours. Playwrights would love to mock them, not only Laberius but 'even our friend Valerius'. Shackleton Bailey has suggested that Gaius Valerius Catullus might be Cicero's 'Valerius'. 'But the theory that he was the poet Caius Valerius Catullus can hardly be taken seriously.'[20]

'Why not?' asked Wiseman. Although no play or mime of his exists except perhaps for *Attis*, of the 109 quotations of his in classical authors such as Horace, Martial and Ovid the majority can be found in the three *Libri*, 'but there is also an irreducible minimum of 17 which evidently refer to works that have *not* come down to us', and which may have come from dramatic pieces now lost. Juvenal wrote of an 'actor playing the screaming *Ghost* of Catullus' and of 'a *farce* like that of the witty Catullus'. A mime by a playwright of the same name was performed on the day that the emperor Caligula was assassinated. He may have been the poet. The name could be a coincidence.[21]

What have come down to us, almost by a literary fluke, are the three *Libri*. The three are very different. Books *I* and *III* contain short, personal, often offensive verses; *II* perhaps contains the poems of which the poet was most proud. Catullus probably edited *Libri I* and *II* but if he had died suddenly, maybe only two-thirds of the way through III, his death could explain the sometimes awkward placing of poems such as [116].

The final editing may have been undertaken posthumously by a friend such as Gaius Helvius Cinna – or, more probably, Cornelius Nepos, as poem [1] implies. Whoever it was, it must have been done very quickly as the poems influenced the succeeding Augustan poets.[22]

Catullus died young. At the end of the first century BC Ovid said so.

> Yet if human survival means more than a ghostly reputation,
> Tibullus must surely dwell in Elysium,
> Welcomed by young Catullus, ivy-garlanded, poet and scholar ...
>   Ovid, *Amores III*, 9, 62[23]

How he died, where or when, is not known. There have been timid murmurs that he might have been killed at the command of some powerful man, angered by the vituperative attacks – Julius Caesar perhaps. But Suetonius' anecdote of Caesar forgiving the poet and inviting him to dinner seems to argue against the idea.

In the first printed edition of his poems of 1472 there is a brief epitaph. It mentioned his jests, the erotic pieces, the marriage poems, and ended, 'He died at Rome in the thirtieth year of his age, with public mourning at his funeral.'

That was written 1,500 years after his death. Five hundred years later, the jokes, the erotic verses, the *epithalamia*, the *Attis* are all admired, but it is for the poems to Clodia that he is best remembered.

No woman can truly say that she was ever loved
as my Lesbia was loved by me.
No faithfulness in any covenant was so honoured
as mine was in my love for you.

[87]

8

POSTMORTEM – 53-30 BC

It was like the last act of a Jacobean tragedy, bodies everywhere on the stage, not a soul stirring. Not a man in this story of Catullus died peacefully in bed.

Marcus Licinius Crassus, 'Dives', the Rich, was the first to go. Vaingloriously he decided to invade Parthia, a country friendly to Rome. It was so unpopular a venture that a tribune publicly cursed him, invoking 'strange and terrible deities ... The Romans believe that no one who had them laid upon him can escape'. [1]

Crassus ignored the maledictions, took his army, plundered Jerusalem and, ill-prepared, entered Parthia. Separated from their Armenian cavalry the Roman legions were attacked by mounted archers with heavy arrows who killed hundreds at the battle of Carrhae in 53 BC. Publius, the son of Crassus, fell and his head was jeeringly displayed out of range of the helpless foot-soldiers. Treacherously talked into surrender, Crassus was murdered and decapitated. His head was taken to the Parthian court. During a performance of Euripides' *Bacchae*, the actor Agave seized it and, instead of the mask of Pentheus, danced wildly with it at the end of the play. He was rewarded with a silver talent from the amused Parthian king Orontes. Some said that in mockery of Crassus' lust for material things molten lead was poured down his throat. Others, more poetically, suggested gold. [2]

There was increasing trouble in Rome. 'The years 54-53 BC were the most anarchic time that had been seen since Catiline's day, and the perpetual riots and affrays stirred up by Clodius and his rival Milo made the city almost uninhabitable. The very consular elections could not be held in 54, so that in the early months of 53 BC the state had no existing supreme magistrate!' [3] Death ended the impasse.

On 18 January 52 BC, the tribune Publius Clodius Pulcher was killed in a skirmish on the Appian Way near Bovillae (Osteria), ten miles south-east of Rome. Oddly, three different forms of transport were involved. Returning on horseback from Aricia where he had been speaking, his party of three comrades and thirty slaves accidentally encountered – or was ambushed by – an armed gang of thugs led by his enemy Milo. Titus Annius Milo was going to Lanuvinium with his wife Fausta, travelling comfortably in a four-wheeled raeda. The two groups met, clashed and stabbed. Slashed with swords, and near death, Clodius was borne to the apparent safety of a nearby house. Men broke in, killed him and dumped the corpse on the road. Hours later, a senator returning to Rome in a litter saw the dead body, got out and had it carried in decency back to the city.[4]

It was rumoured that Milo had him assassinated. What happened was never clear. The corpse of Clodius Pulcher was carried in honour by his supporters to Rome's despised Senate House and cremated on a pyre of ceremonially heaped chairs and benches. No attempt was made to control the fire and the Senate was burnt down.

Milo was tried for causing the death of Clodius Pulcher and was defended by Cicero, 'but the continual clamours of the friends of Clodius, and the sight of an armed soldiery, which surrounded the seat of judgement, so terrified the orator, that he forgot the greatest parts of his argument, and the defence he made was weak and injudicious'. Milo was condemned and exiled to Massilia (Marseilles). The persuasive, well-reasoned speech of Cicero's that exists today is not the one he gave but the one that he would have given had he kept his nerve.[5]

Within a further seven years Pompey, Caelius Rufus, Milo himself, even Mamurra, were dead. Apart from Mamurra, all had chosen the wrong side in the struggle that simmered, seethed and boiled into a civil war between the reactionary Senate and the supporters of Julius Caesar and reform.

In 51 BC Cleopatra and later her half-brother Ptolemy XIII became joint-rulers of Egypt. Both would perish.

In 50 BC the Senate, backed by the ever-conservative Pompey, demanded that Caesar disband the army he had brought from Gaul. Distrusting the honour of the senators he refused and on 11 January 49 BC, accompanied by Mark Antony, he led his one legion across the Rubicon. As a river it was insignificant but politically it was a barrier, the official boundary between Cisalpine Gaul and Italy. To cross it towards Rome, 200 miles to the south, was to declare war. Caesar knew what he had done. '*Alea iacta est*', 'the die is cast', he said.

Gaius Pompeius Magnus, Pompey, accompanied by Cicero, fled to Greece. Caesar defeated his legates in Spain. Next year, 48 BC re-elected as consul, Caesar confronted Pompey in Greece on 9 August and annihilated his army at Pharsalus. Caesar may have lost a thousand men, Pompey fifteen times that number. No longer safe, no longer with a worthwhile legion, Pompey crossed to Egypt only to be stabbed to death on 28 September, his birthday, at the suggestion of Theodotus, a tutor of the ten-year-old pharaoh.[6] 'Dead men do not bite,' he said.

Cleopatra had been deposed early in 48 BC by Theodotus and other courtiers who wanted to take advantage of the amenable boy-pharaoh. She had been forced to escape from Alexandria a few months before Caesar, now master of the world, arrived there. But Caesar preferred Cleopatra to the boy-king and she would soon become his mistress.

One dark October evening a boat passed by the anchored Egyptian and Roman fleets in the harbour. At the wharf a Sicilian, Apollodorus, shouldered a long, bundled carpet which, he told the guards, was a present for Caesar. It contained Cleopatra. Caesar 'is said to have been captivated by this example of daring courage and enslaved by the woman's beauty'. He made Ptolemy XIII accept that his sister was still a co-ruler of Egypt.[7]

In the same year, 48 bc, two men who had judged it prudent to side with Pompey both died. **Marcus Caelius Rufus**, deposed praetor, former lover of Clodia, and a man with huge debts, emptied the gaols of the countryside around Rome, gathered a risible 'army' of slaves and gladiators, hoping to create a riot that would restore him to power. He was killed. Caesar hardly mentioned the incident in his *History of the Civil War*.

The exiled **Titus Annius Milo** returned to Italy, joined Caelius Rufus and attempted to buy the loyalty of Caesar's Gallic and Spanish cavalry. He was arrested by the praetor, Quintus Pedius, and executed at Cosa (Cossano).[8]

Superficially life was peaceful. Egypt was pacified. Cleopatra bore Caesar a son, Caesarion. The two were given a house on the Janiculum, *Mons Aureus*, 'the golden hill of sand', just west of Rome on the far side of the Tiber.

With the guidance of the Greek astronomer-mathematician, Sosigenes, Caesar had the old and inaccurate Roman calendar revised. A 'new' year was created of 365¼ days and the Julian calendar was instituted on the first day of 45 bc.

Life appeared calm. Caesar adopted his great-nephew Octavian, later Augustus, into his family, the Gens Julia, but the peace was deceptive. Octavian was to claim the right to all Caesar's powers, causing a deadly rivalry with Mark Antony.

Death was everywhere. Nothing stood still. Friendship became enmity. Loyalty was exchanged for treason. Men that had been pardoned forgot gratitude and turned to murder. Everywhere there was suspicion and fear.

In the middle of December Cicero visited an indifferent Caesar who kept him waiting for hours. The orator brought him news of the death of **Mamurra**, his former military engineer. 'His face did not change'.[9]

Even Caesar himself was not immune. February 15 was the feast of Lupercalia, when two youths from the Palatine Hill, brows smeared with goats' blood, ran naked around the city walls, lashing out at women with their whips to remove sterility and encourage childbirth. It was on that day in 44 bc that the consul, Mark Antony, offered Caesar the royal crown, an elevation that would have been abhorrent to every educated Roman with a knowledge of the history of the tyrannical kings of Rome. Caesar refused.

Meanwhile a resentful and apprehensive group of sixty senators plotted his death. On 15 March, the Ides, in the Theatre of Pompey, **Gaius Julius Caesar** was repeatedly stabbed by the conspirators, two of whom, Cassius and Brutus, he had spared after the battle of Pharsalus. Astonishingly, according to Suetonius, of his twenty-three wounds only one, the second, to his chest, was mortal.[10]

That the decadent Republic should develop into an imperial power was inevitable, but by their action the assassins precipitated its end. Within seventeen years it had gone. On 17 January 27, BC the Senate proclaimed Octavian the first Roman emperor, Augustus, but none of the tyrannicides lived to see the day.

Cicero had supported them but did not participate. After the murder Cleopatra returned to Egypt, taking Caesarion with her. To ensure her safety she had her co-ruler and little brother Ptolemy murdered. In Rome a revengeful rabble, incited by Mark Antony, rampaged through the streets, searching for the conspirators. They met the tribune, **Gaius Helvius Cinna**, poet and friend of Catullus. Mistaking him for Lucius Cornelius Cinna, an enemy of Caesar's, they mobbed him and tore him to pieces. Over 1,600 years later Shakespeare had one of the ruffians bawl, 'Tear him for his bad verses', which was bad history and worse criticism of a man praised by Catullus for his epic, *Smyrna*. [11]

The murder of Cinna was a classic example of being in the wrong place at the wrong time. It was also a time when to take the wrong side could be fatal. It was dangerously unclear which of four opposing factions – the conspirators, the Republic, Mark Antony or Octavian would be victorious.

Marcus Tullius Cicero, always a defender of the Republic, believed that with the dictator dead political life could return to normality. He advocated a general amnesty for the assassins. It was a misjudgement. As their power declined, Mark Antony's increased, and an outraged and confident Cicero condemned him in fourteen courageous speeches that became known as the *Philippics* for their similarity to those given by Demosthenes in the fourth century against the threat of Philip of Macedon. To Cicero, Mark Antony was an unscrupulous adventurer who was threatening the Republic. 'Mark Antony alone in this city since the founding of the city has openly with him an armed guard: a thing neither our kings ever did, nor those that after the expulsion of the kings sought to seize kingly powers.'[12] Sulla, and now Caesar, did have weapons but concealed them. 'But an army of men-at-arms used to attend this pest . . . displaying their swords.' There were even barbarian archers. 'Is it not better to perish a thousand times than to be unable to live in one's own city without a guard of armed men.' The Senate declared Mark Antony an enemy of the State.

Octavian was ambitious but discreet. In Gaul, Mark Antony had been given the legions of Lentulus and Plancus. Rather than challenging them Octavian proposed unification and in November, 43 BC, a second Triumvirate of Mark Antony, Aemilius Lepidus and Octavian was agreed. Proscriptions were announced and Cicero's name was included. During Catiline's uprising, at Cicero's recommendation, Lentulus, the stepfather of Mark Antony, had been executed. Nor had Antony forgotten the *Philippics*.

Cicero fled on board a ship but rough winter weather and seasickness made him disembark. He went to his villa at Astura near Formiae. Next morning, horrifyingly ominous, a black crow flew on to his bed. Depressed and weary he had his slaves carry him in a litter towards the port but Octavian's soldiers caught up with them. It was 7 December, 43 BC. With uncharacteristic courage Cicero put his head out between the curtains and ordered, the centurion to strike. He died in his sixty-third year, executed near Caieta (Gaetia). His head and his right hand, the one that had written the *Philippics*, were displayed on the Rostra. Antony's wife, the notorious Fulvia, spat at the face, pulled out the orator's tongue and pierced it again and again with a golden bodkin.[13]

In the autumn of 42 BC the army of one of Caesar's assassins, **Gaius Cassius Longinus**, was defeated at the Battle of Philippi in Macedonia and Cassius killed himself. Three weeks later, also at Philippi, his colleague, **Marcus Junius Brutus**, attacked, lost, and committed suicide. Suetonius mused at the fates of the men who had killed Caesar, all dying shortly afterwards, 'some in shipwreck, some in battle, some using the very daggers with which they had treacherously murdered Caesar to take their own lives'.[14] Triumphant, their enemies slain, the Triumvirate divided up the Roman world: Lepidus received Africa, Mark Antony the East. Significantly, Octavian obtained the West, including Italy. For reasons only guessed at and never convincingly explained, Mark Antony commanded Cleopatra to meet him at Tarsus in Cilicia, now southern Turkey. Cleopatra, twenty-eight years old, experienced, undisputed ruler of Egypt, arrived, sailing up the River Cnydus in her famous royal barge 'with its stern of gold, the purple sail shimmering in the wind, rowers with oars of silver that rose and dipped in time to lutes and harmonious pipes and flutes. Cleopatra, dressed richly in the costume of Aphrodite, lay under a canopy of cloth of gold. Around her with fans stood young pages as Cupids. Some of the loveliest of her handmaidens, apparelled like nymphs and dryads, were at the rudder, others at the tackles of the sails. A rich perfume of incense wafted from the vessel to the riverside.[15]

That evening she gave a banquet. It was epicurean, with course after course of delicacies: fine wines; sea-food, oysters, mussels with asparagus; then capons, pies, fish and venison patties; lobsters, spicy sauces, partridges, deer and gazelle cutlets; pheasants en croute, big game, stuffed piglets, quails, ducks, turkeys, roasted peacocks with feathered tails; woodcocks in sauces, sturgeons, lampreys, patisserie, Eastern fruit. Mark Antony was bewitched.

He went with her to Egypt and passed the entire winter in Alexandria before returning to Italy.

That was in 41 BC. There followed uneasy years of suspicion between the Triumvirate. Lepidus and Mark Antony did little but Octavian steadily strengthened his position. In 37 BC Antony invited Cleopatra to Antioch, and they renewed their affair. By 33 BC he was living in Egypt like an indolent Eastern monarch. Then, catastrophically, the pair of them announced that Caesarion, son of Caesar, was the rightful heir to Rome. Octavian, the heir appointed by Caesar, declared war not on Mark Antony but on Cleopatra.

She was denounced in the Senate, 'No accusation was too vile to be hurled at her . . . this accursed Egyptian was a sorceress who had bewitched Antony with drugs; a wanton who had sold herself to his pleasures for power; this one and that one had been her paramours; Caesar's alleged son was the bastard of an unknown father. She was a worshipper of beast-gods, ... a drunkard and a harlot; later she was to be called a poisoner, a traitor and a coward.'[16]

The outcome was decided at the naval battle of Actium on 2 September 31 BC when a cowardly part of the Egyptian force sailed away from the fight. **Publius Gellius Poplicola**, commanding a wing of the Roman fleet, was killed in action. Cleopatra and Mark Antony were forced back to Alexandria where they were besieged. Caesarion was sent to Antioch.

Marcus Antonius, Mark Antony, wrongly informed that Cleopatra had killed herself in the refuge of her mausoleum, tried to commit suicide in August, 30 BC. Falling in Roman fashion on his sword he failed to kill himself. Servants carried him to Cleopatra's refuge in her ornate burial chamber where he died.[17]

Cleopatra VII then took her own life on 10 August. Guards permitted her women to take a basket of lusciously rich figs into the mausoleum. In it, concealed, were one or more asps, venomous *Viperae asperis*, long-fanged and deeply poisonous. By experimenting Cleopatra knew by then that only that type of snake 'brought on without spasms and groans a sleepy numbness and drowsiness'.

She was bitten on the arms and died immortal, as befitted a death caused by a snake. The serpent was the emblem of Isis, a goddess with whom Cleopatra had always identified herself When her body was examined 'two small indistinct marks' could just be seen. In October Caesarion was lured from Antioch back to Alexandria and killed on the orders ofOctavian.[18]

This litany of death ends with Clodia. In Rome she was the owner of a fine suburban property that Cicero had coveted for retirement in his old age. From 49 to 44 BC he had pestered her to sell it to him. By early May in 45 BC he was pessimistic. 'I don't think she will sell (she likes the place and has plenty of money)'. A fortnight later he was confident that she would accept. Unsurprisingly, she never did.[19]

Cicero was always curious about her. In 59 BC 'I'm all agog', he had written to his friend Titus Pomponius Atticus, 'about your talk with Lady Ox-Eyes, and about that delectable entertainment'. He mentioned her again on 16 April 44 BC. 'Please let me know what Clodia has done.' No answer survives.[20]

At the end of this book – its poetry, its deaths and the love of a beautiful woman that brought such anguish to Catullus – there is something that Clodia never knew as she disappeared into the lost pages of history. Fausta, Ipsitilla, Mucia, Palla, Sempronia, Valeria are wraiths.

Catullus made the patrician Claudia Metelli immortal.

SOME POEMS BY CATULLUS
TRANSLATED BY HUMPHREY CLUCAS

2

Sparrow, my love's pet, her favourite playmate,
The one she holds in her lap, provokes to peck
At her fingertip with a sharp bill (hoping,
I think – bright lady of my desire –
To gain some small relief from love's burning),
If I could make such sweet sport as she does,
Lighten the black load that weighs my mind . . .

2b

... welcome as the golden apple, thrown
To the girl in hot pursuit, her maiden girdle
Loosening for the first time around her.

3

Mourn, Amores, Venus; mourn,
All whom they love. My lady's sparrow,
The bright spark of a starry eye,
Is dead. He was her sweetest honey,
Loving his mistress like a girl
Her own mother. He never flew
Far from her lap, but – here, there –
Hopped and chirped for her only.
Now he travels the dim road
From which, they say, there's no returning.
Cursed be the shades of hell that take
Such beauty. My fine sparrow's gone.
Cruel death. Poor bird. And because of you
My lady's eyes are red with weeping.

4

This pinnace, friends, shall make her boast:
The swiftest ship afloat. Never
A vessel sped beyond her reach
With sails or oars. The Adriatic –
Furious sea – supports her claim,
And the island Cyclades, Thrace's
Wild Propontis, famous Rhodes,
The unpredictable gulf of Pontus
Where she stood once in a leafy
Forest – unmade boat, a whisper
On Cytorus' heights. Pontic Amastris,
Cytorus thick with green box,
She says you know this, too; here
She had her roots, and dipped her oars
First in these waters, leaving
To bring her master over the rough
Seas (wind from lee or larboard,
Jupiter in the sheets astern).
She asked the shore-gods no quarter –
A long haul to this limpid lake.

Such things are done now. She rests
In her old age – retired, at ease –
And dedicates herself to you,
Castor, and to Castor's twin.

5

Let's live and love, my love,
Ignore the snide talk
Of all these crabbed old men.

The sun sets, and rises:
Once our candle's snuffed,
We're out for a long night.

A thousand kisses, then,
A hundred thousand thousand,
Till we lose count.

Don't keep score, for no
Evil eye can blight us
If our love seems infinite.

7

How many kisses satisfy,
You ask; how many overwhelm?

As if you'd make reckoning
Of the grains of Libyan desert sand
In Cyrene, where the sylphium grows,
Between the oracle

Of sweltering Jove and the sacred tomb
Of old Battus – or catalogue
The stars that watch our stolen love
These quiet nights. Only

Infinite kissing satisfies
(And more) your mad Catullus – kisses
Beyond the range of an evil eye
Or a wicked tongue's bewitching.

8

Time that you stopped this foolishness, Catullus,
And gave up hoping for what has gone.
Your days have burned brightly: you went once
Wherever your mistress took you – she you loved
As none will be loved now. Such appetite,
Such glad sport; you made your desire known,
And the girl was not backward. Sun-drenched days.
Now she no longer wants it; you, poor fool,
Must think the same. Give up the chase, then –
No regrets. You must be firm, endure.
Farewell, love: Catullus' mind hardens.
He'll not beg favours against your will.
And you'll be the loser – on the shelf, unwanted.
What will you do now? who'll come visiting?
Who'll find you beautiful? whom will you love?
Who'll possess you? whose lips for your kisses?
Whose nibbling lips?

Harden your mind, Catullus:
No regrets. You must be firm. Endure.

11

Furius and Aurelius, my comrades,
Who'd travel with me whether we made our way
To furthest India where the shore's battered
By shattering surf,

Or to Hyrcania and soft Arabia,
To the Scythiads or the Parthian archers,
Or to the plains which sevenfold Nile darkens
With a rich flood,

Or whether we trudged over the massive Alps
To see those monuments to great Caesar,
The Gallic Rhine and the formidable
Outlandish Britons –

Friends, ready to run these risks with me
Whatever the gods' will might bring to us,
Take my mistress a plain message now,
And not a kind one:

Tell her to live, enjoy all her lovers,
Take at once the whole three hundred of them,
Withholding true love, but time after time
Sapping their strength,

And let her not look to my love again;
Through her fault, it's faded like a small
Flower at the field's edge, snapped in passing
By a careless plough.

31

Sirmio, the brightest jewel
Of all peninsulas and islands
That Neptune throws up in limpid lakes
Or the vast ocean, with what joy
Have I disembarked, hardly believing
I've left Thynia and flat Bithynia

And am here, safe. Nothing more sweet
Than to put cares beside us, let
The mind lay down its load, tired with the trouble
Of long miles, and come again
To our own homes, sink in the beds
Our limbs ached for. This pays all the rest.
Welcome, wonderful Sirmio;
Enjoy my happiness. And you,
Lapping waters of the Lydian lake,
Ripple with all the laughter of my home.

33
First of all the bath-house filchers –
Father Vibennius, and son.
One's an itchy-fingered lecher,
One's a randy-ended queer.
The devil take them: everyone's
Disgusted by those groping fingers,
No one wants that hirsute bum.

34
Girls and chaste boys,
Diana's servants, let us
Sing to Diana, girls
And chaste boys.

Latona's child, offspring
Of high Jove, your mother
Bore you under the olive-
tree on Delos

To be the honoured lady
Of mountains, green woods,
Secluded glades, and clear
Sounding streams.

Labouring mothers call you
Juno Lucina; Hecate
At the cross-ways; Luna
With borrowed light.

Month by month, goddess,
You measure the turning year.
From you the barn receives
Its rich harvest.

Sacred under whatever
Name you will, keep safe,
As in the ages past,
Our Roman race.

38

Things aren't well with me, friend –
Not well at all. They're pretty rough,
In fact, and worse daily. Hourly,
I should say. And though a morsel
Of comfort wouldn't cost much,
What have you done about it? No
Word? I'm losing patience, friend.
Console me – send me a few lines.
Fill them with crocodile tears.

39

Egnatius of the white teeth
Is always smiling. If they stand
By the prisoner's bar and hear his counsel
Moving the crowd to tears – he smiles.
If they mourn at a young boy's
Funeral, and the stricken mother
Grieves for her only son – he smiles.
Wherever he is, whatever he does,
On every conceivable occasion,
He smiles. It's a disease, neither
Elegant, nor in good taste.
Here's some advice, my dear Egnatius.
Roman, Sabine, or Tiburtine,
Umbrian pig, or plump Etruscan,
Swarthy, massive-toothed Lanuvian,
Or (to include my own people)
Transpadane – were you *any*
Of these, or anyone else who cleans
His teeth with fresh water, still

I'd bar that everlasting grin.
Nothing's worse than a fool's laughter.
As it is, you're Celtiberian:
The natives there scrub their teeth
And gums with what their bladders pass.
The more dazzling your smile,
The more you've swilled your mouth with urine.

40

What madness, my poor Ravidus,
Drives you headlong into the path
Of my lampooning? What god,
Invoked in an evil hour, stirred up
Such argument? Do you like
To be talked about? What do you want?
To be well-known, no matter what?
And so you shall. You chose to love
My lady. Long may you suffer for it.

46

Now Spring comes, and the warm breezes
Hush these furious equinoctial skies.
Time to leave the Phrygian plains, Catullus,
Nicaea's rich and sweltering farm-lands; time
For the bright Asian cities. Mind in a ferment,
Racing ahead, I'm restless here; my feet
Ache to be off. Farewell, you fellow-travellers;
We came to a distant country, far from home,
And return now, each by a different route.

48

Three hundred thousand times, Juventius,
I'd kiss your sweet eyes; never enough
Kissing – thick as the ripe ears
Of corn in a good harvest. If you'd yield.

50

A day that was all holiday,
Licinius; a day of games –
Sophisticated, by arrangement;
A day scribbling epigrams.

Each followed his quick fancy,
Now one metre, now another,
Taking turns, while the wine and laughter
Flowed. I came away so roused
By your sharp wit, Licinius,
That I couldn't eat, or sleep either.
Open-eyed, I spent a restless
Night tossing around my bed,
Longing for dawn – another meeting,
More talk. But when at last
I could lie still, half-alive
And quite exhausted, I wrote this,
My friend, so that you'd know my need.
Don't be proud – and don't refuse
My invitation. Nemesis
Is a strict goddess, quick to punish;
Take care not to offend her.

51

God-like he seems to me, or happier still,
More than god-like – if that's not sacrilegious –
The man who sits at your side, time after time
Transfixed, pierced through

With your sweet laughter. Misery, how such things
Deprive me of all sense. Whenever I'm with you,
Lesbia, my voice dies in my throat,.'
My tongue falters,

A current of flame rushes through all my limbs,
My ears reverberate to their own echo,
And my poor eyes are cowled in thickening darkness
Like a twofold night.

51b

Idleness, Catullus, degenerate sloth;
It does you no good – and you revel in it.
Idleness: the wrecker of great cities,
The bane of kings.

53

A chap in the crowd really made me laugh
When my dear Calvus was rolling out the charges
Against Vatinius – in splendid style.
'Great gods!' he says, raising his arms in wonder,
'How the old cock spouts!'

56

What an absurd thing, Cato!
You'll laugh. Laugh with Catullus, then.
Cato, it's too ridiculous.
I found a boy banging his girl;
I was so stirred – forgive me, Venus –
That I drew my own rod, and served him right.

58

My Lesbia, Caelius, that same Lesbia
Whom once Catullus loved more than himself
And all his own, now in the alleyways
And at street corners milks with a practised hand
The upright members of magnanimous Rome.

61

Haunter of Helicon, Urania's
Child, you who carry the soft
Virgin to her bridegroom – O
Hymen, marriage-god,
O great Hymen!

Bind your brow with majoram,
That fragrant flower, assume the orange
Veil, joyfully come now
Wearing on white feet
The saffron sandal,

And wakening on this glad day
Sing with a high voice the marriage-
Song, dance with a stamping foot,
Shake with a cheerful hand
The torch of pine.

For Junia weds Manlius,
Junia, fair as Venus when
She came from her Idalian home
To please the Trojan judge,
A bright virgin

Of favourable auspice – like
The Asian myrtle, dazzling
With a flesh bloom, which Hamadryads
Feed on dew nightly
For their own delight.

Come then, come hurrying here;
Leave behind Aonian caves,
Thespian rocks which Aganippe,
The springing nymph, sprinkles
With her cold streams,

And call the bride home, desire
For a young lord warm within her;

Twine her heart with love, as here
And there the clinging ivy
Clutches the tree.

And you, innocent girls, you
Whose nuptial day approaches, come,
Sing in a measure now: 'O
Hymen, marriage-god,
O great Hymen,'

So that the call to play his part
Hastens the god's presence here,
The harbinger of kindly Venus,
Knitter of heart with heart
In wedded bliss.

Which of the gods can best deserve
A lover's invocation? Which
Receives devoutest worship? O

Hymen, marriage-god,
O great Hymen!

Elderly fathers call on you
To bless their children; girls for you
Let loose their maiden girdles; listening
Bridegrooms wait your footfall
With an anxious ear.
You that carry the budding maiden,
Fresh from a mother's breast, into
A young man's hot embraces – O
Hymen, marriage-god,
O great Hymen!

No good comes from Venus' sports
Without your blessing, no honour there
But all is well, if you approve it.
What god can match himself
With this god?

No house without you fills with offspring,
No prop for a father's fond age –
But all is well, if you approve it.
What god can match himself
With this god?

No defence for the country, no
Fresh-sprung troops to guard our borders –
But all is well, if you approve it.
What god can match himself
With this god?

Fling wide the doors, then.
See, the bride is coming.
Look how the torches shake
Their flaming hair. But modesty
Delays her, starts her tears;
Her time has come.

No tears now, Aurunculeia:
What danger that a maid more perfect

Ever shall stand and watch the dawn
Spreading its bright path
Across the ocean?

You stand like blue larkspur gracing
A wealthy master's flower-filled garden.
But while you wait here, the hour
Passes, daylight fades. Come out, bride.

Come out, bride, show yourself;
Our clamorous words command you now.
Your time has come. Look how the torches
Shake their golden hair. Come out, bride.

Your bridegroom is no adulterer,
Lightly following shameful ways;
Tonight, he longs to lie beside you,
Never to lift his head
From your soft breast,

And like the tender vine clutching
The strong tree that stands beside it,
So shall you clasp him. But the hour
Passes, daylight fades. Come out, bride.

O bed with white feet, what joy
For your lord this ranging night, what joy
In the high morning! But the hour
Passes, daylight fades.
Come out, bride.

Youths, shake out your flaming torches;
Welcome the orange veil among us!
Sing in a measure now, 'Hail
Hymen, marriage-god,
O great Hymen!'

The bawdy song must not be silenced,
And let the bridegroom's favourite boy
Throw nuts to the slaves; outgrown now
That childish love, his lord
Has left such things.

Throw the slaves their nuts, you pampered
Child; your time is past. Too long
You've played with nuts; and now you,
Too, must become the slave
Of great Hymen.

Yesterday, this morning even,
You mocked at country matrons; now
The barber comes to shave your cheek.
Throw your nuts, you wretched
Pampered boy.

And next they say the spruce bridegroom
Won't abstain from an old pleasure.
Give up your smooth-cheeked boy; hail
Hymen, marriage-god,
O great Hymen!

Your amorous secrets broke no laws;
We allow this. But wedlock brings
To an end all such freedoms. Hail
Hymen, marriage-god,
O great Hymen!

And you, bride, do not refuse
Your husband's claim, or then he'll make it
In other sheets than yours. Hail
Hymen, marriage-god,
O great Hymen!

See how prosperous, how fine
Is your lord's house, and be contented.
Rule as the mistress here (hail
Hymen, marriage-god,
O great Hymen!)

Till grey old age shall set your head
Trembling; so shall you nod at last,
Give your consent always. Hail
    Hymen, marriage-god,
      O great Hymen!

Lift high the saffron sandal; cross
The threshold with this good omen;
Enter the polished doors, and hail
    Hymen, marriage-god,
      O great Hymen!

See how your lord awaits you, leant
On a couch of Tyrian purple; see
His bursting eagerness, and hail
    Hymen, marriage-god,
      O great Hymen!

Searing, the flame that stirs within him.
You are on fire, too, but his
The stronger burning. Come; hail
    Hymen, marriage-god,
      O great Hymen!

Let go, youth, the maiden's smooth
Arm, for she must come now
To a husband's white-foot bed. Hail
    Hymen, marriage-god,
      O great Hymen!

And you; matrons, you whose elderly
Husbands proved your worth, instruct
The girl in right ways, and hail
    Hymen, marriage-god,
      O great Hymen!

Bridegroom, now your time has come.
Go to her; she is there in the bride-
chamber, radiant as a flower,
Face white as the daisy,
With a poppy's bloom.

She is as fair as you yourself
Are handsome – may the gods protect me.
Venus has blessed you both. But the hour
Passes. Go to her:
No more delay.

Indeed, you are not lingering;
You're there before me. Now may kindly
Venus come to your aid, since your
Desire is open; no shame
In an honest love.

He that would know the number of
Your myriad joys, let him count up
Grains of sand in African deserts,
Or make reckoning
Of the brilliant stars.

Sport as you will, then – and bring forth
Children. Such an ancient name
Should not lack heirs; as the years pass,
It should renew itself
From the same stock.
Soon I'd see a young Torquatus
Reaching out with small hands
From his mother's lap, a sweet smile
For his proud father half-
Parting his lips.

Let him resemble Manlius
His father, recognized by all –
By those, even, who do not know them,
And let his face speak
For his mother's name.

May his praises prove descent
From one so spotless; such, too,
Was the honour Telemachus took
From chaste Penelope,
His perfect mother.

Virgins, close up the doors now;
Enough of such things. And you, most happy
Pair, be true; life is before you.
In wedded bliss use well
Your vigorous youth.

63

Carried over the deep seas in a swift vessel,
Attis arrived eagerly at the Phrygian wood,
Entering with quick foot the place of the goddess,
Dense and filled with shadow; there, goaded by madness,
Confused in mind, he cut with a sharp flint the hanging
Weight of his male members. When she felt then
That her limbs had lost their old masculinity,
Her fresh blood dribbling over the ground, swiftly
She seized a light timbrel into her snowy hands,
Such as is used – Cybele, Mother – at your mysteries,
And shaking the hollow ox-hide with her soft fingers,
Quivering, she sang to her followers in this strain:
'Come, Gallae – off to Cybele's mountain forests,
Off together now, you wandering herd of Dindymus.
Exiles seeking alien homes, swiftly you followed
The appointed way, endured the truculent salt sea,
Unmanned yourselves through utter hatred of love. Come,
Gladden your lady's heart with wild wanderings;
Together, unreluctant, to Cybele's Phrygian shrine,
To the forest where cymbal sounds, and timbrel echoing answers,
Where Phrygian flautist blows deep on a curved reed,
Where Maenads toss their heads violently, ivy-covered,
Shaking with shrill yells their sacred ritual emblems,
Where followers of the goddess meet in a congregation –
There we must go together now with our swiftest dances.'
As soon as Attis, woman but no woman, ceased
Her song, the troupe of revellers raise tumultuous tongues
In a sudden shrieking; the hollow cymbals clash, the light

Timbrel sounds once more; swiftly to green Ida
They charge in a rout with feverish footsteps: Frenzied then,
Panting, distracted, breath dragged from her lungs, Attis
Leads them, striking the timbrel, through the shadowy branches –
A young heifer still to be broken, starting aside
At the yoke's weight. Swiftly the Gallae plunge after
Her quick lead. Reaching at last Cybele's temple,
Faint and leg-weary, they rest with no food,
Stupor over their eyes, the mind's madness lost
In a drooping sleep. But when the sun's eye flashed,
A golden face lighting again the clear heaven,
The firm land and the raging sea-eager horses
Driving away with fresh hooves the night's darkness –
The god of sleep abandoned Attis, hurrying on
To Pasithea's fluttering bosom. Calm now,
Soothed by a soft slumber, Attis knew in her heart
All that was done; with a clear mind she reviewed her loss,
Her whereabouts. She ran to the shore, her thought surging.
Over the wide sea she gazed with streaming eyes,
And piteously addressed her country, shaking with grief.
'Country that gave me life, child-bearer! Wretch
That I am, I ran headlong like a fugitive slave
To the snowbound forests and the lairs of the wild beasts,
Visiting all their dens in a mad fury. Where
Did I think you were, my country? Now that my mind clears
For a while, my eyes ache to see you. Shall I be left
In these forests, far from home and my own land,
Possessions, friends and parents? far from the racetrack, forum,
Wrestling-place, gymnasium? Wretched heart, complain,
And again complain. What human shape have I not had?
I am become woman, who was a boy once,
Youth, and man; I was the best of all the wrestlers,
First among athletes; there were crowds at my door;
Their sleep warmed my threshold; my house was hung with garlands
Whenever I left my bed at dawn. And what am I now?
The gods' handmaid? Cybele's slave? A Maenad,
Less than myself, impotent? Shall I remain here
On the freezing slopes of green Ida, wasting my life
Under the high Phrygian summits, haunting the woods
Like a doe or a wild boar? I regret my deed now,
Now; I wish now, now, it had not been done.'

As these words fell from her rosy lips, bearing
A new message to the ears of the gods, Cybele
Loosened the lions' yoke, urging on with her cries
The beast at her left hand, the herd's fiercest foe.
'Come then,' she said, 'drive him back to his madness,
Send him insane to the forests, he that presumed freedom
To break from my hard rule. Come, let your tail lash
At your back, scourge yourself, shake the sky with your roaring;
Let your tawny mane vibrate on your muscled neck!'
Thus Cybele, threatening, while her hand releases
The lion's yoke. The beast rouses his courage, stirs
His fierce spirit; he runs, he roars, with a ranging foot
He breaks the brushwood. When he comes to the waves' edge,
And sees Attis weeping down by the marbled sea,
He charges; Attis, demented, flees to the wild woodland.
There she lived out her whole life – a slave, always.
Great goddess, goddess Cybele, lady of Dindymus,
Goddess, keep your frenzy far from my own house.
Incite others to wildness. Drive other men mad.

65

I'm worn with incessant grief, Hortalus;
It's keeping me and my muse apart.
I've no mind for my writing, tossed
On such difficult waves. The Lethean flood
Laps at my brother's pale feet;
The Trojan earth lies heavily on him
Under Rhoeteum's shore. He's gone.

I'll never talk to you now, nor hear
Your voice; I'll not see you again,
My brother – dearer than life. Surely
I'll love you for ever, make songs
For your death, as under the branches' shade
The swallow Procne sang of the fate
Of lost Itylus. But in my grief,
Hortalus, I've sent you these verses –
My own, versions of Callimachus –
So that you wouldn't think your words
Blown on the wind, forgotten. Like
An apple, sent as a secret gift

To a young man's first love, tumbling
Out of her chaste bosom – poor girl,
She pushed it into a dress's fold
And forgot it there; her mother comes,
She starts, and it shakes free. Look:
Swiftly it runs along, away –
And a blush spreads over her rueful cheek.

70

No one she'd rather marry, my love says –
Even if Jupiter himself came courting.
Fine. But what they say in a fond moment
Is written on rushing water, scrawled in the wind.

72

You claimed Catullus as your one friend,
Lesbia – dearer than Jupiter.
And then I loved you, not as a common mistress,
But as a father cares for his own sons.
I know you now, and though desire burns
Hotter than ever, you've lost your old value.
Why? you ask; Because such injuries
Stir the passions, but turn friendship cool.

75

My mind thins to a point, Lesbia,
Ruined by your guilt, and its own devotion:
I could not wish you well, though you were perfect,
And if you were worse yet, I'd want you still.

81

Couldn't you find in all Rome, Juventius,
Someone a little smarter than your friend
From back-of-beyond – that hole Pisaurum –
To shower your favours on? He's pale yellow,
Like a gilded statue. And you'd prefer
Him, to me? With an unjaundiced eye?

86

Beautiful Quintia, they say:
I call her straight, tall, fair,
And sexless – not a grain of it!

Lesbia has that Venus touch,
The finest parts of all women.
She steals their graces, one by one.

93

I've no great desire to please you, Caesar –
Or even to know the colour of your hair.

96

If there is pleasure in the quiet grave
At human grief, Calvus – grief
That brings old love to life, and weeps
For past friendship – surely Quintilia
Bears the weight of her lost years lightly.
Such is your love.

100

Caelius is mad about Aufillenus:
Aufillena's sending Quintius crazy.
Each of them, the cream of young Verona.
One's after the brother, one the sister –
Family solidarity, they call it.
Who's my money on? It's you, Caelius;
You showed such firm friendship when the dementing
Flame was licking around my own vitals.
Be happy, Caelius. Good luck to your love.

101

Journeying over many countries,
Many seas, I've come, my brother,
To perform this last, sad rite,
A final gift for the dead. I speak
Vainly, to silent ashes; fortune
Has taken away your real self –
Cruelly snatched away, my brother.
Accept these offerings – my own

Sad tributes, ancestral customs –
As a funeral sacrifice.
Take them, wet with a brother's tears,
And oh my brother, hail and farewell, for ever.

106

A pretty boy – with an auctioneer.
Bargaining there, I fancy.

109

Dearest, you make promises: our love
Is mutual happiness, and lasts for ever.
Great gods, grant that she keep her word.
Make her sincere, and let that luck hold
For a lifetime, our pacts unbroken yet.

110

An honest mistress earns a man's praises;
Charging a fair price, she keeps her bargain.
But not you; you're a man-hater. You break
Rules and promises – take, and give nothing.
To yield is generous; not to yield is chaste.
But to go for the highest bidder, and then withhold
What a man's paid for, makes you, Aufillena,
Greedier than the whore who sells her all.

111

Contenting a single husband, Aufillena,
Is a wife's greatest glory. But better she splayed
Her thighs for the whole town than let her uncle
Come between them – getting her bastard cousins.

113

When Pompey was first consul, Cinna,
There were two men who shared Maecilia's favours.
Now in his second consulship,
It's the same two – but with three noughts added.
Adultery: it's such a fruitful seed.

116

I've racked my brains trying to placate you.
I thought that the works of Callimachus
Might prevent your wretched missives
Showering my head; but I see now
What a waste of time such gifts are.
Gellius, I'll stop your shafts of wit:
I'll wrap my cloak around my shoulders.
Meantime, watch it. Mine shall pierce you.

EPILOGUE
CATULLUS TODAY

Despite the inexplicable early twelfth-century allusion to some words by Catullus in William of Malmesbury's *History of the Kings of England*, and in spite of John Skelton's *Phyllyp Sparowe* of about 1508, the Roman poet was not well known in Britain until the early seventeenth century when Sir Walter Ralegh made his delicate part-translation of poem [5]:

> The Sunne may set and rise:
> But we contrariwise
> Sleepe after our short light
> One everlasting night.
> (*The History of the World*, 1614)

He was the forerunner of a sequence of distinguished enthusiasts that included Ben Jonson, Thomas Campion, Robert Herrick, Richard Lovelace, Lord Byron, Samuel Taylor Coleridge, Thomas Hardy and Ezra Pound. A judicious selection of translations from 1614 to the late twentieth century can be found in Julia Haig Gaisser's *Catullus in English*, 2001. The musical Campion's free version of [5] is one of its delights.

> When timely death my life and fortune ends,
> Let not my hearse be vext with mourning friends,
> But let all lovers, rich in triumph come,
> And with sweet pastimes grace my happie tombe;
> And, Lesbia, close up thou my little light,
> And crowne with love my ever-during night.
>   Thomas Campion (1567-1620)

Most popular of the poems (with eight translations) was [3] about the death of Clodia's sparrow. Other favourites included seven of [5] about the number of kisses, and [51] about the man who looked like a god when close to her. There were six renditions of [43], the anonymous (?) girl with a bent nose, and

[101], the dirge for his brother, five versions of [32], concerning the attractions of Ipsitilla, and [46], Catullus leaving Troy.

There have been novels written about Catullus, Clodia and Caelius Rufus: Kenneth Renton, *Death On The Appian Way*, 1974; Sir Pierson Dixon, *Farewell, Catullus*, 1953; W. G. Hardy, *Turn Back The River*, 1938, and *City of Libertines*, 1957; Benita Kane Jaro, *The Key*, 1982; Jack Lindsay, *Rome For Sale*, 1934, *Despoiling Venus*, 1935, and *Brief Light*, 1939; Robert de Maria, *Clodia*, 1965; and Steven Saylor, *A Murder On The Appian Way*, 1997, and *The Venus Throw*, 1999.

Thornton Wilder's *The Ides Of March*, 1953, about Julius Caesar includes many references to the poet.

In 1942, following the success of his *Carmina Burana* of 1935/6, the German composer Carl Orff wrote *Catulli Carmina*, 'Songs of Catullus', with roles for Catullus, Lesbia, Caelius Rufus, Ipsitilla, and the questionable Ameana as 'a worn-out whore'. The opera contains parts that sound like angry fishmongers bellowing at each other in an open-air market, with housewives mumbling in the background that no one was attending to them.

Orff's *Trionfo di Afrodite*, 'the Triumph of Aphrodite', of 1950-1 is quieter and lovelier, based on two wedding-songs of Catullus, [61] and [62], including some poems by Sappho and ending with a chorus from Euripides, the full orchestra playing Orff's typically dry and staccato music with care and precision.

It is regrettable that so often composers have failed to capture the music of a poet with their own compositions. Debussy's three songs from Villon are pale. Bartok's *Herzog Blaubarts Burg*, 'Bluebeard's Castle', is a thin thing when contrasted with the dreadful crimes of Gilles de Rais, murderer of children.

Claudio Monteverdi was an exception. Much of his *Favolo di Peleo di Theti*, 'the fable of Peleus and Thetis', of 1617 is lost. So is the greater part of what was only his second opera, *Arianna*, 1608. But its *Lamento d'Arianna*, 'Ariadne's lament', survives and the lovely sadness of it haunts the ear. Catullus would surely have approved.

Very much in keeping with the contradictions that were Catullus was the elegiac poem by Walter Savage Landor (1775-1864), who had lived for years in Italy. Catullus was his favourite poet despite his 'uncleanly wit'.

Tell me not what too well I know
About the bard of Sirmio –
Yes, in Thalia's son
Such stains there are –
as when a Grace
Sprinkles another's laughing face
With nectar and runs on.

PELEUS AND THETIS

Technically the longest of all the poems, *Peleus and Thetis*, [64], is a masterpiece of craftsmanship, virtually a perfect chiasmic construction of a later section counterpointing an earlier. Composed as a short epic or epyllion it is possibly the poem of which Catullus was most proud.

In poem [95] he praised Cinna for spending nine years composing and revising his long narrative, *Smyrna*. Being a similar neoteric poet and therefore attentive to detail and form, Catullus was probably as conscientious. He was certainly adding and rewriting parts of [64] as late as 54 BC as eleven references to the recently completed *De Rerum Natura* of Lucretius prove.[1]

It is not a long poem like traditional Roman epics with their books and thousands of solemn lines, and contains only about 400 lines, approximately the same length as T. S. Eliot's *The Waste Land* and just as full of learned asides. It is possibly the survivor of several other mini-epics by Catullus that time and neglect have obliterated. It could have been through these that the poet imagined he might survive posthumously. The German scholar Wilamotz-Moellendorff believed so. 'This poem is the work in which Catullus wanted to write his masterpiece.' Yet even the original title, if there was one, is unknown. The poem is less the story of Peleus and Thetis than an elegy for the world's fall from grace akin to Milton's *Paradise Lost*.[2]

Peleus and Thetis is artistically arranged, filled with classical allusions, a triumph of organization, and although far from the poet's conversational style it was much admired. Virgil borrowed freely from it. The poem is also impersonal, studied. Jenkyns termed it a masterpiece but acknowledged that it 'had not been universally admired'. Fordyce was lukewarm. Quinn equivocated. Robinson Ellis considered it too long and repetitious. Auguste Couat found no dominant theme in it, nor inspiration or unity. Predictably, that advocate of Catullus as a lyric poet, Havelock, complained, 'The poem is read for the emotional episodes and semi-lyrical passages that it contains ... These are strung together with a minimum of hasty narrative into an ill-assorted series.'

The poem is a story within a story, in Jenkyns' words, 'a gallery of tableaux or set pieces; it aims to dazzle metaphorically and almost literally, so full it is of light and colour and precious substances'. It was rococo, baroque, full of gaiety, beauty, mannerisms, it is polished, brilliant with controlled ostentation, ornamental and extravagant. And, significantly, it descends from light into darkness.[3]

It is a tale of a lost Golden Age, the heroic times of Minoan Crete, more than a millennium and a half before Catullus, a long-departed mystical Elysium to a disillusioned Roman, a period of primitive simplicity, gone for ever, when gods walked the earth and mingled with mortals. It was the time when the mythical Cretan king Minos demanded human sacrifices from his conquered lands and when the Greek hero, Theseus, one of its intended victims, killed the murderous half-man, half-bull Minotaur that waited hungrily in the labyrinth below the palace of Knossos. It was an age long before the siege of Troy. Its imagined glory contrasted with the ugly corruption that Catullus knew.

Anyone today smiling patronizingly at such credulity should remember that the palace age of Minoan Crete collapsed a full 1,500 years before Catullus lived. A similar period would return Britain to the Anglo-Saxon invasions and the controversial war-leader, Arthur, a man whose clouded figure is half-hidden in the dream-land magic of Merlin and Morgan la Fay. After more than a century of scholarly research it is still debated whether Arthur was historical or a chimera, an incarnation of wishful thinking. His existence is unproven. Quite differently, the decline of the Minoan civilization, the labyrinth at Knossos and a bull-cult on Crete, have all been proved. Catullus is owed neither pity nor derision.

The architecture of poem [64] was flawless, with the romance of Peleus and Thetis framing and contrasting the tragedy of Theseus and Ariadne. It begins with Peleus sailing with the argonauts in search of the Golden Fleece, being seen by Thetis, daughter of a sea-god, the pair falling in love and marrying. Their son is to become the greatest hero of Greece. The Fates decreed it:

> To you, a son, Achilles, a man who will know no fear,
> whose enemies will not see his back, only his valiant chest ...
> run, spindles, run, make the threads that wait the loom
> (lines 338-9, 342)

It was a well-known tale from antiquity but there was nothing straightforward in the narrative Catullus offered. On the contrary, his version contained allusions to other well-known works, including those of Pindar, Euripides and Apollonius Rhodius. It was a display of learning to reassure and delight his audiences.[4]

In contrast the long centre of the poem, parts 3 to 6, concerned the journey to Crete of Theseus of athens, one of thirteen companions to be sacrificed to the Minotaur, half-man, half-bull, in its labyrinth at Knossos from which no person could find the exit.

Theseus chose to offer his own body
rather than other living corpses went from Athens
to Crete. And in a swift vessel under quiet winds
came to the towered palace of almighty Minos.
(lines 81-4)

Ariadne, daughter of the king, gave him a ball of yarn to guide him back to safety.

How pale she was, whiter than purest gold
when eager to assault the ghastly monster
Theseus departed in search of death or the prize of glory.
(line 100-2)

He slew the Minotaur, found his way out, and took Ariadne to the island of Dia near Crete, where they passed the night together. Next morning Theseus abandoned her, leaving her to her grief. But hurrying back to Athens he forgot to replace the black sails of mourning on his ship with white to announce his safe return. His father Aegeus, fearing Theseus was dead, committed suicide. On Dia Ariadne was saved by Bacchus.

The dark mood of the poem darkened further. The son of the happy Peleus and Thetis, Achilles, became a psychopathic killer. The Parcae, the three Fates of Clotho the spinner, Lachesis the decider and Atropos the unavoidable, ordained it:

currite ducentes subtegmina, currite, fusi.
run, spindles, run, make the threads that wait the loom.

Trojan mothers grieved for their sons as, like a harvester, Achilles reaped the golden youth of Troy. He choked the seething Hellespont with the bodies of the dead. Even after his own death he demanded more, that a princess of Troy should be sacrificed upon the crown of his tomb:

When trickery gave the weary Greeks entry
through the long-protected walls of Troy
They vowed the grave would drip with Polyxena's blood.
Struck down, a victim to the double-bladed axe,
Knees buckling, she fell a headless corpse.
Run, spindles, run, make the threads that wait the loom.
(lines 366-71)

Turning the Greek Achilles into an anti-hero would have pleased the Romans, very conscious of and proud of their supposed Trojan ancestry. Theoretically they were descended from Aeneas who had escaped from Troy and after many years settled in Italy. According to Virgil and other authorities the origins of Rome could be traced back to him.

The poem is a hall of mirrors, full of reflections, each section a reverse image of its counterpart, part 1 in contrast to 8, 2 to 7, 3 to 6 and 4 to 5. Each part links with its opposite:

1. The heroic argonauts and the courtship of Peleus and Thetis. (lines 1-30)
2. The wedding of Peleus and Thetis. Aristocratic human guests. (lines 31-49)
   Tapestry on the bridal bed. The heroic mortals of antiquity. (lines 50-1)
3. Ariadne's search for Theseus. (lines 52-115)
4. Her lament for his betrayal. (lines 116-201)
   Bridge. Zeus grants Ariadne revenge. (lines 202-6)
5. Lament of Aegeus, father of Theseus. (lines 207-50)
6. Search by Bacchus for Ariadne. (lines 251-64)
   Tapestry on the bridal bed.
   Drunken satyrs and followers of Cybele. (lines 265-6)
7. Wedding feast of Peleus and Thetis. Men depart,
   gods arrive. Fates and Achilles. (lines 267-381)
8. The end of the Heroic Age. (lines 382-418)
   They disdain to attend the gatherings of men
   nor ever let themselves be touched by mortal sunlight. (lines 407-8)

His own world was, wrote Catullus, an unheroic period of immorality, an age when brother killed brother, when a father longed for the death of a son to obtain his attractive young widow, when mothers slept incestuously with sons, when men ignored the will of the gods. It was a time when gods no longer came to earth.

Peleus and Thetis is quite unlike the short poems of Catullus. But it is, as Jenkyns argued, 'a masterpiece'.

THE RECOVERY OF THE POEMS OF CATULLUS

FROM HIS DEATH TO AD 1472

Despite his fame and popularity Catullus became a forgotten poet. His colloquial language and unambiguous descriptions of sexual encounters did not appeal to readers of the more prudish Augustan age shortly after his death. For hundreds of years he became a literary ghost.

A fifth-century Christian poet, Paulinus of Nola, had hardly heard of him. A seventh-century Spanish bishop quoted some poems. The sixteenth-century French historian, Jacques de Thou, possessed a late ninth-century anthology known as Codex 'T' for Thuaneus. It contained one Catullan poem, the epithalamium [61]. In the 840s Hildemar, a monk at Brescia not far from Verona, knew some Catullan verses.

A bishop of Verona called Rather read the pagan poems and apologized in a sermon of AD 966 for having seen them, although he may surreptitiously have kept them when he moved to the Belgian abbey of Lobbes, eighty miles north of Reims, in 968.[1]

In the silent years that followed the bishop the poet almost disappeared. Long before then, even in his own city of Rome, it had only been fellow-poets who had admired and respected him. Virgil, 70-19 BC, writer of the magnificent Aeneid, had come to Rome when he was about seventeen years old, a year or so after the poet's death 'and it is a great pity that they never met'. Horace, 65-8 BC, despised third-rate imitators who could only 'croon like Calvus and Catullus' (*Satires I, X, 19*).

A poet lesser than either, Propertius, *c*.50-*c*.2 BC, used Catullus as a means of praising Cynthia, his own mistress, whose beauty:

... shall be made world-famous by my book –
your pardon, Calvus – by your leave, Catullus
Poems, II, 252

A greater poet than Propertius, Ovid, 43 BC-AD 17, grieving the death of another, writing a tender elegy to him, believed that in death Tibullus would be:

welcomed by young Catullus, ivy-garlanded, poet and scholar
>> *Amores III*, 61 [3]

The most enigmatic comments were those by Juvenal, *c.*AD 55–*c.*130.

the girl who wept, red-eyed, for the sparrow's death
>> *Satires VI*, 6

was a straightforward reference to Clodia and poem [3] but Juvenal added controversial lines that have been hopefully taken as evidence that Catullus in his last years had turned from poetry to the writing of mimes and plays for the stage:

playing the screaming *Ghost* of Catullus
>> *Satires VIII*, 186

and

a *farce* like that of the witty Catullus
>> *Satires XIII*, 111

leaving a mystery that remains unresolved.[4]

Of all the poets, however, it was Martial, *c.*AD 40 – 104, who cited Catullus most frequently and always with unconditional respect. In epigram after epigram there are half-quotations, oblique references, imitations such as *nugae*, 'trifles', after Catullus [1] in *Epigram XII*, 94, 9 or 'limp wrapping made for mackerel' in *IV*, 86, 8, which was a direct copy of Catullus' 'roomy coats for mackerel' [95], 8.

And it was probably Martial who by his enduring popularity over the centuries helped to preserve the endangered poems. Churchmen liked his ribald verses:

We're told that Galla's services as a whore
cost two gold coins. Throw in two more
And you'll get the optional extras too ...
>> *Satire IX*, 4

and

'No sodomy!', states my wife. Yet proud Cornelia abided,
so did Portia and Julia, what their husbands had decided.
The goddess, Juno, accepted mighty Jove that way.
>> *Satire XI*, 104[5]

Martial 'was plagiarized and imitated by both pagan and Christian poets. Of course, the darkness that descended outside the monasteries on once popular authors fell also upon Martial ... [but] in the twelfth century Martial provides quotations and even vicious turns of phrase for such learned wits as John of Salisbury, 1100-80.'[6] His fame endured. In 1470 he was one of the first Latin poets to be printed, by coincidence in Verona, two years before Catullus.

Martial's uninhibited wit explains how a few poets survived. Christianity and sexual abstinence were the unlikely saviours of a pagan poet. Learned monks of high rank travelled freely in Britain, Ireland and the European mainland. In Paris, John, Bishop of Salisbury, met the monk and scholar Peter Abelard, lover of Heloise; he also witnessed the murder of Thomas à Becket in Canterbury. He became Bishop of Chartres.

Even after the wreckage of the Dark Ages there were libraries everywhere, in monasteries, priories and abbeys. They contained collections of holy works, of philosophy and of classical authors, some of whose writings were at the very edge of Christian acceptability. But they were enticingly readable and, like closet-pornographers, having renounced sexual intercourse, privileged brethren could compensate by reading bawdy literature in the privacy of their monastic cells.

It explains why the tenth-century bishop of Verona had access to the work of Catullus. And it would explain how an early twelfth-century English cleric, William of Malmesbury, was able to repeat words from Catullus. He had read them somewhere in a collection of antique erotica. Translated from the Latin of his *History of the Kings of England*, the Malmesbury chronicler wrote, 'a maiden neither deficient in elegance nor in understanding'. The same negative description occurs twice in Catullus, poems [6] and [10] 'a girl not without wit or charm'. Both he and William used the unusual and distinctive words *inelegantum* and *illepidum*.[7]

There was a reason for William to choose words from poems [6] and [10]. In the first poem Catullus laughingly reproved a friend, Flavius, for his furtive nights with a secret lover. In [10] another girl was quite bright and graceful but 'a proper tart'. William's woman was an innocent maiden of elegance and sense upon whom King Edgar, 'notoriously libidinous in respect of virgins', had forced himself. The contrast between the love-making of Flavius and the rape by Edgar may have constituted a moral judgement in William's monastic mind.

It is an irony that more than a thousand years after the death of Catullus his licentious poems lived in religious safety, not in cumbersome and decaying rolls but in books. Whereas a word or two here, a few lines there offered little assistance in recovering Catullus, technology as well as monasteries were to rescue him. Early in Christian times bound books replaced the awkward rolls. Known as a codex, an early volume was made first of papyrus, later of more durable sheep – or goatskin parchment, the sheets cut up, folded and stitched together inside a sturdy cover that stood comfortably on a shelf.[8]

How many codices of Catullus there had been is unknown. Only one was ever found. Known as 'V', shorthand for Verona, it may have been the copy shamefacedly read by Bishop Rather of Verona. What matters is that 300 years after the bishop's pulpit confession a codex 'from a far frontier' appeared between AD 1311 and 1321 in Verona, the home town of Catullus.

Legend has it that it was wedged in the bung of a wine cask. In reality it may have been in a measuring vessel, or was one of the volumes in the castle library of Sirmione, acquired from a set given to the canons of Verona by archdeacon Pacificus 500 years earlier. Delightfully the corpus was complete except for a dozen or so lines. Less delightfully, it was full of errors.[9]

It was perhaps discovered by the young, wealthy, poetry-loving Francesco Can Grande della Scala, warlord of Verona, patron of Dante and Giotto, as he browsed through books appropriated for his forty-year-old pseudo-battlemented castle, Castello Scaligero, in Sirmione. By poetical coincidence it was just half a mile south of the ruined villa, reputed home of Catullus, at the tip of the narrow peninsula.

The discovery of the book was celebrated in an enigmatic verse with as many false clues in its six lines as a full-length Agatha Christie murder mystery. In it every 'obvious' answer is a mirage:

The verses of Master Benvenuto Campesani of Vicenza
on the Resurrection of the poet Catullus of Verona.
I come back from exile in a far-off land.
A fellow-countryman was the cause of my return.
A man to whom France gave a name from reeds,
And who watches as the crowds pass by.
With all your joy and gladness, celebrate Catullus,
Whose papyri, like an obscured lamp, lay underneath a bushel.

The verse is cryptic and controversial. The 'distant land' may have been France. 'Fellow-countryman' may refer to Can Grande living near Verona. His town, Sirmione today but Sirmio at the time of Catullus, is by Lake Garda only twenty miles west of Verona.

'A name from reeds' was probably a pun on Can Grande. 'Canne' was Old French for the Latin *canna* 'reed'. 'France' is a double exercise in duplicity, a pun on the name Francesco and a hint about the origin of the codex. Textual analysis showed it to be written in a late twelfth-century French hand.

'Watches the crowds' plausibly refers to the equestrian statue of Can Grande in Verona rising high above the church-door of Santa Maria Romanus Antica,

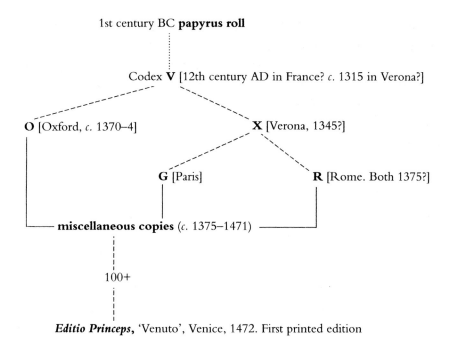

1st century BC **papyrus roll**

Codex **V** [12th century AD in France? *c.* 1315 in Verona?]

O [Oxford, *c.* 1370–4]   **X** [Verona, 1345?]

G [Paris]   **R** [Rome. Both 1375?]

miscellaneous copies (*c.* 1375–1471)

100+

Editio Princeps, 'Venuto', Venice, 1472. First printed edition

looking down at the passers by. 'Bushel' is not a nonsensical wine-cask but a biblical allusion to *Matthew* 5: 15, in which men do not conceal a candle beneath a bushel 'but on a candlestick, and it giveth light unto all that are in the house', rejoicing that Catullus had emerged from the darkness to lighten the world.[10]

The elation of discovery was short-lived, almost tragic. The celebrated codex 'V' vanished. Like will o'the wisps other codices had been made of it, promised to be immortal then flickered into instant obliteration like a series of Houdini disappearing acts.

All nine Muses, led by Erato, protectress of lyric poetry, must have guarded Catullus. He survived. 'V' had gone but two copies had been made. One, codex 'X', was transcribed by the poet Petrarch, client of Can Grande, around 1345. A second and better version was carefully composed by an unknown enthusiast around 1370-4. His codex, 'O' for Oxford, is in the Bodleian Library. Petrarch's 'X' soon joined 'V' in oblivion but luckily had been recorded twice in 1375. One of the two versions is in Paris, 'G' for *Codex Sangermanensis*, named after the Abbé St-Germain-des-Prés. The second is in Rome, codex 'R' for *Romanus*. Many copies were made. Today, everything comes partly from 'G' and 'R', mainly from the more reliable 'O'. Such was the fortuitous survival of a genius.[11]

There were problems. 'V' contained a thousand mistakes. It was only by the end of the nineteenth century, after long years of study and correction by scholars across Europe, that generally reliable editions became available. Today, they are abundant. That they survived was owing to coincidence, to Martial, the monasteries, and the miracle of one impermanent manuscript.

In poem [1] Catullus had pleaded for his little book:

| ... *ut ergo* | ... that it may |
| *plus uno maneat perenne saeclo* | Live more than one brief generation. |

> Wherefore to you, my friend, I dedicate
> This so indifferent booklet. Yet I pray
> Poor as it is – O goddess of my fate,
> Let it outlive the writer's transient day.
>   (James Elroy Flecker, 1884-1915)

Catullus knew that he had lost his woman and dreaded that his poems would also disappear. He grieved for both. He struggled to be firm.

Miser Catulle, desinas ineptire	Poor Catullus, stop being such a fool
et quod vides perisse perditum ducas	and accept as lost what is lost,
fulsere quondam candidi tibi soles	there was a time when the bright sun shone.
.....	...
at tu, Catulle, destinatus obdura!	You, Catullus, be resolute, be hard.
	[8] (p. 169)

Only Clodia was lost. And in his poems even she has survived the centuries. Catullus has remained unbroken.

NOTES

PREFACE

1   T. Nashe, *Summer's Last Will and Testament*, 1592.
2   R. G. C. Levens, 'Catullus': in ed. K. Quinn, *Approaches to Catullus*, Heffer, London, 1972, p. 5.

INTRODUCTION

1   Fragmentary lines of Roman poets: Courtney.
2   Life: Wiseman, 1987, pp. 189-90, 207. Background: Goold, pp. 1-2; Havelock, pp. 79-82; Wray, p. 3.
3   The Capitol and lightning: Taylor, p. 86.
4   Cannae: A. Goldsworthy, *Cannae*, Cassell, 2001, p. 95. Executions: Livy, *History of Rome XXII*, vol. 56, pp. 4-5, vol. 57, pp. 2-9; Polybius, *Histories V*, vol. 56, pp. 6-12; H. Lamb, *Hannibal: One Man Against Rome*, Hale, London, 1959, 104.
5   Wiseman, 1987, p. 4. Ancient Rome: Shelton, pp. 4-16, 59-71, 123-37; Household rubbish: Casson, 1998, pp. 39-40; Human hand: Suetonius, *The Twelve Emperors, Vespasian, V.*
6   Horace, *Satires I*, 10, lines 18-19; Rudd, 1997, p. 79:
7   Library, Alexandria: Casson, 2001, pp. 46-7; MacLeod et al., 2001. Caesar: Meier, pp. 410-11.
8   Forgotten poets: Volumnius: Courtney, p. 234. On Verrius, ibid., p. 291.
9   Octavian's epigram: Courtney, pp. 282-3; Lindsay, 1965, p. 175; Martial, *Epigrams XI*, line 20; Bailey, 1993, pp. 20-1.
10 Octavian/Augustus: Suetonius, *Augustus, LXVIII-LXIX*; Plutarch, *Mark Antony, XXX*, p. 2. On Manius, see Lindsay, 1971, p. 172. See also G. Foster, *Augustus Caesar's World, BC 44 to 14 AD*, Charles Scribner, New York, 1947.
11 François Villon and his editor, Clement Marot: Burl, 2000, pp. 105-6.

12   Pompeii and Catullus: Goold, p. 9. Lindsay, 1960, with references to other poets: Ovid, lines 110, 127, 163, 247; Martial, line 265; and Horace, lines 182, 241.

13   'Intellectual pygmy': *Cambridge History of Classical Literature, II*, 1982, p. 116; *Oxford Classical Dictionary*, 1996, 'Cornelius Nepos'.

14   The poems of Catullus: Gaisser, 2001, pp. xviii-xix. On mistakes in 'V' see Goold, pp. 11-13. In 1554 an editor, Marc-Antoine de Muret, added three Priapic epigrams [18-20] of which only [18] may be genuine: Gaisser, 1993, pp. 166-7; Swanson, pp. 19-21. There are also fragments: Lindsay, 1948, p. 7.

15   Errors in the poems: Quinn, 1970, pp. xxii-xxvii.

16   Hortentius, Volusius and Hatriensis: Munro, pp. 209-14; also Courtney, pp. 230-1; Goold, pp. 207, 261-2; Lee, 1990, pp. 135, 137; The name Hortentius may be corrupt. Catullus is his friend in poem 65, line 180; Lindsay, 1929, 'Note', p. 120; Lindsay, 1948, 77. On Livy's provincialism: Garrison, p. 169. Tanusius Geminus of Padua as 'Volusius', see Simpson, p. 95.

17   First edition 1472: Gaisser, 1993, pp. 24-65.

18   Sir Richard Burton, 1894, p. 184: Lady Burton, pp. v, ix, xvii. On poem [28], see Burton, ibid. pp. 52-3.

19   Verres: Moore, pp. 125-7; Haskell, pp. 139-43.

20   Martin, 1992, p.14. Ezra Pound, *Literary Essays of Ezra Pound*, New Directions, New York, 1968, p. 41.

1 – CHILDHOOD, YOUTH AND WAR

1   Learning from a lost book of Suetonius that Catullus had died at the age of thirty, St Jerome deduced that the poet had been born in 87 BC, the year when Cinna was consul. But poem [11] refers to Caesar and the 'dreadful Britons', probably written in 54 BC. The problem is resolved because Cinna was consul for a second time in 54 BC.

2   Marius: Plutarch, Marius, I-XLVI. *The Bardiaei*, ibid., XLIV, p. 281.

3   Status of Verona: Fitzgerald, p. 203f; Wiseman, 1987, pp. 107, 110; Wray, p. 43.

4   Citizens of Verona: Lindsay, 1929, pp. 3-4. Cisalpine Gaul: Levi, pp. 198, 16-18.

5   The family of Catullus: Wiseman, 1987, p. 100. Valerius: ibid. p. 109.

6   Business in Bithynia: Wiseman, 1987, p. 101; The abacus: Goold, p. 2; Lee, 1990, p. xviii.

7   Jugurtha: Sallust, *The Jugurthine War*, Handford, pp. 39-148.

8   Mithridates: Grant, 1978, pp. 158-60, 166-7; Perowne, pp. 101-3.

9   Mithridates and poisonous herbs: Edwards, p. xxv.

10   Caesar with Minucius Thermus. The three Mithridatic Wars began in 89 BC, 83 BC and 73 BC, respectively. All were unsuccessful.

11   Cicero and Sextus Roscius: Grant, 1990; 'Trial of Sextus Roscius', pp. 23-110; Everett, pp. 54-7.

12   Sulla: Plutarch, *Sulla, I-XXXVIII*; Oman, pp. 116-61.

13   The birth dates of the four men are not certain but were probably: Crassus, *c.* 115 BC; Pompey, 106 BC; Cicero, March 106 BC; Caesar either 12 July 102 BC or 100 BC.

14   Crassus and Licinia: Plutarch, *Crassus, I*.

15   Caesar's description: Suetonius, *Caesar, XLV*. It is regrettable that only fragments of another work, *De Viris Illustribus*, 'The Lives of Great Men' survive. Almost certainly amongst the anecdotes and physical descriptions there was the life of Catullus.

16   Calvus and Pompey: Lindsay, 1929, p. 24; Courtney, p. 210; Quinn, 1969, pp.110-11.

17   For Asinius Pollio see Wray, p. 59, note 77. Aelius Saturninus: Bauman, p. 60.

18   Caesar in Bithynia: Suetonius, *Caesar, LXIX*; Fitzgerald, p. 62; Walter, I, p. 23.

19   The moods of Lake Garda: Whigham, pp. 44-5.

20   A fresco of Catullus: Martin, 1992, p. 40.

21   Caesar and the pirates: Suetonius, *Caesar, IV, LXXIII*; Perowne, p. 140.

22   Pompey and the pirates: Southern, 2002, pp. 59-65; Grant, 1978, pp. 165-6.

23   Cicero as quaestor: Cowell, pp. 221-2.

24   Quaestors: Cowell, pp. 166-71, 173. Praetors ibid., pp. 173-5. Consuls: ibid., pp. 166-71.

25   A sketch of Spartacus? Shaw, p. 15.

26   The authority of pirate captains: A. Burl, *That Great Pyrate. Bartholomew Roberts and His Crew, 1718-1723*, Port Talbot, 1997, pp. 44-5.

27   The son of Publius Gellius Publicola: Quinn, 1970, pp. 404-5, 425-6.

28   Karl Marx: Shaw, p. 15.

29   The third Servile War: Sallust, *The Conspiracy of Catiline*, Handford, pp. 151-232; Plutarch, *Crassus, VIII-XI*. Classical accounts of the first and second Servile Wars and translations of authors describing the war against Spartacus, ranging from Sallust, first century BC to Orosius, fifth century AD, can be found in Shaw, 2001.

30   Capua and perfumes: H. Fast, *Spartacus*, Fast, New York, 1951, p. 4.

31   Crassus and the Appian Way crucifixions: A. Koestler, *The Gladiators*, 1939, pp. 213-15. Roman measures: The foot was about 11.65 inches (29.6 mm), the pace, 4 ft 10 ins (1.47 m), the mile, 1,618 yards (1,480 m). R. E. Zupko, *British Weights and Measures. A History from Antiquity to the Seventeenth Century*, University of Wisconsin, Madison, 1977, pp. 6-7.

32   Reforms: Grant, 1978, p. 165; Perowne, pp. 130--1; Scullard, pp. 93-5.

33   On Verres and his courtesans: see Lyne, p. 10. For Cicero: see Haskell, p. 362.

34   Togas and manliness: Wray, p. 60.

35   The toga: A. Marks and G. Tingay, *The Romans*, Usborne, London, 1990, p. 53. Juvenal, *Satire 3*, lines 171-2.

36   Valerius Cato: Levi, 1998, p. 24. Callimachus: Lyne, 1995, pp. 100-1; MacLeod, pp. 67-9, 97-8; Whigham, pp. 28-9. Also: F. Nisetich, pp. 62-3.

37   Callimachus, 'The Lock of Berenice', Aitia 4, 7. Garrison, pp. 143-7, Map 6; Havelock, p. 77; Lee, 1992, pp. 171-2; Quinn, 1972, pp. 265-6; Nisetich, pp. 167,286-9.

38   Harrington, pp. 6-7.

39   Charles Badham, 1813-84, in Gaisser, pp. 129-30.

40   Catullus: Goold, p. 240. The ritual: Quinn, 1970, pp. 145-54.

41   Poem [17]: Fitzgerald, p. 204; Lee, 1992, p. 191; Quinn, 1970, pp. 145-54; Williamson (his poem 100), p. 81. Metre, Garrison, p. 175.

42   Milesian tales and Roscius: Plutarch, *Crassus XXXII*. 43 Poem 67: Fitzgerald, pp. 205-7; Garrison, pp. 147-8; Goold, p. 256; Havelock, pp. 76-7; Quinn, 1972, p. 368.

44   Caesar and the Subura: Suetonius, *Caesar, XLIV*. The Domus Publica: Platner & Ashby, pp. 440-3.

2 – NEW POETS, OLD ENEMIES AND SCANDAL

1   Writers from northern Italy: Havelock, pp. 163-8; Lindsay, 1929, pp. 27-33 (pages unnumbered after the poems); Lindsay, 1948, pp. xiii-xix.

2   'Spring season': Levi, 1998, p. 4.

3   'New' metres: Garrison, pp. 171-5; Goold, pp. 19-37; Michie, 1981, pp. 12-15.

4   William Harvey and the Neoterics: O. L. Dick, *Aubrey's 'Brief Lives'*, Secker & Warburg, London, 1949, p. xliv.

5   Cicero and the Neoterics: Cicero, Letters, *Atticus*, pp. 7, 2, 1; Fitzgerald, p. 6; Klostenko, pp. 53, 114; Quinn, 1969, pp. 44-8; Raphael & McLeish, p. 13.

6   A year of 'signs and portents': Hardy, p. 20.

7   The trial in 65 BC: Gruen, pp. 42, 217, 271. Catiline: Hardy, pp. 6-11.

8   Election, 63 BC: Gruen, p. 130; Klostenko, p. 5.

9   Sallust and 64 BC instead of 63 BC: Hardy, p. 28, note 6.

10   Sempronia: Sallust, *XXV, 5*.

11   Killing of senators: Hardy, p. 28, note 6; Suetonius, *Caesar, IX*.

12   Plots and accusations: Sallust, *XLII, 2-XLV, 1*; Gruen, pp. 280-1; Hutchinson, pp.69-105.

13   Cato and Caesar: Sallust, *LII, 8 – LIII, 4*.

14   The Tullianum (now known as the Mamertine): Sallust, *LV, 6*; Hutchinson, pp. 14-3-59; Platner & Ashby, pp. 509-10; G. Lugli, *The Roman Forum and the Palatine*, Bardi, Rome, 1958, pp. 14-17; Sallust: Lemprière, pp. 540-1; Handford, pp.7-11.

15   His description of Catiline: Sallust, pp. 184-5, *V, 1, XVI, 4*. See also P. McGushin, *Sallust. The Conspiracy of Catiline. A Companion to the Penguin Translation*, Bristol Classical Press, London, 1987.

16   OK Corral: F. Waters, *The Earp Brothers of Tombstone*, Transworld, London, 1963, pp. 129, 131; J.M. Myers, *Doc Holliday*, Arrow, London, 1958, pp. 170,171.

17   Robin Hood: S. Knight (ed.) *Robin Hood. An Anthology of Scholarship and Criticism*, Brewer, Cambridge, 1999, pp. 17, 22. R. B. Dobson & J. Taylor, *Rymes of Robyn Hood. An Introduction to the English Outlaw*, Heinemann, London, 1976, p. 119.

18   Criticisms of Catiline: Cicero, Grant, 1989, p. 82, who remarked of 'horrible Sallust' and the, 'one-sided vituperation of Cicero', p. 73. Plutarch, *Cicero, X*. Juvenal, *Satire 8*, lines 231-3.

19   Pistoia and its aftermath: Sallust, *LVIII, 6 – LXI, 9*. Cicero: January, 62, Bailey, Letters, pp. 31, 32-5; Whigham, p. 16; Wiseman, p. 64.

20   Metellus Celer in Cisalpine Gaul: Garrison, p. 167; Goold, p. 3; Lee, 1990, p. xiii; Quinn, 1972, p. 139; Whigham, pp. 16-17.

21   Plato and Sappho: Reynolds, p. 70. Strabo: Saklatvala, p. 15. Lord Byron: 'Dark Sappho', *Childe Harold's Pilgrimage* 2, line 76; the Isles of Greece, *Don Juan* 3, line 86. The death of Sappho: Reynolds, pp. 7, 71, 74. For a discussion of Sappho's poetry, see Jenkyns, pp. 1-84. The complete fragments can be found in Carson.

22   Lesbos: Roche, p. xi. Pace: Powell, p. 42. Simplicity: E. Morwitz, quoted in Roche, p. xxiv. 'Luminous': Jenkyns, p. 62.

23   Moon and the Pleiades: Fragment 168B, Bing & Cohen, p. 81; Reynolds, note 21, pp. 4-5. Jenkyns, p. 77, doubted its authenticity. See also Greene, 1996a, 1996b.

24   Suidas: Harvey, p. 409. For Callimachus, see Nisetich, pp. xviii-xxi, xxiv.

25   Kerkylas: Greene, 1996b, pp. 146-7. Bawdy plays: Sharrock & Ash, p. 25.

26   Lesbianism: Greene, 1996b, pp. 15-16; Saklatvala, note 21, p. 11; Snyder, note 23, p. 36. The phallus: Roche, note 22, p. xiv. Fragment no. 99 see Vanita, pp. 37-61. See also Carson, p. x.

27   John Donne, 'Heroicall Epistle. Sapho to Philaenis'; J. Carey, *John Donne. Life, Mind and Art*, Faber & Faber, 1990, pp. 256-7.

28   Catullus, Poem 11, and Sappho, Fragment, 105A: Quinn, 1970, p. 129, n.23; Jenkyns, pp. 45-8. Virgil's simile: 'like a white poppy', Levi, 1998, p. 208.

29   R. Bums, 'Grizzel Grimme', in *The Secret Cabinet of Robert Burns*, Paul Harris, Edinburgh, 1979, p. 47. W. Barnes, 'The Wife A-Lost'. Aeolian and Attic speech: Powell, p. 36; Reynolds, p. 18.

30   Grenfell, Hunt and papyri: Reynolds, pp. 19-21; Roche, pp. xxi-xxii. Parkinson & Quirke, pp. 73-4, Fragment 57: *Times Literary Supplement*, 25 June 2004. For Tithonus, see under 'Eos' in: S. Price & E. Kearns, *Oxford Dictionary of Classical Myth and Religion*, Oxford University Press. Oxford, 2003, 188.

31   Philodeinus. 'Charito': Paton, V, line 135, no. 13. Retranslated in W. R. Paton, 'Philodemus the Epicurean', *Edinburgh Review* 237, 1923, 306-18; Obbink, 1995.

32   Herman Goering: Deiss, p. 29.

33   Pompeii and Herculaneum: Grant, 1976; A. de Franciscus, *The Buried Cities: Pompeii and Herculaneum*, Orbis, London, 1978; Etienne; A. Maiuri, *Herculaneum*, Instituto Poligrafico dello Stato, Roma, 7th ed., 1954.

34   Alcubierre and crabs: Deiss, pp. 27-8.

35   Excavation of the Villa of the Papyri: Parslow, pp. 77-106. Deep shaft: ibid, p. 85.

36   Paul Getty: Deiss, pp. 74-82.

37   Library: Casson, 2001, p. 75; Unrolling the papyri: Wright, p. 308; Etienne, pp. 150-3. Piaggio: Deiss, pp. 70-1. Slicing the rolls: R. Janko, in Obbink, p. 70; Philodemus and Sappho: *Literary and Linguistic Computing* 12 (3), Oxford University Press, 1997, pp. 159-62. Late twentieth-century excavations by building firms with no archaeologists, resumed properly, 2002. *Daily Telegraph*, 26 March, 18 May 2002, see also, Gigante, v-viii.

38   Poems: Philodemus, *Loeb*, note 28, V, lines 151-3, no. 46. On Sappho's Fragment 121, see Carson, pp. 246-7; Powell, note 22, p. 9; Roche, note 22, p. 113; Snyder, note 23, p. 99.

39   Bona Dea: Kiefer, pp. 132-4, Ogilvy, p. 97.

40   Juvenal, *Satire 6*, lines 314-51; Pomeroy, pp. 209-10. Black stone blocks: *Archaeologia* 57, 1900, 175-84.

41   Cicero to Atticus: Everitt, pp. 112-13.

42   The Bona Dea affair: Gruen, p. 248; Haskell, pp. 212-13; Taylor, p. 87.
     Cicero to Atticus: Bailey, 1999, I, p. 59. *Nifas*: Bailey, 1999, I, p. 63.

43   For an account of the life of Sappho, see Sharrock & Ash, pp. 24-31. For
     the blank page, see M. Wittig & S. Zeig, *Lesbian People: Material for
     a Dictionary*, Avon, New York, 1979, cited by Jack Winkler in Greene,
     1996a, 89.

44   Martin, 1992, p. 37.

45   Havelock, pp. 79-82.

46   Roman roads: Hazlitt, 1851, pp. 369-70. On Via Aemilia, see
     Warrington, p. 10; on Via Appia, ibid., p. 55; Via Flaminia, ibid., p. 235.
     See also *Atlas of the Classical World*, ed. A. A. M. van der Heyden & H.
     H. Scullard, Nelson, London, 1959, Map 53, p. 128.

47   Roman vehicles: Balsdon, p. 213; Casson, 1998, pp. 115-16.

48   Pompeii: Casson, 1998, pp. 117-18.

49   Catullus on 'cobwebs' in poem [13]; on houses in poem [44]; on yacht,
     poem [4].

50   Possesion of slaves: Hutchinson, p. 24.

51   Homosexuality. Greeks and Romans: Garrison, p. 104. Pedagogical
     pederasty: B. Sergent, *Homosexuality' in Greek Myth*, Boston, 1986, p.
     3. Cato: C. Miles, *Love in the Ancient World*, Seven Dials, 1997, p. 134.
     Petronius, *Satyricon X*: Arrowsmith, pp. 9, 11; Lisieux, pp. 16,18; Sullivan,
     pp. 33-4. Homoerotic love: Bing & Cohen, pp. 7-11. Sallust, *Catiline XIII*.

52   Philodemus: W. R. Paton, 'Philodemus the Epicurean', *Edinburgh
     Review 237*, 1923, 314; D. Snider, in Obbink, 1995, p. 47. Catullus,
     poem [13].

3 – A DAY IN ROME

1   Sabine women: Plutarch, *Romulus, XIV-XV*. Tarpeia: *Romulus, XVII-XX*.

2   Lemures: Ogilvie, pp. 85-6,; Persius, *Satire V*, line 185; Horace, *Epistle
    II*, 2, line 208.

3   Roman upper-class society: Havelock, p. 100.

4   The Roman day: Adkins & Adkins, pp. 338-9; Balsdon, pp. 16-19;
    Shelton, pp. 123-4; Candles: Grant, 1976, p. 122.

5   Fires in Rome: Adkins & Adkins, pp. 66-7; Casson, 1998, p. 40.

6   Catullus and bookshops: *'Ad librariorum'*, [14A]; *'omnibus libellis'*, [55].

7   Early libraries in Rome: Casson, 2001, pp. 78-81.

8   Marrucinus Asinius and napkins: Catullus, [12], lines 1-4, 10-11.
    Martial and Hermogenes, *Satire XII*, no. 28. Martial's bookseller: *Satire
    I*, no. 117.

9   Private libraries: Casson, 2001, pp. 69-79; Cicero and Atticus: Pentroski, pp. 27-8.

10   Lucullus: Plutarch, *Lucullus, XXIV-XLIII*. On his own: ibid., *XLI*. Five thousand cloaks: Horace, *Epistle, I, 6*, lines 41-4.

11   Roman names: Adkins & Adkins, pp. 243-4; Grant, 1986, p. 232; Speake, p.427.

12   The *Venatio*: Auguet, pp. 83-8.

13   Rufa and the cemetery: *Corpus Inscriptionum Latinarum* 4, 2421; Quinn, 1970, p. 262; Lindsay, 1960, p. 268.

14   Foodstalls: H. Fast, *Spartacus*, Fast, New York, 1951, p. 182. Dangers in the streets. Cicero: Casson, 1998, p. 38. Juvenal, *Satire III*, lines 268-77. Dog-collar: Casson, 1998, pp. 46-7. Darkness: Petronius, *Satyricon*, 79; Sullivan, p. 89.

15   The protective phallus: Adkins & Adkins, p. 301. On house walls: A. de Simone & M. T. Merella, in Grant, 1997, pp. 108-9.

16   Brothels in Pompeii: Lindsay, 1960, pp. 239-48. Houses with sexual murals: A. de Simone & M. T. Merella, 'The Collection', in Grant, 1997, pp. 85-166; Clarke, 1998, pp. 59-142, 145-240, map 146; Plates 1-16. Villa of Farnesina: Clarke, 1998, pp. 93-107.

17   Murals in Pompeii: B. Conticello, *Pompeii. Archaeological Guide*, Novara, 1987; Lucretius Frontone: Lindsay, 1960, f. 183. Terentius Neo: ibid., pp. 83-4.

18   Chariot-races: M. Junkelmann, 'On the starting block with Ben Hur: chariot-racing in the Circus Maximus' in E. Kohne & C. Ewigleben (eds), pp. 86-114. Starter's white cloth: ibid., p. 99; Auguet, p. 135. See also Balsdon, pp. 314-24; Carcopino, pp. 20-1; Casson, 1998, pp. 101-3.

19   Caesar and gladiatorial shows: Grant, 1969, p. 42; Meier, I, p. 48; Walter, I, pp. 54-6; Plutarch, *Caesar, V*; Suetonius, *Caesar, X*. 46 BC: Walter, II, pp. 181-2; Plutarch, *Caesar, V*.

20   Pompey's games: Beacham, pp. 63-4. Cicero: Cicero to M. Marius, August, 55 BC, Bailey, *Letters*, pp. 85-7; Pliny, *Natural History, VIII*.

21   Leisured study: Auguet, p.207. 21 Crispinus: Horace, *Satire I, 4*, lines 13-16.

22   Catia: Rudd, 1997, p. 47; Horace, *Satires I, 2*, lines 101-3.

23   Adultery in Rome: Assa, p. 92; Carcopino, p. 94; Quinn, 1972, pp. 233-7; Speake, p. 6.

24   Caesar's love-affairs: Suetonius, *Caesar, L-LII*; Plutarch, *Caesar, XLII*.

25   Postumia: Burton, 1894, p. 52; Williamson, p. 125; Lee, 1990, pp. 155-6. Mucia: Quinn, 1970, pp. 451-3.

26   Voluptas: G. G. Fagan, p. 76.

27   Latin proverb: Carcopino p. 263.

28   Murals in the suburban baths: d'Ambra, pp. 76-8; Clarke, pp. 212-40.

29   Catullus, [33], after Sisson, pp. 26-7.

30   Martial about Menogenes: Fagan, p. 23. Lavatories: Martial, *Satires XI*, 77, lines 1-3.

31   Catullus, [13]. *Cenabis bene, [name 'mi Fabulle'] apud me paucis si tibi favent, diebus . . .*

32   Juvenal, *Satires V*, lines 24-106. Cruelty to slaves: Kiefer, pp. 90-3.

33   The triclinium and dinner: Balsdon, pp. 32-54; Carcopino, pp. 265-76.

34   The wine of Trimalchio: Balme, p. 17; Arrowsmith, pp. 32, 192, note 32.

35   Gemellus' orgy: Valerius Maximus, *Facta et Dicta Memorabilia, Libri IX, I*, 8, 'Nine Books of Memorable Deeds and Sayings'; Lindsay, 1929, p. 8; Lyne, 1980, p. 15. Fulvia: Warrington, 1969, p. 238.

36   Richard Lovelace, Poem 48; Gaisser, 2001, p. 27. Symons, 1924, p. 27.

37   Mary Stewart, Poem 34; Gaisser, 2001, p. 139.

38   Quintus Arrius: Williamson, pp. 94-5, (his Poem 19). See also Harrington, p.208.

4 – POETRY AND PASSION

1   Aurelia and Clodius: Grant, 1969, p. 54.

2   The Bona Dea trial. Cowell, pp. 243-4; Gruen, p. 248; Taylor, 1984, pp. 87-8.

3   Hortensius: Williamson, p. 103. On the promise of a poem, no. 65, Gaisser, 2001, p. 225.

4   Political rivalry: Gruen, p. 273.

5   Terentia and Clodius: Plutarch, *Cicero XXIX*.

6   Cicero to Atticus, early July, 61 BC: see Bailey, *Letters*, p. 46; Perowne, pp. 174-5.

7   Corrupt jurors: Cicero, Bailey, Letters, pp. 42-6; Lindsay, 1929, pp. 8, 20-1.

8   The scandal and Caesar's reply: Walter, I, pp. 85-91.

9   Guard for the jury: Haskell, p. 216.

10   Credit: Krostenko, p. 216; Bailey, 1999, I, p. 97.

11   Incest: Cicero, De Domo Sua, in Watts, p. 243; Everitt, p. 114; Haskell, p. 217; Krostenko, pp. 182-3.

12   The new poetry: Fitzgerald, p. 6; Garrison, pp. xi-xii; Michie, 1981, pp. 12-13.

13   Laevius; Gerard Manley Hopkins: Copley, p. xii.

14   On metres: see Goold, pp. 19-27; Michie, 1981, pp. 12-15. Gallic rather than Latin: Ulrich von Wilomowitz-Mollendorff, *Geschichte Verkunst*,

Berlin, 1921, p. 139. On lost poets: see Lindsay, 1929, pp. 26-9; Martin, 1992, p. 19. See also Courtney, 1993, for Bibaculus, pp. 192-200, and Cornificius, pp. 225-7.

15   Licinius Calvus: Ovid, *Tristia*; Propertius, *Book II*, 25, line 4: Lee, 1994, p. 55. Surviving poetry: Courtney, pp. 201-11. Quintilia, ibid., p. 209. See also, Catullus [96].

16   Speech in Catullus: Copley, p. xv; Whigham, p. 45.

17   Frances P. Simpson. Goold, p. 7, quoting from 'the old school edition' of 1879.

18   The miller's donkey: Quinn, 1970, p. 434; Martin, 1990, p. xi.

19   Punishment for adultery: Burton, 1894, p. 301, note 19.

20   Fordyce and censorship: Wiseman, p. 242.

21   Homer: George Chapman, 1611, *The Odysseys of Homer, II*, London, 1907, pp. 205, 207-8.

22   Poem [32]: George Lamb, 1821, I, 'The Rendezvous', pp. 63-4. Merritt, 1893, p. 59. Invitation to tea: Gaisser, 2001, p. 116. *Fututiones*: Adams, pp. 118-22.

23   Coinage and wages: Baldson, p. 354; Shelton, pp. 129-32,327.

24   Pompeii: Lindsay, 1960; on Druca, p. 240; on Attice, p. 243. Mule and hay: *Corpus Inscriptionum Latinarum*, 9, 2689; Lindsay, 1965, 98. Prostitutes: Kiefer, pp.59-63.

25   Noses: Catullus, [41]; Villon, Burl, 2000, p. vii; Dale, 2001, pp. 124-5. Brevity: Catullus, [85]; Villon, 'Ballad from the contest at Blois', Dale, 2001, p. 220. Plays: Villon, Burl, 2000, pp. 223-5. Catullus, Bailey, Cicero: *Epistulae Ad Familiares*, 1977, p. 338; Catullus, Wiseman, pp. 187-9.

26   A young life of intensity: Havelock, p. 2; Swanson, 1959, p. vii.

27   Papyrus rolls: Casson, 2001, pp. 24-6; Parkinson & Quirke, pp. 13-19.

28   The arrangement and editing of the poems: Quinn, 1972, pp. 1, 10-20.

29   *Chiasmus*: Martin, 1992, pp. 35-6, 61-8, 172-84.

30   Harold Nicolson, *Diaries and Letters, 1945-1962*, London, 1968, 31 March 1957, p.305.

31   Censorship: Williamson, p. v; Arnold, Aronson & Lawall, p. 1.

32   Catullus as a lyric poet: Havelock, 1939, pp. 166, 183; Kiefer, pp. 185-92.

33   Poem [55]: Garrison, pp. 121-2, 123-4. Ovid, *Ars Amatoria III*, line 337.

34   The brassière: Pliny the Elder, *Natural History VIII*, Book 28, line 76; Amy Richlin, 'Pliny's Brassière', in Hallett & Skinner, pp. 197-220. Catullus' Greek pun was deliberate. Elsewhere he used the Latin *strophium* for brassière: '*non territi strophio lactentes vincta papillas*', [64], line 65.

35   Roman attitudes to homosexuality: Bing & Cohen, pp. 7-11; Garrison, pp. 104 [15],105, note 2; Martin, 1992, pp. 139-41.

36 The background to the First Triumvirate: Marsh, pp. 170-6; Perowne, pp. 175-8.

5 – CLODIA

1 'Stupid': Lindsay, 1929, pp. 7,9. Naevius: Quinn, 1972, pp. d3-4. Desertion: A. Goldsworthy, *Cannae*, 2001, pp: 160-1. Metellus and Cicero: Cicero, *Selected Letters*, January, 62 BC, lines 32-5. 'Barren seashore': Lindsay, 1929, p. 20.

2 Varus: Suetonius, *Augustus, XXIII*; Grant, 1978, p. 208.

3 Clodia: Highet, p. 25. 'Ox-Eyes': Bailey, 1999, I, pp. 161, 167, 173, 207, 211. Tortolian Maiden: d'Ambra, p. 29.

4 Vettius: Fitzgerald, p. 64; Gruen, pp. 286-7, note 103, p. 525; Lyne, pp. 15-16; Wiseman, pp. 38-9; Plutarch, *Cicero, XXIX*; R. Gardner, pp. 495, 497. *In triclinio* ..: Quintilian, 'The Orator's Education', *Institutio oratoria VIII*, 6, 54.

5 Circe and Encolpius: Arrowsmith, pp. 153-62.

6 Incest: Sextus Marius: Tacitus, *Annals of Imperial Rome VI*; Bauman, p. 60; Cicero and Claudius: Lindsay, 1929, p. 21.

7 Juvenal: Rudd, 1992, p. 54. Cruelty to slaves: Kiefer, pp. 90-3.

8 A lady's morning toiletry: Assa, pp. 59-69; Carcopino, pp. 168-9. Neumagen: Adkins & Adkins, p. 346.

9 The Clodia sisters: family tree, Wiseman, pp. 16-17. Clodia Metelli: Mulroy, pp. xiii-xvi. Character: Cicero, 'In defence of Marcus Caelius Rufus', Grant, 1989, pp. xvii, 201. Not a real love affair: Fitzgerald, p. 27.

10 Archilochos: Todd & Todd, I, p. 78; Sharrock & Ash, pp. 18-24. Philodemus' opinion: Obbink, pp. 9, 27, 272-3.

11 Chronological order: D. Bray, *The Original Order of Shakespeare's Sonnets*, Methuen, 1925. Villon and Catullus: P. Levi, *The Life and Times if William Shakespeare*, Macmillan, 1988, p. 93. 'Mr. W. H.' J. Michell, *Who Wrote Shakespeare?*, Thames & Hudson, 1996, p. 181.

12 Apuleius and his pseudonyms: Quinn, 1972, pp. 134-5. Suetonius: Lee, p. xix. Hyginus: Casson, 2001, pp. 93-4. Petrus Victorius: Quinn, 1972, pp. 134-5. Rule for pseudonyms: Bing & Cohen, p. 17; Gaisser, 1993, p. 13; Lindsay, 1929, pp. 10-11, 102. 'Corinna': P. Green, 1982, pp. 22-3. Trial: P. Ward, *Apuleius on Trial at Sabratha*, Oleander, Cambridge, 1968.

13 Legendary island: Havelock, p. 130. Fragment 5: Reynolds, p. 11.

14 Clodia's poems: Grant, 1989, p. 204; Cicero, 'In defence of Caelius'.

15 Negligée and armour: Martin, 1992, pp. 43-4. The first poet: Lyne, 1980, p. 60.

16   Sappho, Fragment 31V in Carson, pp. 62-3; Greene, 1996a, pp. 66, 129-30; 1996b, pp. 68-78; Powell, pp. 23-4; Roche, pp. 44-5; Snyder, p. 72. Catullus and Sappho: Reynolds, pp. 72, 75-6; References such as [51, 51B] refer to the poems translated by Clucas on pp. 221-48. For the original Latin, see: Quinn (1950).

17   The ending of [51]: Garrison, p. 120; Lindsay, 1948, p. 107, his poem 1; Michie, p. 212, note 83; Williamson, pp. 110-11; (his poem 36); Wiseman, pp. 151-7.

18   Skelton. Poems by John Skelton, ed. R. Gant, Grey Walls Press, London, 1949.

19   'Basia': Martin, 1972, p. xv. The Lesbias and courtship: Quinn, 1970, p. 112. Classical references in [7]: Fordyce, pp. 108-10, J. Hollander & F. Kermode, *The Literature of Renaissance England*, O. U. P., 1973: Campion, 510; Daniel, 409; Jonson, 577, 581.

20   Right foot first: Arrowsmith, p. 190; Sullivan, p. 47. Brides and the threshold:
S. Baker, 'Lesbia's foot', Classical Philology 55, 1960, 171-3; Fitzgerald, p. 208; Fordyce, p. 385; Quinn, 1970, p. 272 [61].

21   Cicero, 'Pro Caelio'; Grant, 1989, pp. 201-2. Poison: Lee, p. xxvii; Whigham, p. 17.

22   Poisons: Cleopatra: Plutarch, *Mark Antony LXXI*; Ivar Lisser, *Power & Folly. The Story of the Caesars*, Jonathan Cape, 1958, pp. 78-9. Claudius: Tacitus, *Annals XII*, p. 66; A. Massie, *The Caesars*, Seeker & Warburg, 1983, p. 148. Britannicus: Tacitus, *Annals XIII*, p. 14; M. Grant, *Nero*, Weidenfeld & Nicolson, 1970, pp. 46-7; Lissner, pp. 122-3; Massie, p. 154. Locusta: Suetonius, Nero, 33; Tacitus, *Annals XIII*, p. 14.

23   Funerals: Harlow & Laurence, pp. 135-41; Adkins & Adkins, pp. 356-8.

24   Baiae: Baldson, pp. 201, 204, 221; Casson, 1998, pp. 112, 113, 145. Propertius, *Poems, I,* 11, lines 27-30. Laevina: Martial, *Satires, I,* line 62, Ker, 1969, p. 69.

25   Publius Clodius Pulcher: Gruen, pp. 97-8. As tribune: Grant, 1969, pp. 77-9.

26   Cyprus, Cato and talents: Oman, pp. 218-19. The banishment of Cicero: Cowell, pp. 244-6; Everett, pp. 138-40; Haskell, p. 237f. Speech of Clodius: Hutchinson, p.174.

27   Caelius Rufus on Pompey: Haskell, p. 272. Wiseman on Caelius Rufus, p. 63.

28   The career of Caelius Rufus: Haskell, p. 43; Wiseman, pp. 42, 62-8.

6 – BITHYNIA, VERONA, ROME

1   Bithynia and business. Wiseman, pp. 100-1; Goold, p. 2; Lee, pp. xviii-xix.

2   Gaius Memmius: Latham 'Appendix B', pp. 251-4. See also Hazel, p. 194; Highet, p. 23; Lee, p. xxviii; Lindsay, 1929, p. 115; Williamson, p. 4. Poem: Courtney, p.233.

3   Extortion of provinces: Gruen, pp. 502-6.

4   Journeys by sea: Balsdon, pp. 226-7.

5   Corruption: Marsh & Scullard, pp. 336-9; McDonald, pp. 151-4; Moore, pp.47-9.

6   Galli: Sir J. G. Frazer, *The Golden Bough, IV, I, Adonis, Attis, Osiris*, pp. 265-8, 277-80.

7   British gallus: P. R. Wilson (ed.), *Caractonium. Roman Catterick and its Hinterland, I, II*, Council for British Archaeology, York, 2002, II, pp. 41-2, 467; grave, p. 951, site, p. 46.

8   Artis: Grant & Hazel, pp. 59-60.

9   Pergamum and parchment: Casson, 2001, pp. 48, 52.

10 Livy, *Ab Urbe Condita*, 'From the City's Foundations', Book XXIX, 'The War with Hannibal', B. Radice (ed.), Penguin, 1972, pp. 578-80.

11 Claudia Quinta: Livy, ibid., note 10, p. 584; Ovid, *Fasti, IV*, lines 275-336; Vermarseren, pp. 41-2.

12 Hannibal's gesture: E. Bradford, *Hannibal*, Macmillan, 1981, pp. 191-2, 203; S. Lancel, *Hannibal*, trans. A. Nevill, Blackwell, 1998, p. 146. Caesar, coins and elephants: J. Addison, *Spectator 59*, 11 May, 1711; '*Elephantus* in Punic was pronounced "Caesar"', F. C. Sillar and R. M. Meyler, *Elephants Ancient and Modern*, Studio Vista, 1968, p. 29.

13 Cybele's Temple, *Aedes Magna Mater*, Platner & Ashby, pp. 324-5; Vermaseren, pp.42-56.

14 Acrostics: Jonson, 'Volpone' in: *Three Comedies*, Penguin, 1985, p. 49. Newton: *Poetry Today 5*, 1952, p. 9. Villon: Burl, 2000, pp. 119-30; Dale, 2001, p. 126.

15 Catullus [60]: The acrostic was first noticed by Goold, p. 248. See also Martin, 1992, p. 72.

16 Cicero's welcome: to Atticus, 10 September, p. 57; Bailey, *Letters*, p. 68.

17 Rome: Oman, p. 277. Cicero and disorder: Bailey, 1999, I, p. 301; Plutarch, *Cicero XXXIII*; Everett, pp. 136-47; Gruen, pp. 440-1. Cicero's three houses: Bailey, 1999, I, p. 297.

18 Ptolemy Auletes. Historians disagree on whether he was Ptolemy XI or XII. He was XII. His removal and restoration: Gruen, pp. 306-8; Perowne, pp. 161-2. Lightning: Perowne, p. 185.

19 Caelius Rufus accused of crimes and the murder of Dio: Gruen, pp. 305-6.

20 Jupiter, lightning and the Sibylline Books: Perowne, p. 185.

21 Cleopatra as ruler of Egypt: Southern, 2000, pp. 20-5.

22 Shambles: Gruen, p. 146, Lucca: Perowne, pp. 186-7; Marsh, pp. 192-3; Gruen, pp. 100-1, 146-7.

23 On poem [101], Fitzgerald, pp. 185-9; Garrison, pp. xiii, 98, note 11.

24 The voyage: Garrison, p. 96; Goold, p. 227; Quinn, 1970, p. 230; Whigham, p. 14. P. d'Epiro and M. D. Pinkowish, *What are the Seven Wonders of the World?*, 1999: Ephesus, pp. 148-9; Colossus of Rhodes, pp. 150-1. Temple of Aphrodite, Corinth: Lemprière, p. 172. Xenophon: Miles & Norwich, pp. 77-8.

25 Family deaths: Lee, 1990,:pp. 115, [68A], 22; [68B], 94; 12,31.

26 The trial: Cicero, 'In defence of Marcus Caelius Rufus', Grant, 1989, pp. 165-214; Highet, pp. 45-51; Wiseman, pp. 62-90. There is a good translation of Cicero's speech in Steven Saylor's *The Venus Throw*, 1999, pp. 316-38.

27 Husband/brother: Grant, 1989, p. 184. Friend of all men: Saylor p. 323, note 26.

28 Character of Clodia: Grant, 1989, p. 199.

29 Clodia and her slaves: Saylor, p. 331, note 26.

30 Messalina: Juvenal in P. Green, 1974, p. 131; S. Perowne, *The Caesars' Wives. Above Suspicion?*, Hodder & Stoughton, 1974, pp. 59-69. A relation of Clodia's: see family tree, Wiseman, pp. 16-17.

31 Caesar, *The Gallic War, III*, trans. H.J. Edwards, Heinemann, 1979, pp. 147-61; Tumiac: Burl, *Megalithic Brittany*, Thames & Hudson, 1985, pp. 108-9.

32 Poem [10]: Fordyce, pp. 116-24.

7 – FINAL YEARS

1 Election: Taylor, pp. 143-4.

2 Catullus, a traditional background: Fitzgerald, p. 29; Wiseman, pp. 110-13, 118-21.

3 Catullus and marriage: Martin, 1995, p. 175.

4 Martin, 1990, p. xiii.

5 Tanusius Geminus as Volusius: 'Thinly disguising his name', Fordyce, p. 179; Simpson, p. 95. A historian: *Suetonius, The Twelve Caesars. Julius Caesar, IX.*

6 Mamurra: Garrison, p. 123; Quinn, 1970, p. 258. Caesar and Catullus: Suetonius, *The Twelve Caesars. Julius Caesar, LXXIII.*

7 Ameana: Martin, 1992, pp. 60-4. Garrison, pp. 116-17; Lee, 1990, p. 160; Quinn, 1970. Ten thousand *sestertii*: Legionary: Shelton, p. 452. Clivus Victoriae: Grant, 1989, p. 175; R. G. Austin, *Cicero. Pro Caelio*, Oxford University Press, 1988, pp. 7, 17, '*decem milibus [dixistis]*'.

8 Lucius Gellius Poplicola and Crixus: Shaw, pp. 133, 139, 151.

9 Gellius 'poems: [88]: Fitzgerald, p. 81; Poem [80], Wray, p. 157; Poem [78], Copley, p. 100.

10 The 'trial' of Gellius Maximus *Nine Books of Memorable Deeds and Sayings*, V, 9,1; Gruen, pp. 33n, 306n, 527.

11 The tradition that Persian magi ... practised incest with their mothers is reported by Strabo, *Geography, XV*, p. 735.

12 On poem [116] and its place in the canon see Garrison, p. 163, 'a vain attempt to make peace'; Goold, p. 264, 'last, not by any design of Catullus', but simply because it was the last epigram to come to the editor's desk'; Quinn, 1970, p. 455, 'Is Poem 116 a prelude to the savage attacks ... rather than a last word?'; Williamson (his poem 10), p. 89, 'hurling at his enemy's head five unprintable poems'.

13 On translations of *glubit*, [58]: 'deepthroat', Raphael & McLeish, p. 63; 'husk', 1894, p. 100; 'milking', Michie, 1981, p. 89; 'peel', Fitzgerald, p. 76, Lee, p. 55; 'public lips', Symons, p. 31; 'rub up', Swanson, p. 50; 'sap', Goold, p. 105, Wiseman; p. 156; 'shuck', Martin, 1990, p. 59, Wray, p. 45; 'skin', Mulroy, p. 43; 'suck', Lindsay, 1929; 'toss off, Whigham, p. 118; 'gluts', Benita Kane Jaro, *The Key*, 1988, p. 229, 'A Note', p. 239.

14 *Attis*: Garrison, pp. 133-3. Galliambics: Tennyson, 'Boadicea', Gaisser, pp. 282-3.

15 The consular elections for 54 BC: Gruen, p. 54.

16 Death of Julia: Southern, 2001, pp. 56, 79.

17 Caesar in Britain, 54 BC: Fuller, pp. 125-7; Southern, 2001, pp. 76-7. The Armada: G. Mattingly, *The Defeat of the Spanish Armada*, Cape, 1959, p. 189.

18 Disease and doctors: Balsdon, p. 111; Adkins & Adkins, pp. 261, 354-5.

19 Public performance of *Attis*: Wiseman, pp. 200-3.

20 Catullus as a playwright: Wiseman, pp. 188-9; Bailey: 'Two studies in Roman nomenclature', *American Classical Studies 3*, 1976, 71.

21 Possible lines from plays by Catullus: Wiseman, p. 192, and Appendix, 'References to Catullus in ancient authors', pp. 246-60. Juvenal, *Satires VIII*, line 186; XIII, line 111; on Caligula, Wiseman, pp. 188-9.

22 Arrangement of the *Libri*: Goold, pp. 8-9; Quinn, 1972, pp. 277-82.

23 Ovid and the early death of Catullus: Green, 1982, p. 156.

8 – POSTMORTEM

1   Crassus. The curse: Warner, 1972, p. 133.
2   Parthia: Plutarch, *Crassus, XVI-XXXIII*; Oman, pp. 197,202.
3   Riots in Rome: Oman, p. 277.
4   Clodius and Milo: transport, Balsdon, p. 213. Cremation of Clodius, Millar, pp. 181-3.
5   Cicero and Milo: Lemprière, p. 370; Grant, 1989, pp. 215-78; ibid., 1990, pp. 295-6; Millar, pp. 182-5.
6   Pompey's last years and murder: Southern, 2002, pp. 125-41; Plutarch, *Pompey, LXXVIII-LXXX*; Oman, p. 287. Birthday, Plutarch, *Camillus, XIX*.
7   Cleopatra, the carpet and Caesar: Plutarch, *Caesar, XLIX*.
8   Caelius Rufus and Milo: Caesar, *The Civil War, III*; Oman, pp. 332-3.
9   News of Mamurra; Cicero to Atticus, 19 December, 45 BC: Bailey, Letters, p.193.
10 The death of Caesar: Plutarch, *Caesar, LXVI*. One fatal wound: Suetonius, *Caesar, LXXXII*.
11 Death of Cinna: Plutarch, *Caesar, LXVIII*; Shakespeare, *Julius Caesar, III*, 3, 34.
12 Cicero and Mark Antony: Cicero, *Philippics V*, line 18; W. C. A. Ker, Cicero. Philippics, Heinemann, London, 1969, p. 273.
13 The death of Cicero: Cowell, pp. 265-8; Everett, pp. 298-310; Haskell, pp. 345-50.
14 Deaths of the conspirators: Suetonius, *Caesar, LXXXIX*
15 Cleopatra's barge: Plutarch, *Mark Antony, XXVI*; Southern, 2000, pp. 78-80; L. Foreman, *Cleopatra's Palace: In Search of a Legend*, Discovery, London, 1999, pp. 196-7.
16 Cleopatra's reputation: M. P. Charlesworth, quoted in, J. F. C. Fuller, *A Military History of the Western World I*, Cassell, London, 1954, p. 219.
17 Death of Mark Antony: Plutarch, *Mark Antony, LXXVI-LXXVII*.
18 Cleopatra's asp: Plutarch, *Mark Antony, LXXI*. Death: J. Lindsay, *Cleopatra*, Constable, 1971, pp. 420-37; Southern, 2000, pp. 144-5. Death of Caesarion: Plutarch, *Mark Antony, LXXXII*.
19 Clodia and Cicero: Wiseman, pp. 42-3; Bailey, 1999, I, p. 173. Her suburban property: Bailey, 1999, I, pp. 301, 305; III, pp. 339, IV, pp. 282-8,288. Pessimism and optimism: ibid., IV, pp. 3, 35, 37; Lindsay, 1929, pp. 101-2.
20 'What Clodia has done': Bailey, 1999, IV, p. 155. Death of Clodia: Whigham, p.19.

APPENDIX I – PELEUS AND THETIS

1   Lucretius, *De Rerum Natura* in Goold, p. 250.

2   Ulrich von Wilamotz-Moellendorff, *Hellenistische Dichtung in der Zeit von Callimachus*, ('Hellenistic poetry in the time of Callimachus'), 2 vols, Berlin, 1924, pp. 2,298. 'Staked his reputation': 'What would we make of Shakespeare if we had only the Sonnets and one play?', Michie, 1981, p. 8.

3   On poem [64]: 'Catullus and the idea of a masterpiece', Jenkyns, pp. 85-150; Havelock, p. 77; Martin, 1992, 'On passionate virtuosity', pp. 151-71, 'Lifting the poet's fingerprints', pp. 172-85.

4   References to earlier stories of the Argonauts and the Golden Fleece: Pindar, *Fourth Pythian Ode*; Euripides, *Medea*; Apollonius Rhodius, *Argonautica*.

APPENDIX II – THE RECOVERY OF THE POEMS OF CATULLUS

1   The monk, Hildemar: Gaisser, 1993, p. 17, also p. 283, note 70. Bishop Rather of Verona and Lobbes: ibid., p. 17.

2   Virgil: Levi, p. 19. Horace: Rudd, 1997, p. 79. Propertius: Lee, 1994, p. 55.

3   Ovid: P. Green, 1982, p. 156.

4   Juvenal: P. Green, 1974, pp. 127, 183, 253.

5   Martial, *Satire XI*; line 104: Cornelia, Portia and Julia were the well-born wives of the patricians: Sempronius Gracchus, Brutus and Pompey the Great. What Martial states as fact about male-female sodomy is unproven. Prostitutes preferred anal intercourse to avoid pregnancy. Whether it became fashionable for high-class women is unclear. See Clarke, 1998, pp. 84-7, 229-31, Plate 14; Miles & Norwich, pp. 74, 75.

6   Martial's influence: Whigham, 1985, p. 18.

7   William of Malmesbury, *Gesta Regum Anglorum*, c.1142, Book 2, part 159, Llanerch Press reprint, 1989, pp. 140-1. Catullus, poems [6], line 2; [10], line 3.

8   The development of the codex: Casson, 2001, pp. 124-35; Martin, 1992, p. 31.

9   Codex 'V'. Chapter library, Verona: Gaisser, 1993, p. 17. Not in the bung of a wine-cask: Raphael & McLeish, p. 11. Archdeacon Pacificus: J. E. Sandys, *A History of Classical Scholarship, I*, Cambridge, 1903, p. 603.

10   On the poem of Benvenuto Campesani: the puns: Lindsay, 1929, p. 115. History: Goold, 29; Martin, 1990, p. xx; Matthew, 5, 15; Wray, pp. 6-10. Can Grande: Goold, p. 235.

11   Codices 'V', 'X', 'O', 'G' and 'R': Fordyce, 1978, pp. xxv-xxviii; Gaisser, 1993, pp. 18-23; Lee, 1990, pp. ix-xi; Primacy of 'O': Quinn, 1970, p. xxiii.

BIBLIOGRAPHY

Adams, J. N. (1982) *The Latin Sexual Vocabulary*, Duckworth, London

Adkins, L. and R. A. (1994) *Handbook to Life in Ancient Rome*, Oxford University Press, Oxford

Ambra. *see* d'Ambra

Arnold, B., Aronson, A., and Lawall, G., (2000) *Love and Betrayal. A Catullus Reader*, Prentiss Hall, Upper Saddle River

Arrowsmith, W. (trans.) (1962) *Petronius. The Satyricon*, University of Michigan, Ann Arbor

Assa, J. (1960) *The Great Roman Ladies*, trans. A. Hollander, Evergreen, London

Auguet, R. (1975) *The Roman Games*, trans. George Allen & Unwin, Panther, St Albans

Bailey, D. R. Shackleton (trans.) (1986) *Cicero. Selected Letters*, Penguin, London

—(1993) *Martial. Epigrams III, Books XI-XIV*, Harvard University Press, Cambridge, Mass.

—(trans.) (1999) *Cicero. Letters to Atticus, I-IV*, Heinemann, London

Baker, A. (2000) *The Gladiator*, Ebury Press, London

Balme, M. G. (1974) *The Millionaire's Dinner Party*, Oxford University Press, London

Balmer, J. (1992) *Sappho. Poems and Fragments,* Bloodaxe Books, Tarset.

—(2004a). *Chasing Catullus, Poems, Translations and Transgressions.* Bloodaxe Books, Tarset

—(2004b). *Catullus. Poems of Love and Hate.* Bloodaxe Books, Tarset

Balsdon, J. P. V. D. (2002) *Life and Leisure in Ancient Rome*, Phoenix, London

Bauman, R. A. (1996) *Crime and Punishment in Ancient Rome*, Routledge, London

Beacham, R. C. (1999) *Spectacle Entertainments of Early Imperial Rome*, Yale University Press, London

Bing, P. and Cohen, R. (eds) (1991) *Games of Venus. An Anthology of Greek and Roman Erotic Verse from Sappho to Ovid*, Routledge, London

Bradford, E. (1971) *Cleopatra*, Penguin, London

Braund, S. and Mayer, R. (eds) (1999) *Amor Roma. Love and Latin Literature*, Cambridge Philological Society, Cambridge

Burl, A. (2000) *Danse Macabre. François Villon. Poetry and Murder in Medieval France*, Alan Sutton, Thrupp

Burton, Sir R. F. and Smithers, L. C. (trans.) (1894) *The Carmina of Gaius Valerius Catullus. Englished into 'Verse and Prose*, Privately printed, London (1928) *The Carmina of Gaius Valerius Catullus*, illustrated, privately printed, New York

Caesar, Gaius Juiius (1967) *The Civil War . . .*, trans. J. F. Gardner, Penguin, London

—(See also Fuller; Grant, 1969; Meier; Oman, pp. 289-340; Southern, 2001; Walter)

Callimachus, *see* Nisetich

Campbell, D. A. Trans. (1990) *Greek Lyrics, I. Sappho and Alcaeus*. Harvard University Press, Cambridge, Mass.

Carcopino, J. (1992) *Daily Life in Ancient Rome*, trans. E. O. Lorimer, Yale University Press, London

Carson, A. (trans.) (2002) *If Not, Winter. Fragments of Sappho*, A. A. Knopf, New York

Casson, L. (1998) *Everyday Life in Ancient Rome*, Johns Hopkins University Press, Baltimore

—(2001) *Libraries in the Ancient World*, Yale University Press, New Haven

Catiline (Lucius Sergius Catilina), *see* Handford (Sallust); Hardy; Hutchinson

Cicero, Marcus Tullius, *see* Bailey 1986, 1999; Cowell, 1956; Everett; R. Gardner; Grant, 1989, 1990; Haskell; Ker, 1968, 1969; Macdonald; Watts

Clarke, J. R. (1998) *Looking at Love. Constructions of Sexuality in Roman Art, 100 BC-AD 250*, University of California Press, Berkeley

Cleopatra, *see* Bradford; Foss; Lindsay, 1971; Southern, 2000; Walker & Higgs

Clucas, H. (trans.) (1985) *Versions of Catullus*, Agenda Editions, London

Copley, F. O. (trans.) (1964) *Gaius Valerius Catullus. The Complete Poetry*, University of Michigan Press, Ann Arbor

Corelis, J. (trans.) (1995) *Roman Erotic Elegy*, University of Salzburg, Salzburg

Cornish, F. W. (trans.) (1938) *The Poems of Gaius Valerius Catullus*, 2nd ed. G. P. Goold (ed.), Heinemann, London (with Tibullus; Pervigilium Veneris)

Coulston, J. and Dodge, H. (eds) (2000) *Ancient Rome. The Archaeology of the Eternal City*, Oxford University School of Archaeology, Oxford

Courtney, E. (1993) *The Fragmentary Latin Poets*, Clarendon Press, Oxford

Cowell, F. R. (1956) *Cicero and the Roman Republic*, Pelican, Harmondsworth

—(1962) *The Revolutions of Ancient Rome*, Thames & Hudson, London

Crassus, Marcus, Licinius, *see* Oman, pp. 162-203

Dale, P. (trans.) (2001) *Poems of François Villon*, Anvil Press Poetry, London

D'Ambra, E. (1998) *Art and Identity in the Roman World*, Weidenfeld & Nicolson, London

Davies, Rev. J. (1898) *Catullus, Tibullus and Propertius*, Blackwood, London

Deiss, J.J. (1985) *Herculaneum. Italy's Buried Treasure*, Harper & Row, New York

Dinnage, P. (trans.) (1999) *Petronius. Satyricon*, Wordsworth, Ware

Duff, P. W. (1971) *Personality in Roman Law*, A. M. Kelley, New York

Edwards, J. (trans.) (1988) *The Roman Cookery of Apicius*, Rider, London

Etienne, R. (1992) *Pompeii. The Day a City Died*. trans. C. Palmer, Thames & Hudson, London

Everett, A. (2001) *Cicero. A Turbulent Life*, John Murray, London

Fagan, G. F. (1999) *Bathing in Public in the Roman World*, Michigan University Press, Ann Arbor

Fitzgerald, W. (1999) *Catullan Provocations. Lyric Poetry and the Drama of Position*, University of California Press, Berkeley

Fordyce, C.J. (1978) *Catullus. A Commentary*, Clarendon Press, Oxford

Foreman, L. and Goddio, F. (eds) (1998) *Cleopatra's Palace. In Search of a Legend*, Discovery Books, London

Foss, M. (1977) *The Search for Cleopatra*, Michael O'Mara, London

Fuller, J. F. C. (1965) *Julius Caesar: Man, Soldier and Tyrant*, Eyre & Spottiswood, London

Gaisser, J. H. (1993) *Catullus and His Renaissance Readers*, Clarendon Press, Oxford

—(ed.) (2001) *Catullus in English*, Penguin, London, 2001

Gardner, J. F. (trans.) (1967) *Caesar. The Civil War. ..*, Penguin, London

Gardner, R. (trans.) (1965) *Cicero. Pro Caelio . ..*, Heinemann, London

Garrison, D. H. (1989) *The Student's Catullus*, Oklahoma University Press, Norman

Gigante, M. (2002) *Philodemus in Italy. The Books from Herculaneum*, trans. D. Obbink, University of Michigan Press, Ann Arbor

Godwin, J. (trans.) (1999) *Catullus. The Shorter Poems*, Aris & Phillips, Warminster

—(trans.) (2002) *Catullus. Poems 61-68*, Aris & Phillips, Warminster

Goold, G. P. (trans.) (1989) *Catullus*, 2nd edition Duckworth, London

Grant, M. (ed.) (1958) *Roman Readings*, Pelican, Harmondsworth

—(1960) *The World of Rome*, Weidenfeld & Nicolson, London

—(1969) *Julius Caesar*, Chancellor Press, London

—(1971) *Gladiators*, Pelican, Harmondsworth

—(1976) *Cities of Vesuvius. Pompeii & Herculaneum*, Penguin, Harmondsworth

—(1978) *History of Rome*, Weidenfeld & Nicolson, London

—(trans.) (1989) *Cicero, Selected Political Speeches*, Penguin, London

—(trans.) (1990) *Cicero. Murder Trials*, Penguin, London

—(trans.) (1996) *Tacitus. The Annals of Imperial Rome*, Penguin Classics, London

—and Hazel, J. (1993) *Who's Who in Classical Mythology*, Routledge, London

—and Mulas, A. (1975) *Eros in Pompeii. The Erotic Art Collection of the Museum of Naples*, Stewart, Tabori & Chang, New York

Graves, R. (trans.) (1957) *Suetonius. The Twelve Caesars*, Penguin, Harmondsworth

Green, P. (trans.) (1974) *Juvenal. The Sixteen Satires*, Penguin, Harmondsworth (trans.) (1982) *Ovid. The Erotic Poems*, Penguin, London

Greene, E. (ed.) (1996a) *Reading Sappho. Contemporary Approaches*, University of California Press, Berkeley

—(ed.) (1996b) *Re-Reading Sappho. Reception and Transmission*, University of California Press, Berkeley

Gregory, H. (trans.) (1931) *The Poems of Catullus*, Covici-Friede, New York

Gruen, E. S. (1974) *The Last Generation of the Roman Republic*, California University Press, Berkeley

Hallett, J. P. and Skinner, M. B. (eds) (1997) *Roman Sexualities*, Princeton University Press, Princeton, New Jersey

Handford, S. A. (trans.) (1963) *Sallust. Jugurthine War; The Conspiracy of Catiline*, Penguin, Harmondsworth

Hardy, E. G. (1924) *The Catilinarian Conspiracy in its Context: a Re-Study of the Evidence*, Blackwell, Oxford

Harlow, M. and Laurence, R. (2002) *Growing Up and Growing Old in Ancient Rome*, Routledge, London

Harrington, K. P. (n. d.) *Catullus and his Influence*, Harrap, London

Harrisson, J. A. B. (trans.) (1980) *Catullus. A Brief Memoir*, Southwold Press, Southwold

Haskell, H.J. (1942) *This Was Cicero. Modern Politics in a Roman Toga*, Secker & Warburg, London,

Hazlitt, W. (1851) *The Classical Gazetteer. A Dictionary of Ancient Sites*, Whittaker, London

Havelock, E. A. (1939) *The Lyric Genius of Catullus*, Blackwell, Oxford

Hazel, J. (2001) *Who's Who in the Roman World*, Routledge, London

Highet, G. (1959) *Poets in a Landscape*, Pelican, Harmondsworth

Horace (Quintus Horatius Flaccus), *see* Lyne, 1995; Rudd, 1997; West, 1997; Lyne, 1980

Howatson, M. C. (1989) The Oxford Companion to Classical Literature, Oxford University Press, Oxford

Hutchinson, L. (1966) *The Conspiracy of Catiline*, Anthony Blond, London

Jaro, Benita, Kane (1988) *The Key*, Dodd, Mead & Co., New York

Jay, P. & Lewis, C. ed. (1996) *Sappho Through English Poetry*. Anvil, London.

Jenkyns, R. (1982) *Three Classical Poets. Sappho, Catullus and Juvenal*, Harvard University Press, Cambridge

Johns, C. (1982) *Sex or Symbol. Erotic Images of Greece and Rome*, Colonnade, London

Jones, P. (1998) *Classics in Translation. From Homer to Juvenal*, Duckworth, London

Juvenal (Decimus Junius Juvenalis), *see* Green, 1974; Jenkyns; Rudd, 1992

Kebric, R. B. (1993) *Roman People*, Mayfield Publishing, Mountain View, California

Ker, W. R. A. (trans.) (1968) *Martial. Epigrams, I*, Heinemann, London

—(trans.) (1969) *Cicero. Philippics, I-XIV*, Heinemann, London

Kiefer, O. (trans.) anon., *Sexual Life in Ancient Rome*, Abbey, London

Kohne, E. and Ewigleben, C. (2000) *Gladiators and Caesars*, trans. A. Bell, British Museum, London

Krostenko, B. A. (2001) *Cicero, Catullus and the Language of Social Performance*, University of Chicago, Chicago

Kyle, D. G. (1998) *Spectacles of Death in Ancient Rome*, Routledge, London

Lamb, Hon. G. (trans.) (1821) *The Poems oj Caius Valerius Catullus, with a Priface and Notes, I, II*, John Murray, London

Latham, R. E. (trans.) (1994) *Lucretius. On the Nature of the Universe*, Penguin, London

Laurence, R. (1999) *The Roads of Roman Italy. Mobility and Cultural Change*, Routledge, London

Lee, G. (trans.) (1990) *The Poems of Catullus*, Clarendon Press, Oxford

—(trans.) (1994) *Propertius. The Poems*, Oxford University Press, Oxford

—(trans.) (2000) *Ovid in Love*, John Murray, London

Lemprière, J. (n.d.) *A Classical Dictionary . . .*, Routledge, London

Levi, P. (1998) *Virgil. His Life and Times*, St Martin's Press, New York

Lindsay, J. (trans.) (1929) *Gaius Valerius Catullus. The Complete Works*, Fanfrolico Press, London

—(trans.) (1948) *Catullus. The Complete Poems*, Sylvan Press, London

—(1960) *The Writing on the Wall. An Account of Pompeii in its Last Days*, Muller, London

—(trans.) (1965) *Ribaldry of Ancient Rome. An Intimate Portrait of Romans in Love*, Frederick Ungar, New York

—Cleopatra, (1971) Constable, London

Liseux, I. (trans.) (1889) *The 'Satyricon' of Titus Petronius Arbiter*. Complete Translation, Liseux, Paris

Lucretius (Titus Lucretius Cams), *see* Latham; West, 1994

Lugli, G. (1958) *The Roman Forum and the Palatine*, Bardi Editore, Rome

Lyne, R. O. A. M. (1980) *The Latin Love Poets. From Catullus to Horace*, Clarendon Press, Oxford

—(1995) *Horace. Behind the Public Poetry*, Yale University Press, London

McDonald, A. H. (1966) *Republican Rome*, Thames & Hudson, London

Macdonald, C. (ed.) (1986) *Cicero. De Imperio Cn Pompei ad Quirites Oratio*, Bristol Classical Press, Bristol

MacLeod, R. (ed.) (2000) *The Library of Alexandria. Centre of Learning in the Ancient World*, R. B. Tauris, London

Maiuri, A. (1954) *Herculaneum*, Instituto Poligrafico Delio Stato, Rome

Marshall, F. B. and Scullard, H. H. (1963) *A History of the Roman World from 146 to 30 BC*, Methuen, London

Martial (Marcus, Valerius Martialis), *see* Bailey, 1993; Ker, 1968; Michie, 1978,2002; Whigham, 1985

Martin, C. (trans.) (1979) *The Poems of Catullus*, Johns Hopkins University Press, Baltimore

—(1992) *Catullus*, Yale University Press, London

Meier, C. (trans.) (1996) *Caesar*, D. McKlintock, Fontana Press, London

Merritt, E. T. (1893) *Catullus. Edited with Commentary and Critical Appendix*, Harvard University Press, Cambridge, Mass.

Michie, J. (trans.) (1978) *Martial. The Epigrams*, Penguin, Harmondsworth

—(trans.) (1981) *The Poems of Catullus*, Folio Society, London

—(trans.) (1996) *From Bed to Bed. Catullus*, Phoenix, London

—(trans.) (2002) *Martial. Epigrams*, intro. S. Bartsch, Modern Library, New York

Miles, C. with Norwich, J. J. (1997) *Love in the Ancient World*, Seven Dials, London

Miles, G. B. (1995) *Livy. Reconstructing Early Rome*, Cornell University Press, Ithaca

Millar, F. (1998) *The Crowd in Rome in the Late Republic*, Michigan University Press, Ann Arbor

Moore, R. W. (1942) *The Roman Commonwealth*, Hodder & Stoughton, London

Mulroy, D. (trans.) (2002) *The Complete Poetry of Catullus*, University of Wisconsin, Madison

Munro, H. A. J. (1938) *Criticisms and Elucidations of Catullus*, Stetchert, New York

Myers, R. and Ormsby, R. J. (trans.) (1972) *Catullus. The Complete Poems for Modern Readers*, Unwin, London

Nisetich, F. (2001) *The Poems of Callimachus*, Oxford University Press, Oxford

Obbink, D. (ed.) (1995) *Philodemus and Poetry. Poetic Theory & Practice in Lucretius, Philodemus and Horace*, Oxford University Press, Oxford

Ogilvie, R. M. (1969) *The Romans and Their Gods*, Charto & Windus, London

Oman, Sir C. (1902) *Seven Statesmen of the Later Republic*, Arnold, London

Ovid (Publius Ovidius Naso), *see* Green; Lee, 2000

Parkinson, R. and Quirke, S. (1995) *Papyrus*, British Museum

Parslow, C. C. (1995) *Rediscovering Antiquity. Karl Weber and the Excavation of Herculaneum, Pompeii, and Stabiae*, Cambridge University Press, Cambridge

Paton, W. R. (trans.) (1993) *The Greek Anthology, Bks. I-VI*, Loeb Classical Library, Harvard University Press, Cambridge, Mass.

Payne, R. (1964) *The Roman Triumph*, Pan, London

Perowne, S. (1969) *Death of the Roman Republic. From 146 BC to the Birth of the Roman Empire*, Hodder & Stoughton, London

Petronius, Gaius, *see* Arrowsmith; Balme; Lisieux; Sullivan; Walsh

Petroski, H. (1999) *The Book on the Bookshelf*, Knopf, New York

Philodemus, *see* Obbink; Wright

Platner, S. B. and Ashby, T. (1929) *A Topographical Dictionary of Ancient Rome*, Oxford University Press, London

Plutarch, *see* Stewart and Long; Warner

Pomeroy, S. B. (1994) *Goddesses, Whores, Wives, and Slaves. Women in Classical Antiquity*, Pimlico, London

Pompey (Gnaeus Pompeius, 'Magnus'), *see* Oman, pp. 234-88; Southern, 2002

Poole, A. and Maule, H. (eds.) (1995) *The Oxford Book of Classical Verse*, Oxford University Press, Oxford

Powell, J. M. (trans.) (1993) *Sappho. A Garland. The Poems and Fragments of Sappho*, Farrar Straus Giroux, New York

Propertius (Sextus Aurelius Propertius), *see* Lee, 1994

Quinn, K. F. (1969) *The Catullan Revolution*, University of Michigan, Ann Arbor

—(1970) *Catullus. The Poems*, Macmillan, London

—(1972) *Catullus: an Interpretation*, Batsford, London

Rakos, S. (1989) *Catullan Games*, trans. J. Kessler and M. Korosy, Marlboro Press, Marlborough, Vermont

Raphael, F. and McLeish, K. (trans.) (1978) *The Poems of Catullus*, Jonathan Cape, London

Rayor, D. J. and Batstone, W. W. (eds.) (1995) *Latin Lyric and Elegiac Poetry*, Garland, New York

Reynolds, M. (ed.) (2000) *The Sappho Companion*, Chatto & Windus, London

Roche, P. (trans.) (1966) *The Love Songs of Sappho*, New English Library, London

Rubinstein, W. Z. (1987) *Spartacus' Uprising and Soviet Historical Writing*, trans. J. G. Griffith, Oxbow Books, Oxford

Rudd, N. (trans.) (1992) *Juvenal. The Satires*, Oxford University Press, Oxford

—(trans.) (1997) *Horace: Satires and Epistles.*

Persius: *Satires*, Penguin, London

Saklatvala, B. (trans.) (1968) *Sappho of Lesbos. Her Works Restored*, Skilton, London

Sallust (Gaius Sallustius Crispus), *see* Handford

Salmon, E. T. (1950) *A History of the Roman World from 30 BC-AD 138*, Methuen, London

Sappho, *see* Carson; Greene; Powell; Reynolds; Roche; Saklatvala; Snyder; Vanita

Scarre, C. (1995) *The Penguin Historical Atlas of Ancient Rome*, Penguin, London

Sesar, C. (trans.) (1974) *Selected Poems of Catullus*, Mason & Lipscomb, New York

Sharrock A. and Ash, R. (2002) *Fifty Classical Authors*, Routledge, London

Shaw, B. D. (trans.) (2001) *Spartacus and the Slave Wars. A Brief History with Documents*, Bedford St Martins, Boston

Shelton, J-A. (1998) *As the Romans Did. A Sourcebook in Roman Social History*, Oxford University Press, Oxford

Simpson, F. P. (1879) *Select Poems of Catullus*, Macmillan, London

Sisson, C. H. (trans.) (1966) *Catullus*, Macgibbon & Kee, London

Snyder, J. M. (1995) *Sappho*, Chelsea House, New York

Southern, P. (2000) *Cleopatra*, p/b, Tempus, Stroud

—(2001) *Julius Caesar*, Tempus, Stroud

—(2002) *Pompey the Great*, Tempus, Stroud

Speake, G. (1995) *The Penguin Dictionary of Ancient History*, Penguin, London

Stewart, A. and Long, G. (eds) (1883) *Plutarch, Lives, I-IV*, George Bell, London

Suetonius, Gaius Tranquillus, *see* Graves

Sullivan, J. P. (trans.) (1997) *Petronius. The Satyricon; Seneca, The Apocolcyntosis*, Penguin, Harmondsworth

Swanson, R. A. (trans.) (1959) *Odi Et Amo. The Complete Poetry of Catullus*, Liberal Arts, New York

Symons, A. (trans.) (1924) *From Catullus. Chiefly Concerning Lesbia*, Seeker, London

Tacitus, Publius, Cornelius, *see* Grant, 1996

Taylor, L. R. (1984) *Party Politics in the Age of Caesar*, University of
    California Press, Berkeley & Los Angeles

Todd, J. And J. M. (1960) *Voices From the Past, I, II*, Grey Arrow, London

Vanita, R. (1996) *Sappho and the Virgin Mary. Same-Sex Love and the
    English Literary Imagination*, Columbia University Press, New York

Vennarseren, M.J. (1977) *Cybele and Attis, the Myth and the Cult*, Thames
    & Hudson, London

Villon, François, *see* Burl; Dale

Virgil (Publius Vergilius Maro) *see* Levi; West, 2001

Walker, S. and Higgs, P. (eds) (2001) *Cleopatra of Egypt. From History to
    Myth*, British Museum, London

Walsh, P. G. (trans.) (1997) *Petronius. The Satyricon*, Oxford University
    Press, Oxford

Warner, R. (trans.) (1972) *Fall of the Roman Republic. Six Lives by Plutarch*,
    Penguin, London

Walter, G. (1953) *Caesar, I, II*, trans. E. Craufurd, Cassell, London

Warrington, J. (1969) *Everyman's Classical Dictionary, 800 BC - AD 337*, J. M.
    Dent, London

Watts, N. H. (trans.) (1965) Cicero, 'De Domo Sua' in: *Pro Archia Poeta ...*,
    Heinemann, London

West, D. (1994) *The Imagery and Poetry of Lucretius*, Bristol Classical Press,
    London

—(trans.) (1997) *Horace. The Complete Odes and Epodes*, Oxford
    University Press

—(trans.) (2001) *Virgil. The Aeneid*, Penguin, London

Whigham, P. (trans.) (1966) *The Poems of Catullus*, Penguin,
    Harmondsworth

—(trans.) (1985) *Letter to Juvenal. 101 Epigrams from Martial*, Anvil Press
    Poetry, London

Williamson, G. A. (1969) *Poems of Catullus*, Bristol Classical Press, London

Wiseman, T. P. (ed.) (1985) *Roman Political Life, 90 BC-AD 69*, Exeter
    University Press, Exeter

—(1987) *Catullus and his World. A Reappraisal*, Cambridge University
    Press, Cambridge

Wray, D. (2001) *Catullus and the Poetics of Roman Manhood*, Cambridge
    University Press, Cambridge

Wright, F. A. (1923) 'Philodemus the Epicurean', Edinburgh Review 237,306-18

INDEX

Please note all poems are referred to as numbers in square brackets.
A page number after the bracket refers to a poem in this book
translated by Humphrey Clucas.

Also available from Amberley Publishing

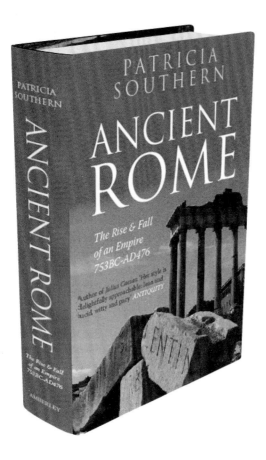

Ancient Rome
Patricia Southern

ISBN: 978-1-84868-100-2
Price: £20.00

Hardback 480 pages
80 illustrations and maps
62 colour photographs